ENDURING LOSS

ENDURING LOSS
Mourning, Depression and Narcissism through the Life Cycle

Editors

*Eileen McGinley
and Arturo Varchevker*

KARNAC

First published in 2010 by
Karnac Books Ltd
118 Finchley Road
London NW3 5HT

British Library Cataloguing in Publication Data

A C.I.P. for this book is available from the British Library

ISBN-13: 978-1-85575-692-2

Typeset by Vikatan Publishing Solutions (P) Ltd., Chennai, India

Printed in Great Britain

www.karnacbooks.com

CONTENTS

ACKNOWLEDGEMENTS

Some of the chapters in this book were previously published in the following journals, and are reprinted by the kind permission of the publishers, Taylor & Francis Ltd. (http://www.informaworld.com).

Polmear C. (2004). "Dying to live: mourning, melancholia and the adolescent process", in *Journal of Child Psychotherapy*, vol. 30, (3) 263–274.

Waddell M. (2006). "Narcissism: an adolescent disorder?", in *Journal of Child Psychotherapy*, vol. 32, (1) 21–34.

Flynn D., Skogstad H. (2006). "Facing towards or turning away from narcissism", in *Journal of Child Psychotherapy*, vol. 32, (1) 35–48.

Bolognini S. (2008). "Reconsidering narcissism from a contemporary, complex psychoanalytic view", in *International Forum of Psychoanalysis*, vol. 17, (2) 104–111.

Rhode M. (2005). "Mirroring, imitation, identification: the sense of self in relation to the mother's internal world", in *Journal of Child Psychotherapy*, vol. 31, (1) 52–71.

CONTRIBUTORS

Anne Alvarez, PhD, M.A.C.P., trained as a clinical psychologist in Canada and the USA before training as a child and adolescent psychotherapist in the UK. She is an honorary consultant child and adolescent psychotherapist and retired co-convener of the autism service at the Tavistock Clinic, London. She is the author of *Live Company: Psychotherapy with Autistic, Borderline, Deprived and Abused Children,* and has edited with Susan Reid, *Autism and Personality: Findings from the Tavistock Autistic Workshop.* A book in her honour, edited by Judith Edwards, entitled *Being Alive: Building on the work of Anne Alvarez,* was published in 2002.

Stefano Bolognini is a training and supervising analyst of the Italian Psychoanalytic Society (SPI) and works and lives in Bologna. He is currently co-chair for Europe for the IPA CAPSA committee and chair of the IPA 100th anniversary committee. He has published widely and two of his books have been translated into English: *Psychoanalytic Empathy* (London: Free Associations), and *Like Wind,*

Like Wave. Fables from the Land of the Repressed (New York: Other Press).

Denis Flynn is a fellow of the British Psychoanalytical Society and a child analyst. He was head of child and adult psychotherapy at the Cassel Hospital, and for ten years consultant head of the inpatient adolescent unit. He has written two books, *Severe Emotional Disturbance in Children and Adolescents: Psychotherapy in Applied Contexts* (Brunner Routledge, 2004) and *The Internal and External Worlds of Children and Adolescents: Collaborative Therapeutic Care* (Karnac, 2003, L. Day & D. Flynn, Eds.), He currently works in private practice with adults, children and adolescents, and is involved in teaching and training in psychoanalysis.

Eileen McGinley is a member of the British Psychoanalytical Society. She works as a consultant psychiatrist in psychotherapy in the psychotherapy unit at the Maudsley Hospital, and as a psychoanalyst in private practice in London. She is currently honorary secretary of the scientific committee of the British Psychoanalytic Society.

Caroline Polmear is a training and supervising analyst of the British Psychoanalytic Society. She worked at the Brent Centre for Young People and retains an interest in psychoanalytic work with young people through supervision of therapists in university student counselling services. She co-wrote *A Short Introduction to Psychoanalysis* (Milton, Polmear & Fabricius) and has also published on the subject of the psychoanalytic treatment of Aspergers syndrome. She is currently centrally involved with the psychoanalytic training at the Institute of Psychoanalysis in London.

Maria Rhode is professor of child psychotherapy at the Tavistock Clinic where she co-convenes the autism workshop. She is co-editor of *Psychotic States in Children* (1997) and *The Many Faces of Aspergers Syndrome* (2004), both in the Tavistock Book Series, and of *Invisible Boundaries: Psychosis and Autism in Children and Adolescents* (Karnac, 2006). She works as a psychoanalytic psychotherapist in private practice with children and adults.

Ken Robinson is a member of the British Psychoanalytical Society and works as a psychoanalyst in private practice in Newcastle-upon-Tyne.

Before training as a psychoanalyst, he taught English literature at university. He is honorary archivist of the British Psychoanalytical Society and the IPA.

Margaret Rustin is a consultant child psychotherapist at the Tavistock Clinic, London, and an honorary affiliate member of the British Psychoanalytical Society. She has written widely on child psychotherapeutic practice, co-editing and contributing to *Closely Observed Infants* (1989), *Psychotic States in Children* (1997), and *Assessment in Child Psychotherapy* (2000). She is co-author, with Michael Rustin, of *Narratives of Love and Loss: Studies in Modern Children's Fiction* (1987/2001), and *Mirror to Nature: Drama, Psychoanalysis and Society* (2002). They have jointly published articles on the three volumes of Philip Pullman's *His Dark Materials* trilogy, in the *Journal of Child Psychotherapy*, 29, 1, 2, & 3, (2003), and have recently written about the revived television series of *Doctor Who*.

Michael Rustin is professor of sociology at the University of East London, and a visiting professor at the Tavistock Clinic. He is an honorary affiliate member of the British Psychoanalytical Society. He has written widely on psychoanalytic topics. He is author of *The Good Society and the Inner World*__(1991), and *Reason and Unreason: Psychoanalysis, Science and Politics*_(2001), and, with Margaret Rustin, *Narratives of Love and Loss: Studies in Modern Children's Fiction* (1989/2001) and *Mirror to Nature: Drama, Psychoanalysis and Society* (2002).

Helga Skogstad trained as a psychiatrist and psychoanalytic psychotherapist in Germany. She is a member of the British Psychoanalytical Society and works as a psychoanalyst in private practice in London. She is currently head of adult psychotherapy at the Cassel Hospital in Richmond and has worked with severely disturbed adults, adolescents and families in inpatient and outpatient settings. She is involved in teaching and training in psychoanalysis in England and abroad.

Arturo Varchevker is a fellow of the British Psychoanalytical Society. He trained as a psychoanalytic psychotherapist at the Tavistock Clinic. He works in private practice in London as a psychoanalyst and family therapist, and in the NHS where he developed an interest in Domesti Violene and Trauma. He co-edited a book with Edith Hargreaves entitled *In Pursuit of Psychic Change: The Betty Joseph Workshop* (Brunner Routledge, 2004).

Margot Waddell is a fellow of the British Psychoanalytical Society and a consultant child psychotherapist in the adolescent department, Tavistock Clinic, London. She edits the Tavistock Series and has published widely. She is the author of *Inside Lives: Psychoanalysis and the Development of the Personality* (Karnac, 2002), and *Understanding 12–14 year olds* (Jessica Kingsley, 2005).

Sally Weintrobe is a ellow of the British Psychoanalytical Society. She was a member of the teaching staff at the Tavistock Clinic, an honorary senior lecturer at UCL in the Department of Psychoanalytic Studies, and was part of the young adult project at the Anna Freud Clinic. She works full time in private practice as a psychoanalyst in London.

Arturo Varchevker

This book comprises a selection of papers initially presented as a series of lectures organised by the Psychoanalytic Forum of the British Psychoanalytical Society. The contributions, by well known clinicians and theoreticians in their respective fields, seemed to capture certain important themes which we thought worthwhile to put together having in mind two main incentives: first, that the mental states of mourning, depression and narcissism constitute the basic fabric of psychoanalytic theorizing. Secondly, to illustrate a particular way of understanding mental functioning by locating these mental states within the life cycle frame. By exploring these states at different stages of the individual's development one can obtain a wider and at times different perspectives.

Awareness of the overall life cycle also provides a natural framework to explore human behaviour and deepens our understanding of the complexities of mental life and emotional relationships. For example, the apparently similar actions in a child, an adolescent, an adult or an elderly person may have quite different significances. An anxious interaction in front of a mirror could point to some form of pathology in one phase of development, whereas in another phase, it could be symptomatic of the way an adolescent, or a woman approaching menopause, expresses a natural interest and preoccupation with biological and physical change.

Considering mourning and narcissism in a continuum from birth to death enables us to imagine the phases of the life cycle, with all its physical, biological and psychological changes, being like the "stations"of a life journey. Each "station" is like a geographical place that differs from the previous one. We often share the experience of longing or dreading to reach a particular "station" in life, like the child who wants to be a grown-up or the adult fearing old age. Negotiating these phases means that an individual has to make transitions, which involve choosing what to leave behind and what to acquire, and therefore having to deal with the interaction of new and old emotions and fantasies. A person struggling with entering older age may feel that adolescence has not yet ended. Similarly an adolescent may avoid entering the next phase of development, and taking responsibility as an adult. Family therapists have been familiar with, and have used, the individual and family life cycle for some time. One of the main benefits of family therapy is that it widens the angle of observation by providing a natural frame to explore human behaviour in relational terms. However, there are considerable differences in the approach used in psychoanalysis and psychoanalytic psychotherapy, where the emphasis is on mental processes and how the individual perceives and deals with various pressures coming from outside and from within. There are always different interacting contexts, which make human behaviour and its conscious and unconscious meaning complex, and it is this complexity that the authors expand on in their chapters.

At one level, we can simplify the understanding of the process of mourning by relating it to the natural process of growing up.

At every stage of the life cycle the individual has to deal with two basic types of anxieties: those aroused by the fear of loss, and those aroused by what is to come in the next phase of development.

This is an important frame for exploration, but is, of course, an oversimplification.

At every stage of development there are important events which activate external and internal reactions that highlight a person's strength, weakness and psychopathology, as the individual has to deal with these anxieties.

For instance, a patient ("A")'s narrative *may* address a *very* important loss in A's adolescence, which has had a significant influence on problems A has encountered and the way A's life has developed. A's apparent free associations flow freely and link with the above. The psychoanalyst notices that A speaks in rather flat voice.

This may trigger several possible questions, for instance, is A trying to draw the analyst and A to work upon the struggles A has had with mourning, or is A trying to seduce the analyst to see a recurrent scenario that has been seen many times in previous sessions. There can be several possible meanings that may support this interaction. But what is going on in the "here and now" *is* often the main gateway to enter and explore what is going on in the patient's mind and in the interaction with the analyst. It can also alert the analyst of a possible partial or total enactment.

Reconstruction is an aspect associated with the work of mourning, but an understanding of how this reconstruction is assembled and co-constructed in the psychoanalytic relations will highlight if the work of mourning is taking place. This is what produces the important cohesion of past and future worked through in the present and therefore emerging with new life in the present.

To be aware of the "total transference" (Joseph, 1989) deepens our understanding of the various interactive contexts that could favour, block, or alter the mourning process to serve other needs. The analyst's response at this point is crucially important. It is useful to remind readers of Bion's important contribution to technique in relation to the analyst's "memory and desire", and personal prejudices. To put a brake on them is not a simple and straightforward recommendation; it activates and really challenges the analyst's sensitivity to become aware and resist the patient's pressure, and, especially his own, when he feels he ought to understand. This is especially relevant when not understanding is difficult to bear. To resist "no memory or desire" may open the road to a new understanding through the freshness of new experience and observation. All the contributors acknowledge the importance of paying close attention to these very important and significant technical issues.

Another aspect that emerges in the clinical examples and some of the theoretical discussions is the exploration of how the patient's mind functions at different stages of the life cycle when confronted by neurotic or psychotic anxieties triggered by external or internal pressures.

Analysts' approaches to this process vary according to their different theoretical stances and techniques. These differences can be observed through how the analyst uses the patient's history in the exploration of the patient's mind and helps the patient to achieve a positive transformation. Notwithstanding these differences, in the last decades, there has been a shared emphasis on focusing on the interaction of patient and analyst. This comes through in the clinical material presented in the various chapters in this book.

Before giving a brief synopsis of the individual papers in this volume, let us consider that Freud's work on *Mourning and Melancholia* (1917) could be regarded as an extension of the paper *On Narcissism* (1914), which was written a year earlier. The history of the theoretical understanding of these two interconnected concepts did not follow a straight line of development; Freud's critical and questioning attitude manifested itself in revisions, further developments related to new discoveries, and different perspectives and emphasis. When Freud first wrote *On Narcissism* in 1914 he was introducing what has remained a difficult, controversial and complicated concept.

As Quinodoz (2005) points out: "The terms 'narcissism', 'primary narcissism' and 'secondary narcissism' are very difficult to define, because they are used in many different ways both by Freud himself and in psychoanalytic literature as a whole." But it is clear clinically that the concepts of narcissism, mourning and depression are intimately linked.

Whether a person is able to deal with the psychic pain of loss, in its many guises, either predominantly through the process of mourning, or through melancholic narcissistic solutions, is what the papers in this book address. In depression, Freud showed how the ego was unable to give up its object choice and instead regressed to narcissistic mechanisms. Each of the authors makes a link between narcissism, mourning and depression in ways that are enriching to the understanding of these concepts and how they interact. They address how the individual can recruit their objects into enacting their phantasy in ways that, although communicative, may be used as an avoidance of the real contact with potentially helpful objects and thus becomes a hindrance to development.

The early contributions of Freud and Abraham on narcissism and melancholia in the early 1920's, and Klein's development of these ideas in some of her seminal work in the 1940's and 1950's, greatly influenced the ideas which were later developed by Herbert Rosenfeld in the Sixties and Seventies, and which most of the contributors to the present volume make reference to. In a highly influential paper, Rosenfeld (1971) drew our attention to the difference between libidinal narcissism and destructive narcissism, which he saw as an expression of the death instinct, and related to envy.

As will be seen from the clinical material presented by the various authors, this destructiveness is also active against the positive and constructive aspects of the patient. Willi Baranger suggested, "Once introduced, narcissism completely overturned the theory of instinct; the ultimate root of psychological conflict now became situated in the struggle between libido and destructiveness: Eros and Thanatos." For instance, Baranger (1991) identified nine meanings to narcissism, which he grouped in three groups of three, and Britton (2003) draws attention to the similarities between Baranger's views of narcissism and his. Ron Britton in the first group describes narcissism as a defence against adverse object relations; the second is narcissism as a basic, hostile expression to object relations. Using Baranger's terminology, he differentiates narcissism firstly as a form of libido, in the second group he refers to the nature of the object, and in the third he refers to the character of the person.

In relation to mourning and depression, Freud introduces the notion of "the work of mourning", implying an active mental process that was partly conscious and partly unconscious. One of the most immediate features that Freud noticed when the individual was experiencing a major loss was the lack of interest in the external world, a withdrawal into an internal preoccupation which, if it reached an extreme and fixed form, became what in those days was called melancholia, and what we would now know as psychotic depression. As Freud highlights (1917, p. 250), "Melancholia, therefore, borrows some of its features from mourning, and the others from the process of regression from narcissistic object-choice to narcissism. It is, on the one hand, like mourning, a reaction to the real loss of a loved object; but over and above this, it is marked by a determinant which is absent in normal mourning or which, if it is present, transforms the latter into pathological mourning."

A few paragraphs later on he adds: "If the love for the object—a love which cannot be given up though the object itself is given up—takes refuge in narcissistic identification, then the hate comes into operation on this substitutive object, abusing it, debasing it, making it suffer and deriving sadistic satisfaction from its suffering."

Freud also mentions that in some cases one can observe gradual differences between mourning and melancholia and he warns us of the importance of recognizing the healthy work of mourning, which requires non-interference, from a pathological one. We often encounter the tendency to deny or diminish the importance of mourning, or pathologize a normal process, or disregard its depth and rigour, following the incorporation of these concepts into everyday language.

The authors in this present volume take up, in their own rich and creative way, some of the complexities in understanding Freud's original ideas in these chapters, and it is a testimony to the depth of Freud's originality that so many ideas can be developed from his thinking.

The contributions

Childhood

Anne Alvarez is a distinguished child psychotherapist, working for many years at the Tavistock Clinic, who has long been interested in the study and treatment of depression in childhood. In the opening chapter, *Melancholia and Mourning in Childhood and Adolescence: Some Reflections on the Role of the Internal Object*, she addresses the complexities aroused by the experience of loss in childhood and concentrates on Freud's work on *Mourning and Melancholia*. She draws our attention to an interesting clinical observation that since 1917 there have been four particular developmental strands that have emerged following the initial description of melancholia. She especially concentrates on considering the perverse and addictive attachment to states of misery that can develop in depression, taking Joseph's ideas on chuntering from her paper, *Addiction to Near Death* (1982). She addresses some of the issues in relation to what handicaps mourning, where depression can lead to apathy and despair, by considering what type of object the child is able to mourn. She puts the emphasis on the distinction between what she refers to as "unvalued objects", as opposed to "devalued objects", where the external circumstances are so extreme that there is an absence of a containing object or containing environment that results in the child being more than "deprived", that is having only a limited experience of a good containing object. This is close to Winnicott's view that there is a difference between "deprived" and the positive experience never existed (personal communication, June 1970). In this chapter, as well as the next, the author keeps in mind the contributions made by deficits, as distinct from psychological defences, on the failure to introject a good object, which determine the psychological outcome of how losses are dealt with.

The second chapter on childhood is by Professor of Child Psychotherapy, Maria Rhodes, whose main area of expertise has been in the psychopathology and treatment of autism and narcissistic disorders in children. She addresses these difficult-to-understand conditions in her paper entitled, *The Lost Child: Whose is the Face in the Mirror?* She describes the lost part of the developing personality of the child who presents with a narcissistic disorder, who is capable of love, but in whom a Mafia-type of internal organization sabotages or attacks the constructive part of the developing personality. She describes the narcissistic features of three children, all of whom present with varying degrees of autistic spectrum disorders. She highlights the nature of the child's intense anxieties, the limited psychic apparatus available to deal with these anxieties so that defences are often concretised into actions, and the affective responses in the transference-countertransference interactions that are so important to understand and manage when working with these difficult-to-reach children.

She draws on the work of Meltzer, Tustin and Rosenfeld in her clinical understanding of autistic and narcissistic states.

Adolescence

In an insightful and challenging understanding of adolescence, as the title suggests: *Dying to Live: Mourning and Melancholia and the Adolescence Process,* Caroline Polmear reminds us of the history of the concept of mourning and melancholia and the various external and internal contexts that might have influenced Freud in arriving at this concept, and the subsequent changes he introduced to his theory. Her clinical examples vividly convey the struggle adolescents goes through in the process of development and the dramatic ordeals that evolve when they cannot mourn their infantile level and when they identify with a melancholic object.

She highlights the crucial role that the adolescent superego plays in their development and anti-development and she also explores the various types of attachment and rebellion that adolescents may experience in the interaction with their parental figures. Another important issue that she touches upon is bullying. This is a phenomenon that is widespread and is the cause of many grievances and disturbances in adolescence and later on in life. All these issues in different ways are part of the struggle that adolescents have as they negotiate their new external and internal space and establish their own identity.

In her chapter, *Narcissism—An Adolescent Disorder?* Margot Waddell enters the world of adolescence to try to reach its essence.

With her literary knowledge she highlights some of the most salient characteristics of the adolescent turmoil. She focuses on what she calls the "adolescent organization" and poses an interesting question in relation to one of the characteristics of this organization. Why is it that in some adolescents, what appear to be very entrenched characteristics get easily modified, even by small external or internal changes, and not in others? Her clinical illustrations show the forces that block development and become anti-developmental; she points out how destructiveness furnishes their superego, ruling in an almost totalitarian way, and how it is possible to observe a positive gradual modification taking place. She illustrates her thinking on the subject using a clinical case of working with an adolescent young woman, and how the analysis of her dream provided a lively demonstration of her inner struggle. This is a vivid account that shows how misleading our impressions could be when we witness similar manifestations in adult patients, but also highlights how difficult and sometimes horrible the experience of treating adolescents can be, and yet also how moving, fascinating and rewarding it can be working with them.

Denis Flynn and Helga Skogstad have extensive experience of working with adolescents within an NHS setting at the Cassell Hospital. In their joint chapter *Facing Towards or Turning Away from Destructive Narcissism*, they address some of the issues concerning both the nature of narcissistic disorders, and how they are manifest in adolescent individuals. They make reference to contemporary contributions and link some of Freud's theories about libidinal narcissism with Rosenfeld's contributions, particularly stressing his later work when he draws attention to the omnipotent destructive parts of the self which are themselves idealized, and therefore incorporated into the narcissistic character structure. They insightfully describe through their clinical material how frightening and difficult these situations are when they emerge in analysis and when they lead to dangerous acting out, which are highlighted in both examples.

Their first example is an assessment of a 17-year-old girl with a history of anorexia, depression, obsessional symptoms and suicidal ideation and their second example is of a 16-year-old girl with anorectic and self-harm symptomatology. The struggle emerges between the destructive states dominated by ruthless omnipotence and narcissism, and a more positive reflective state that gives space to others being acknowledged. It is also an important description of the work carried out in an adolescent inpatient unit where the nursing staff operate as a second container and where other patients bring forward an interesting dynamic in the therapeutic process.

Unfortunately the richness of the container-contained model within the structure of the unit could not be expanded, as it would require another chapter.

Adulthood

In the first of these three chapters on adulthood, the author concentrates on depression and mourning. As the title of Eileen McGinley's paper suggests, *Mourning or Melancholia: What's Love Got to Do with it?* it is an exploration of a particular psychoanalytic interaction when positive connections between the patient and the analyst seem to be present and discernible to the analyst, but are kept hidden to the patient by the expression of only negativity and hostility. Through the various projections and enactments that are activated with intensity and puzzlement in the patient-analyst interaction, she is able to impose clarity on the paradoxical complexities that these situations bring about when they are enacted in the transference. She writes in relation to her clinical example: "… located somewhere behind the open expression of her aggression and hatred, she has real feelings of love, affection and concern for me that seem to cause her considerable problems." This type of phenomenon arouses interesting problems of technique as well as theoretical discussion.

She describes clinical situations in which paradoxical interactions emerge in the clinical material and pose a considerable challenge to the analysis. She puts forward a key question in relation to this: "What is it about love for the object that can be so painful and difficult to tolerate, or acknowledge? This might in part be due to envy of the goodness of the object who is loved, and in part to the capacity to integrate both loving and hateful feelings, but this does not seem sufficient to explain why it is the love for her object that causes her so much difficulty." In some cases these impulses move convincingly into the area of perversions, when the good functions are totally hijacked or misused in order to obtain a sadomasochistic gain, seducing or enticing the analyst, or the external context, to be part of the perverse system. This is important to note because, at one point in time we would be dealing with a healthy narcissism or a mourning process and then imperceptibly it could turn into a pathological one.

Narcissism is the theme of the next chapter by the Italian psychoanalyst, Stefano Bolognini. In his paper, *Reconsidering Narcissism from a Contemporary, Complex Psychoanalytic Perspective,* he uses different clinical examples to highlight some of the characteristics of certain narcissistic disorders and the transference-countertransference pressures that are imposed on the analyst. This is a very interesting text where he considers, in a balanced personal style, the contemporary contributions on narcissism. He writes, "Contemporary psychoanalysis seems to have understood the usefulness of distinguishing, both dynamically and developmentally, the processes of constitution and growth of human beings, also (but not only) in the light of the development of their narcissistic order and equilibrium."

His starting point is Freud's ideas about narcissism and he focuses on some of the main contemporary contributions. Bolognini stresses the general view that "acceptability or lovability of one's own self by others, but also by oneself", is what he calls "*necessary narcissism or ... minimum living narcissism*" and in relation to this it is worth paying special attention to the aspects he lists as "*the narcissistic dimension*".

This is important in relation to establishing different manifestations of narcissistic presentations, where development and pathology can point in quite different directions. Bolognini also manages to use the classic theories of Kohut and Rosenfeld on narcissism in a very complementary and integrative way.

The next chapter by Sally Weintrobe, *Entitlement, the Abnormal Superego and Prejudice,* further develops themes on narcissism, grievances and entitlement that she has previously been published on.

She highlights the three types of phantasies attached to prejudice and their very destructive effect when the three operate together.

When this destructive constellation predominates, the possibility of a lively or more benign form of narcissism emerging is badly handicapped.

This is an area that is addressed by all the contributors. In this chapter, Weintrobe explores how the lively part of the personality is blocked or annihilated by the destructive narcissism and especially when there is an active malignant superego as described by O'Shaughnessy (1999).

Another interesting aspect she draws attention to is the link she makes with intolerance; she reminds us of Bion's contribution to the understanding of this phenomenon when he points out that if the capacity to tolerate meaning is lacking, the link that would make reality meaningful is blocked or disqualified The clinical examples she has chosen illustrate different types of struggles at the various levels of disturbance. She also draws attention to the link that exists between the individual psychoanalytic domain and the group or social domain and relates this to the phenomenon of prejudice at the social level. Past and present history are ongoing examples of the power struggle between the superior, intolerant groups and other groups, whether this takes the shape of discrimination of ethnic minorities, racial prejudices or other forms of discrimination and exploitation. When this acquires malignant characteristics the effect on the subject is catastrophic. As she mentions, this subject has been approached by a number of professionals from a psychoanalytic perspective as well as from a social or anthropological perspective.

Older age

Arturo Varchevker works as a psychoanalyst and a family therapist, and both of these influences can be seen in his paper, *Mourning in Later Years: Developmental Perspectives*, in which he explores how the various interactive contexts facilitate or inhibit the process of mourning that frequently relates to this phase of development. He describes how two aspects of mourning are manifested with various degrees of intensity throughout the individual life cycle: the first refers to the notion of an internal world as described by Melanie Klein and her followers in terms of how the individual copes and relives his early developmental anxieties. The transition in each stage of development in the individual's life cycle brings about changes and losses, which are like possible crisis points and sometimes can be quite traumatic.

The crisis points highlight previous developments in terms of the individual's capacity to deal with them. The second aspect refers to the present in terms of external and internal reality and the links that are activated from early situations, and coping mechanisms which acquire a new version or dimension in older age. When considering gains or losses, there are some interesting similarities and differences with childhood and adolescence, which are explored.

The use of several clinical vignettes serves to illustrate mourning and difficulties in mourning related to the emotional impact that older age has on the individual and its context, including the psychoanalyst's countertransference. Attention is drawn to sexuality in older age. From the point of view of technique, the repetitive use of history and the passivity with those who have encountered multiple external and physical losses is discussed.

The conclusion is that considerable significant psychic changes can be achieved even at this stage of the life cycle.

As well as being a psychoanalyst, Ken Robinson has a background in English literature. He uses one of Shakespeare's great tragic figures, Lear, to think about narcissism and mourning in old age. In his contribution *His Majesty the Ego: the Tragic Narcissism of King Lear's "Crawl towards Death"*, he quotes a famous politician, Tony Benn, referring to the anxieties brought about by retirement. He explores the anxieties of losing important roles in life: in the case of Benn, his role as a politician. This may well activate other losses and narcissistic wounds, or could lead to depressive withdrawal of a melancholic kind, or to a manic reaction, depending on the narcissistic investment in the role and the state of his objects. He draws attention to the high value of the investment that we make in a role. This is a very significant issue that can be explored from various angles and begs further exploration, and it is also linked to the life cycle.

Shakespeare's *King Lear* offers very interesting examples of all these issues and Ken Robinson offers an illuminating analysis of some of the characters, focussing on King Lear's narcissism: his weak ego supported by his grandiose omnipotence that interferes with the possibility of mourning. This is an example of a narcissistic pathology linked to psychotic processes that, as Robinson points out, so vividly comes to life in some of Shakespeare's characters.

The author stresses the links that exist between the two concepts of narcissism and depression.

Culture and society

This final chapter explores narcissism in a societal and cultural context.

In *States of Narcissism*, Margaret and Michael Rustin rightly stress that if we are going to apply our knowledge about narcissism "outdoors", meaning in contexts which are different from the consulting room, it is essential to have a clear theoretical and clinical perspective of narcissism, as previous authors of this book have stated, in terms of its developmental function and its different forms of pathology. Along these lines they assert their view that narcissistic states of mind are primarily modes of defence or strategies for survival when there is a background of external and internal deficiencies or a mixture of both. There is a self-centredness aroused by withdrawal of attention and concern for others and this state of mind develops into different forms of narcissism. They highlight their theoretical understanding of narcissism, which, together with the clinical examples and the reference to Shakespeare characters, provides a sound base to develop their views of "narcissism outdoors".

This is an important contribution that touches on many vital issues that affect us every day, from the moment we open a newspaper, go out to work, or interact in any form of group or social situation.

It is not only a serious and intellectual exploration but also a passionate one.

References

Baranger, W. (1991). Narcissism in Freud. In: J. Sandler, E. Spector Person & P. Fonagy (Eds.), *Contemporary Freud*. The International Psychoanalytical Association.

Bion, W. (1970). Opacity of memory and desire. In: *Attention and Interpretation*. London: Tavistock.

Britton, R. (1998). Subjectivity, objectivity and triangular space. In: *Belief and Imagination*. London: Routledge.

Britton, R. (2003). Narcissism, Part III. In: *Sex, Death and the Superego*. London: Karnac.

Davenhill, R. (Ed.) (2007). *Looking Into Later Life*. The Tavistock Clinic Series. London: Karnac.

Freud, S. (1914). On Narcissism: An Introduction. S.E, *14*. London: Hogarth.

Freud, S. (1917e). Mourning and melancholia. S.E., *14*. London: Hogarth.

Green, A. (1986). *Narcisismo de Vida, Narcisismo de Muerte*. Buenos Aires: Amorrortu.

Green, A. (1983). The dead mother. In: A. Green, *On Private Madness*. London: Hogarth.

Hinshelwood, R.D. (1989). *A Dictionary of Kleinian Thought*. London: Free Association.

Joseph, B. (1989). Transference: the total situation. In: M. Feldman & E.B. Spillius (Eds.), *Psychic Equilibrium and Psychic Change*. London: Routledge.

Muir, B. & Varchevker, A. (1975). Acting out, rebellion and violence. In: S. Meyerson (Ed.), *Adolescence and Breakdown*. London: Allen & Unwin.

Perelberg, R.J. (2004). Narcissistic configurations. *International Journal of Psychoanalysis, 85*: 1065–1079.

Quinodoz, J.M. (2005). *Reading Freud*. London: The New Library of Psychoanalysis.

Segal, H. & Bell, D.L. (1991). The theory of narcissism in the works of Freud and Klein. In: J. Sandler, E. Spector Person & P. Fonagy (Eds.), *Contemporary Freud*. The International Psychoanalytical Association.

Waddell, M. (2002). *Inside Lives: Psychoanalysis and the Growth of the Personality*. London: Karnac.

PART I

CHILDHOOD

CHAPTER ONE

Melancholia and mourning in childhood and adolescence: Some reflections on the role of the internal object

Anne Alvarez

I first read Freud's 1917 paper *Mourning and Melancholia* after reading Melanie Klein's paper, *Mourning and its Relation to Manic-depressive States* (1940). It has been a joy and something of a relief, to go back again to this great work of Freud's: I have been spending much time in recent years studying phenomena in the more paranoid and schizoid states of mind of extremely disturbed children, and although that has been edifying and unfortunately necessary, it was good suddenly to find myself back home, as it were, with this subject (Freud, 1917).

I would like to discuss two very different conditions which interfere with a person's capacity to mourn: protesting too much and protesting too little. In the years since 1917, I will suggest that five particular states of mind, all of which appear in and are foreshadowed in Freud's description of melancholia, have been developed further by subsequent theorists. The first feature is the nature of the paranoid state of mind, (Klein, 1935) and the second is the state of manic contempt (Klein, 1935; Segal, 1964) for devalued objects. The third, developed greatly by Rosenfeld, Kernberg, and Kohut is narcissism. Freud had made note of a narcissistic preoccupation. He does not seem to like these melancholics much. In a way, he is

3

right, because the real mourner evokes our sympathy in a far more powerful way: on the other hand, a psychoanalysis which attends carefully to the nature of the internal object's possible collusive role in all this might lead us to be a bit less impatient.

I shall concentrate on a fourth and a fifth feature. The fourth arises from a concept of Betty Joseph (1982), the process of addictive and perverse chuntering, which under different names was noted both by Freud and also by Abraham as a characteristic of the state of mind of the melancholic. The fifth feature, which arises from our greater understanding nowadays of the preconditions for the work of mourning, was also first described to us by Freud. This feature, which has to do with despair, and with those states which go beyond despair into apathy, concerns the question of the level of development of early introjections and internalisations of, and identifications with, a good object, and the part early development plays in the capacity to mourn. Here I shall also say a word about unvalued, as opposed to devalued objects. The findings from infant observation and infant research and also those from the clinical treatment by child psychotherapists of extremely deprived and traumatized children, support the work of Klein, Bion and the developmentalists. All the newer developments in thinking are underpinned, I suggest, by the greater attention to object relations theory and by the growing understanding of the nature of the difference between pathological and benign projective processes, and pathological and benign introjective ones.

But back to Freud. As with all his great papers, what you get in *Mourning and Melancholia* is Freud thinking on the hoof, telling you what he has observed, what he does know and is perfectly clear about, but always being equally clear about what he and we do not understand yet. Time and again, for example, here and in later papers, he is puzzled about why the work of mourning should be so extraordinarily painful. A theory based on libidinal economics does not explain that, he tells us. We might nowadays point out that a one-person psychology never could. Such pain was not easy to explain until there was a theory that left room for the power of our link to other people, and especially to their representations (or internal objects) set up inside us: that is, the power their sheer otherness exerts on us. (It is interesting that Freud's paper is not painful to read, whereas with Klein, the painfulness of the subject gets further into the prose.) But this is Freud at his tough-minded best: he begins with his usual device of dropping all claims to the general validity of his findings, and then he starts to think. Freud then points out that the external precipitating conditions are the same in both mourning and melancholia: the loss of a loved person, or of some abstraction such as one's country, liberty, or an ideal. The mental features are the same too: he says that both grief and depression involve a dejected mood, a loss of interest in the world, a loss of the capacity to love, and an inhibition of activity. Yet although mourning also involves "grave departures from the normal attitude to life", he points out that it never occurs to us to regard it as a pathological condition, and that we rely on its being overcome after a certain lapse of time.

But there is one important feature in melancholia which is not present in mourning, and this he identifies as the "extraordinary diminution of self-regard" which expresses itself in self-criticism and self-vilification. Freud expands, with a certain distaste, on the nature of this loss of self-respect in the melancholic: he points out that there is a terrible truth in some of the things the melancholic says about herself: she really is as lacking in interest, as petty and egoistic and as incapable of love and achievement as she says. Freud finally concludes (p. 248) that patient listening to all this leads to the impression that the self-accusations, with significant modifications, do fit someone else—someone whom the patient loves or has loved or should love. The key to the clinical picture, therefore, is what look like self-reproaches are in fact reproaches against a loved object which have been shifted away from the object on to the patient's own ego. "The woman who loudly pities her own husband for being tied to such an incapable wife as herself is really accusing her husband of being incapable ... The underlying revolt passes over into the crushed state of melancholia."

Now I would like to turn to the fourth feature of melancholia, that of "chuntering". Freud makes another extremely important observation (p. 247) when he points out that the melancholic does not behave quite like ordinary people crushed with remorse, because feelings of shame seem to be lacking; he is referring to the narcissism. But there is a further point. "Indeed," he adds, "there is almost an opposite trait of insistent communicativeness which finds satisfaction in self-exposure." Note the emphasis on the insistence of the communicativeness. He says also that the complex of melancholia behaves like an open wound, which draws to itself cathectic energies, "... from all directions and emptying the ego until it is totally impoverished". (Later, we can ask, if there is no healing, no normal scarring, what prevents it?)

Here there is a foreshadowing, a long away ahead, of Betty Joseph's concept of addiction to near-death, or chuntering, moaning on about misery in a way which can be both profoundly addictive, and also may be secretly quite masochistically perverse. Joseph's 1982 paper explored not just the phenomenon of a way of talking about misery that could accompany genuine misery, but also the effects on the transference and counter-transference in the relationship with the analyst; that is, the way the analyst could get pulled down into a state of depression where the pulling down was nevertheless felt to be quite sexually and masochistically exciting to the patient. Joseph insists that she is not talking about simple over-dramatization. I think myself there are probably gradations from something which is less perverse but still quite addictive to that which is both addictive and perverse. I shall expand on this continuum later.

Klein did draw attention to sadism and the gnawing of conscience, but was busy exploring the genuine hostility and hatred that interfere with love, real grief, and real reparation toward a loved object. Abraham, however, did draw attention to the masochism accompanying the narcissism hidden in the self-reproaches (Coyne, 1985, p. 39). He refers to the omnipotence of the biggest guilt and secret pleasure, the masochistic tendencies, the pleasure from his suffering and from continuing to think about himself. "Thus even the deepest melancholic distress contains a hidden source of pleasure." Abraham adds that it is an auto-erotic negation of life (p. 40).

I want to think a bit more later about what it is in the personality and inner world that prevents chuntering, or at least enables us to stop chuntering, to allow the processes of mourning to take their natural course and allow us to get back to life. Do our internal objects tell us they have had enough, or does our own self get weary? Either way, something happens to stop us picking and scratching at it, to allow some healing and scarring of the open wound to take place. What is it? In one way, with all the later hindsights from later theories, it is easy to protest the absence, in Freud's description of the work of mourning, of any reference to the reinstatement of the lost object within the ego, a piece of theory so much a part of Abraham's

(1924) and Klein's (1940) work, and also Freud's own later work (1923). Abraham also wrote to Freud about it on reading *Mourning and Melancholia* and we owe to Klein the notion that the loss of the external objects awakens fears of the loss of good internal objects too. Her view was that such reinstatement depended on the balance between love and hate towards internal objects in the internal world. She also saw it as dependent on recognition of the otherness of one's objects and a relative absence of a narcissistic identification with them.

But this was only 1917, and maybe we can look again at Freud's more active vocabulary. What Freud emphasizes here is the way the dictates of reality determine that the libido shall "detach itself" from the object which is now gone (p. 249). He describes the normal process in what might in one way seem to be rather too active terms as: "a withdrawal of the libido from this object and a displacement of it on to a new one, or to life itself" (p. 252). He says, for example, when this work is accomplished the ego will have succeeded in "freeing its libido from the lost object". (Perhaps we could say that even the concept of work is a fairly active one.) This next statement is not quite so active: "Each single one of the memories and situations of expectancy which demonstrates the libido's attachment to the lost object is met by the verdict of reality that the object no longer exists; and the ego, confronted, as it were, with the question of whether it shall share this fate, is persuaded by the sum of the narcissistic satisfactions it derives from being alive, to sever its attachment to the object that has been abolished" (p. 255). He comments that it is remarkable that this painful unpleasure is taken as a matter of course by us, and that the fact is, however, that when the work of mourning is completed, the ego becomes free and uninhibited again.

It is easy to read all this now and agree with Klein: yes, but not so free, free but changed internally, that is, to note the lack of the notion of internalization, the process that we now understand to accompany the so-called detachment of libido. But maybe we should not lose sight entirely of Freud's more active vocabulary. For it is also true that mourning, at least in its heightened form, does not go on for ever. What stops an insistent going over and over of one's loss and misery? Instead of an active concept such as Freud's "severance", we might say there is something about the importance of letting go, and being let go of by the object, which is foreshadowed in

Freud's thinking. Letting go of the object, and letting go of the grief. It is interesting that in the film *Truly Madly Deeply* the permanently grieving woman is as helped as much by her dead husband who returns from the grave to make her tired of him, as by her own growing desire for life. We have to let our objects go, but they have to be felt to let us go too. But maybe we could say with Freud there is also, finally, a wearying or impatience with one's own grief. A little paternal insistence on severance is sometimes good for us.

Clinical work with a depressed adolescent where there were features of both mourning and melancholia

This is a situation where the patient and I came to learn that a type of melancholic rumination did accompany some real mourning. I want to draw, however, particular attention to the role of the internal object, in this case a paternal one, in helping to reduce the rumination. Henri Rey wrote that in borderline patients at least, it was often the case that the internal objects had to get better before the self could (Rey, 1944).

Luisa was referred at the age of 15 for depression, extreme separation difficulties, and various somatic and psychosomatic conditions. Her family was Latin American, but she herself was born and raised in the UK. She was the youngest of three daughters, and many of her extended family lived in England, too. Theirs was an affectionate and devoted family, and Luisa was particularly close to her eldest sister and to her mother. Luisa told me that her extremely happy childhood ended around the age of 13, that she had been feeling unhappy inside since then. Later she added that adolescence itself had probably upset her, because it meant the loss of her wonderful childhood. She often spoke to me very poignantly about the warmth and simplicity of her childhood days; the feeling of loss and grief was real, but it was sad to see how little pleasure she could allow herself in her current life. She did have fun, but somehow she had to steal it and hide it from other parts of herself. Later, it was also sad to see that the prospect of university and the round-the-world travels of the gap year offered no exciting adventures for Luisa: she saw the future as simply grey. She seemed like someone walking backwards into the future, looking longingly at a brightly lit past.

Luisa's fears and griefs about separation were a great problem at the time of referral and for years afterward. Whenever her parents, or she herself, were to go away, however briefly, she imagined them dying, and therefore her own life over. At times she tried to hide her grief and panic from them, but usually failed. Sometimes, instead of the emotional upset, one of the somatic conditions would erupt. It is important to say that her anxieties, whatever unconscious aggression they may have hid, were also accompanied by real love for her parents, who were indeed devoted to her, and very bewildered and worried by the intensity of her distress. They had not had this kind of difficulty with their older girls. To me she was a reliable and cooperative patient—she brought interesting dreams, and helpful associations to them and to my interpretations. Gradually, however, it became clear that the work was being done for me rather than for herself, that she had a fantasy of parental figures as needing her, and of me as needing her confirmations of my ideas. Over the first three years, there grew some signs in dreams and in sessions that parent figures could be seen to be on the side of life—not yet really potent, but not quite so needy either.

And Luisa did seem then, by the age of 18, to be less depressed and persecuted in her outside life. But as the time of her gap year round-the-world travels approached, the phobias about separation recurred with a bang. She was experiencing real depression and grief about leaving the family home and her boyfriend. There was also real phobic and sometimes realistic fear about the dangers of travelling the globe. We had previously learned that she was, however, capable of over-dramatizing such panics and griefs. Yet it was not simple over-dramatization: we could by now both recognize a quality of ruminative dwelling upon, and morbid fascination with, her own grief, depression and panic. We had also begun to learn of the way in which other people could get caught up in escalating her anxiety into ever more vicious circles which somehow got everyone into a heightened state of excitable anxiety. Luisa could indeed `chunter' on to all of us. I believed that in our sessions I was taking account of both; that is, interpreting both the real panic and grief (she was also due to interrupt her psychotherapy for some months) and the driven and addictive quality to her desperate protestations. I had begun to recognize a certain weariness and lack of sympathy at certain moments in my own counter-transference. I tried to detect the moments at which one or the other element, the real anxiety or the rumination, was paramount in the differing quality of Luisa's voice, but it was not easy. A complication was that the condition of depression itself was depressing her! And nothing was changing. The family (and I) were beginning to be afraid that she was actually breaking down.

One day, Luisa suddenly reminded me of the night three years before when her father had taken away her mobile phone after he found her still comforting a bereaved friend at four in the morning. The two young people had been on the phone like this all night for weeks. I felt that she was telling me that I should be firmer about the chuntering, so that she could hear me. I had felt a certain weariness, as I said, but I think my accompanying anxiety about her anxiety had inhibited not only my containment of my weariness, but also, what Bion called the adequate "transformation" of it, that is how I communicated it back to her (Bion, 1965). As I began to use that aspect of my counter-transference more, I think my voice became cooler and drier, and probably less sympathetic and somewhat resigned. Luisa did seem to hear this, and perhaps this helped her to calm down and to some extent even to enjoy the prospect of the trip. Gradually, when she returned, she became better able to catch herself dwelling in a morbid way on things, and the habit became considerably reduced. She considered that her problem then was to learn to think deeply, but in a new way. Needless to say, many of Luisa's other problems remained, but perhaps at least a fall into psychiatric illness was forestalled. There was still much work to be done on her lack of interest in people who were neither fragile nor in great need of her.

A brief word about the continuum from defensive use of rumination on to addictive and to perverse uses of it (clearly, all these gradations on such a continuum need to be carefully distinguished from our patients' genuine grief and genuine despair): I think that some types of repetitive grieving may primarily involve a defensive activity aimed at deflecting or placating envy; when, however, it becomes habitual and addictive, the person may get very stuck, without necessarily getting perverse excitements from it. There may be, as developmentalists note, a type of self-soothing involved. Yet I think there was some excitement involved in Luisa's grieving, though this did not seem to include perverse elements. Where the element of sexual or perverse excitement is added, further technical problems arise, and it is important to show the patient that he has come to get a strange kick out of his misery. Analytic work with the rituals of children with autism—or with the perverse preoccupations of sexually abused children—teaches us that an over-reactive response can feed into and perpetuate the condition—but we have also had to learn that too passive an analytic stance can have a similar result.

I suggest, therefore, that the image of the father removing the phone raises interesting questions about the role of the internal object (and eventually the ego) in preventing a tendency to dwell on things overmuch in the course of childhood development. It also raises issues about whether there is more than one analytic stance. This was no easy natural letting go or relinquishment on Luisa's part, I think: where the internal parents have been felt to be too helpless, or too sympathetic, something stronger may be needed. (Of course, this function is not exercised only by fathers! Mothers, and especially sibling figures, can serve as excellent conduits for letting us know when they have had enough of us.) Our objects need to feel free to communicate to us when we are being boring. And Freud's term severance may not be so irrelevant after all!

This implies, I think, that there is not one but innumerable analytic stances. They have in common the one feature that all involve the feelingful thinking about counter-transference experiences, that is, the digestion and containment of these, but once we arrive at the point of communicating something back to the patient, then the paths of response diverge, for everything depends on the content of the counter-transference, which is different every time. Grief requires one response, rumination another, for example. And when they are mixed which they usually are, things are very difficult!

Depression in earlier childhood: Can we distinguish mourning from melancholia and both from despair or apathy?

I shall say something about depression in childhood before going on to discuss some processes that predate and are preconditions for the capacity to mourn. It is interesting that there is much reference to a depressed mood, to lassitude, and lack of interest in the literature on diagnosis (Coyne, 1985; American Psychiat. Assoc: DSMIV, 1994) but nothing that I could find concerning the more active symptoms of lamentation and protestation seen in the adult melancholic. But perhaps both types need our attention. Children do chunter I believe, or in my Canadian terms, whine. Children cry when they are upset, but there are many kinds of cries and crying. Real misery can be used or rather misused, even by children. One three year old boy was really sobbing one day, the first that his mother had left him alone with me during the consultation period. I became aware that this child with an extremely strong will was really prolonging his tears, which somehow had clearly run their course. He was very controlling and wilful, and when I suggested this to him, he was enraged but stopped crying at once! Another, Julia, when I voiced a similar suspicion, took her hands away from her eyes and said, "Yes I often 'cry' like this at home, it's just my own saliva on my cheeks." That was chillingly psychopathic and sadistic, but the third case was chilling for its masochistic delight: this boy, when challenged, removed his hands, and grinned in a terrible triumph at what he could see was my obvious irritation. Masochism played a major part in his development from very early on.

Probably mothers learn from experience to discriminate the different notes in their babies' cry, i.e., when it is really unbearable and desperate, and when there is a grumbling on, where the baby might fall asleep and indeed be in need of sleep if the parent can resist the temptation to pick it up. Sometimes the more anxious parent is unable to do that, and cannot discriminate between the real thing and the getting stuck. The latter can sometimes lead on to an unfortunate downward spiral. Perhaps our objects need to know when they and we have had enough. Defensiveness and greedy possessiveness can perhaps with time develop into dangerously addictive and even perverse chuntering later in life.

Finally, I would like to move on to the fifth feature, the question of real despair. I want to talk about states of depression which go beyond mourning to chronic despair or even apathy, but which are also different from melancholia. Freud pointed out that if the object does not possess great significance for the ego (p. 256), a significance reinforced by a thousand links, then, "… its loss will not be of a kind to cause either mourning or melancholia". Here we have to address problems of trauma and deprivation (they are different). Klein tells us that the internalization that underlies the capacity for mourning lost objects depends on the balance between love and trust versus hatred and persecution. But what happens with the abused or traumatized child who has not built up the previous introjections, internalizations of and un-narcissistic identifications with a good object and a valued self so essential to that process? A hole in the universe, occasioned by the loss of a loved parent at age 10, say, is very different from the sense a much younger child or baby may have that the universe itself, the universe of smells, voices, shapes, has shifted unalterably. In the novel, *The God of Small Things*, the narrator says, "Some things come with their own punishments." (The main punishment was guilt.) "Like bedrooms with built-in cupboards. They would all learn more about punishments soon. That they came in different sizes. That some were so big they were like cupboards with built-in bedrooms. You could spend your whole life in them, wandering through dark shelving" (Roy, 1998, p. 115).

It is important to say that some even quite ordinary children may be as traumatized by the death of a parent as bereaved by it. This is particularly where the death is slow, and, as is so common, the dying person changes physically, sometimes terribly. One child I treated whose mother had died of cancer spent the first months talking only about horror films. At first I thought this was a kind of defensive excitement, but there was more to it: I think he needed time to process horror, long before grief could be available.

Many borderline traumatized children have suffered severe neglect as well as trauma, and, as I have said, the sense of good objects may be as weak as the sense of bad or abusive objects is strong. Judith Trowell's research on depression in young adolescents warns us to take seriously what it may be like to have not only internal objects who are felt to be too fragile and depressed to be criticized, but possibly also external real ones. Some of her patients seem to have had had nowhere to put it except on themselves (Trowell et al., 2003). Moira McCutcheon's research shows that in very deprived children, those who retained some concept of a good helpful figure were also those who had a stronger identification with the good but damaged and depressed parental figures, whereas those who did not have a concept of a helpful figure had less of an identification (unpublished). A bitter choice to have to make!

In other cases, with certain blunted, empty children, the internal objects are not bad, and not even devalued, they are simply unvalued. There are important differences between children with devalued internal objects, where the disparagement was (or at least began as) defensive, and those whose internal objects, for a variety of reasons, have never been valued or admired in the first place, never respected, nor acquired sufficient elevation, as it were, to be looked up to. I began to think about these issues in, admittedly, a rather literal and concrete manner, after seeing several deprived, apparently severely depressed children regularly placing dolls in horizontal positions, lying about on couches or even the floor in the dolls' house, rarely even placed to watch television, which is in itself a fairly passive activity. (The actual parents in these cases tended to be alcoholic, drug addicted, or severely depressed.) The dolls were usually said to be asleep, but they were certainly never doing anything, and worse, never even standing up. The therapist may be treated with, not contempt, simply indifference. Indeed, in some cases, there was no such concept as that of intelligence and of an interested and interesting mind. Adults were seen as stupid, fundamentally uninteresting, but not necessarily bad. I have heard of many children, suddenly realizing that the therapist could understand their feelings, asking, "How did you know that? Are you a mind-reader?"

The strength of the good or ideal (Klein and Segal often use these terms interchangeably) object is exactly what cannot be taken for granted in the work. (did you leave out the refs deliberately?) Ok by me if you did. And as I say, the interestingness also cannot. Separation and loss occurring in the context of an internal object with practically no constancy, no substantiality, can throw such children terribly. The damage is cognitive as well as emotional. When the disturbance is too great, thoughts about separation may become unthinkable until thoughts about reliable returns can grow. We have much to learn about the conditions under which our patients can begin to think these new thoughts. Patients returning after a holiday may not be in a well enough or integrated enough state to be struggling as yet with feelings of missing or loss. They may have lost contact with any sense of a good or familiar object real enough to be missed. They may need help to find their good object again.

And they may need time to study and process the nature of such an object. Introjection, internalization, and eventual identifications take time, and Bion's concept of alpha function—the function of the mind that makes thoughts thinkable and lends experience meaning—has much to offer in helping us to facilitate this process (Bion, 1962).

Klein pointed out, "There is no doubt that if the infant was actually exposed to very unfavourable conditions, the retrospective establishment of a good object cannot undo bad early experiences. However, the introjection of the analyst as a good object, if not based on idealization has, to some extent, the effect of providing an internal good object where it has been largely lacking"(1957, p. 90).

The following is an example of a child engaging in what appears to be a deeply thoughtful introjective process. A ten-year-old adopted girl, who had been raised in an orphanage in a third world country, was recovering hope and trust thanks to understanding adoptive parents and also to the therapy. In one session, calming down after the first rather desperate 20 minutes of the session, she asked musingly and tenderly of the therapist, "Why are you called Jane?" A little later, she briefly stroked the fuzzy shoulder of the therapist's cardigan and asked, softly, "Why is it so fuzzy?". The language she was using and the question "why" was that of a ten-year-old, but in reality I think she was doing what the baby does when it explores its mother's or father's face with its eyes or hands, getting to know, reflectively and cognitively, as well as emotionally, not the why-ness of his parents, but the what-ness, the is-ness.

Segal's distinction between true symbol formation and the symbolic equation has been enriched and extended by Bion's theory of alpha function. Bion hypothesized "alpha function", a function of the mind which made thoughts "thinkable". He pointed out that thoughts precede thinking, that each thought needs to be thought about and dwelt upon (we might add played with), in order for it to be digested, processed and useful for further thinking and for relating to other thoughts (Bion, 1962). Introjections, internalizations, and alpha functioning begin at birth, if not before. For those children who have not had a decent start, life and psychotherapy may give them a second chance for new introjections to take place. In many instances, we are working at the level of allowing the child to forge the thousand links Freud spoke of, and our task is not easy.

References

Abraham, K. (1911). Notes on the psycho-analytical investigation and treatment of manic-depressive insanity and allied conditions. In: J.C. Coyne (Ed.), *Essential Papers on Depression*. New York: University Press, 1986.

Abraham, K. (1924). A short study of the development of the libido. In: *Selected Papers on Psycho-analysis*. London: Maresfield Reprints.

Alvarez, A. (2006). Narcissism and the stupid object: devalued or unvalued? With a note on addictive narcissism and apparent narcissism. In: O.F. Kernberg and H.-P. Hartmann (Eds.), *Narzissmus: Grundlagen-Storungsbilder-Therapie.* Stuttgart: Schattauer.

American Psychiatric Association (1994). *Diagnostic and Statistical Manual of Mental Disorders*, Fourth Edition. Washington, DC: American Psychiatric Association.

Bion, W.R. (1962). *Learning from Experience*. London: Heinemann.

Bion, W.R. (1965). *Transformations*. London: Heinemann.

Freud, S. (1917e). Mourning and melancholia. S.E., 14: 237–258. London: Hogarth.

Freud, S. (1923). *The Ego and The Id*. S.E., 19: 3–66. London: Hogarth.

Joseph, B. (1982). Addiction to Near Death. *International Journal of Psychoanalysis*, 63: 449–456. Reprinted in E.B. Spillius and M. Feldman (Eds.), *Psychic Equilibrium and Psychic Change: Selected papers of Betty Joseph*. London: Tavistock/Routledge, 1989.

Kernberg, O.F. (1970). Factors in the psychoanalytic treatment of narcissistic personalities. *International Journal of American Psychoanalytic Association, 18*: 51–85.

Klein, M. (1935). A contribution to the psychogenesis of manic-depressive states. *International Journal of Psychoanalysis, 16*: 145–174. Reprinted in *The Writings of Melanie Klein, 1*. London: Hogarth, 1975, 262–289.

Klein, M. (1940). Mourning and its relation to manic-depressive states. *International Journal of Psychoanalysis, 21*: 125–153. Reprinted in *The Writings of Melanie Klein, 1*. London: Hogarth, 1975, 344–369.

Klein, M. (1952). Some theoretical conclusions regarding the emotional life of the infant. In: J. Riviere (Ed.), *Developments in Psychoanalysis*. Reprinted in *The Writings of Melanie Klein, 3*. London: Hogarth, 1975, 61–93.

Klein, M. (1957). *Envy and Gratitude*. London: Tavistock. Reprinted in *The Writings of Melanie Klein, 3, Envy and Gratitude and Other Works*. London: Hogarth, 1975.

Kohut, H. (1977). *The Restoration of the Self*. New York: University Press.

Roy, A. (1998). *The God of Small Things*. London: Harpers Flamingo, 1997.

Rey, J.H. (1988). That which patients bring to analysis. *International Journal of Psychoanalysis, 69*: 457–470. Reprinted in J. Magnana (Ed.), *Universals of Psychoanalysis in the Treatment of Psychotic and Borderline States: Henri Rey*. London: Free Association, 1994.

Rosenfeld, H. (1964). On the psychopathology of narcissism: a clinical approach. *International Journal of Psychoanalysis*, 45: 332–337. Reprinted in *Psychotic States*. London: Hogarth, 1965.

Segal, H. (1957). Notes on symbol formation. *International Journal of Psychoanalysis*, 38: 391–397. Reprinted in *The Work of Hanna Segal*. New York: Jason Aronson, 1981, 49–85.

Segal, H. (1964). *Introduction to the Work of Melanie Klein*. London: Heinemann.

Trowell, J., Rhode, M. & Miles, S. (2003). Childhood depression: work in progress. *Journal of Child Psychotherapy*, 29: 2, 147–169.

CHAPTER TWO

The lost child: Whose is the face in the mirror?

Maria Rhode

In children who are developing well, healthy self-love goes hand in hand with love for others and a lively interest in the outside world. A narcissistic child takes his parents' love as though it were his right and the natural consequence of his own qualities. A child who is himself capable of love, on the other hand, will feel loveable precisely because he can trust in their love for him, in spite of the normal conflicts of the Oedipal constellation. In such a benign cycle, the child's sense of his own goodness reinforces his capacity for love and gratitude, and is reinforced by it.

In contrast, in the situation that Freud (1914c) characterized as secondary narcissism, conflicts arising in relation to others can lead to a turning away from the outside world and to excessive self-absorption. In other words, Freud saw secondary narcissism as a means of safeguarding the self against the hazards of relationships. Equally, in primary narcissism, which Freud postulated as secondary narcissism's normal developmental analogue, he suggested that well-being was linked to the absence of relationships: that is, he thought of object cathexis as draining libido away from the ego. As Britton (2003a) has recently pointed out, Freud's discussion of narcissism tended to emphasize its function in underpinning the sense of identity, whereas Abraham's emphasis (1919) was much more on the negativistic character of narcissistic patients, which led them to attack the possibility of relating to anyone who was not under their control.

This distinction has been carried over into much subsequent work on narcissism. For example, Rosenfeld (1987) contrasted thin-skinned narcissists, who often had a traumatic history and whose pleasure in their own achievements precariously bolstered their sense of a cohesive identity, with thick-skinned narcissists, in whom the growing part of the self was imprisoned by a Mafia-type gang led by a mad aspect of the personality that was opposed to any kind of dependent relationship. While Steiner (1987) proposed that such pathological organizations could serve as a retreat from depressive anxieties as well as from the fear of chaos, Britton (2003a) has contrasted those narcissistic alliances between twin parts of the self where the aim is to preserve the possibility of loving with those where the aim is jointly-executed murder. On the other hand, Kohut (1971, 1977) and analysts whom he influenced, particularly in America, placed far greater emphasis on the patient's need to underpin the sense of self. Stolorow and Lachman (1986), for example, define as narcissistic anything that contributes to a cohesive sense of identity.

Another area of continuing debate that was opened up by Freud's 1914 paper on narcissism has centred on the likely nature of the infant's experience—normal primary narcissism or early object relatedness? It is perhaps worth reminding ourselves of Balint's observation (1969) that Freud himself had more than one theory, and never fully integrated his different formulations. In 1914, he postulated a state of normal primary narcissism; but in the *Three Essays* (1905d), he had written that the baby's first object was the mother's breast, and that this was true from the beginning of life. This statement was not modified when he revised the *Three Essays* in 1915, though was diametrically opposed to his position in the paper *On Narcissism*. Since then, different authors have emphasized the implications of one of Freud's various theories over those of another.

Recent advances in developmental research (see, for example, Stern, 1985; Trevarthen, 2001) have demonstrated that very young babies are capable of intense and complex object relationships—something that psychoanalytic workers had come to realize through the discipline of infant observation (Bick, 1964). This does not, of course, imply that these relationships are sustained at a uniform level: the baby who goes to sleep after a feed with the nipple in its mouth is likely to be experiencing a state in which self and other are far less differentiated than is the case for a baby who is satisfied, alert, and ready to engage with others.

The "lost child" of my title is that part of the child's personality that *is* capable of love, that *does* have potential, but is not given the opportunity to flourish because of the dominance of a Mafia-type organization or gang. This "lost" part, as we know, continues to exist even when a destructive aspect of the personality is in command, although, as Steiner (1982) has described, the loving part may sometimes engage in perverse, collusive submission to the gang leader. The question then is whether and how it may be possible to speak to the growing part of the child's personality. A particular problem arises from the despair and dislike which such children can inspire—and dislike is a sufficiently unusual response to a child to deserve, I think, to be taken very seriously as a pointer to a possible narcissistic organization. Besides, despair and dislike can easily overwhelm the therapist so that their communicative value may be overlooked, and so can the traces, however faint, of a potentially growing part of the child's personality.

Narcissism and autism

The children whose material I wish to discuss in this chapter all had a diagnosis of autistic spectrum disorder, though they withdrew to different degrees from relationships with other people. On a purely behavioural level, children with autism seem to present an extreme degree of the withdrawal from relationships that characterizes the narcissistic states described in adults. However, the structure of the two conditions has generally been approached from different vantage points. Even leaving aside the implication of genetic and neurological factors in autistic spectrum disorders, many authors from Melanie Klein onwards have regarded these as stemming from an inhibition of development rather than from regression (Klein, 1930). In her last book, Tustin (1990) referred to some cases in which she thought that autistic coping strategies were invoked in order to hold a psychosis in check, a formulation that seems to converge with Steiner's (1987) view that psychic retreats can serve as a protection against chaos. However, in the main she viewed autism proper as a sensation—dominated state in which autistic objects and autistic shapes provided, respectively, hard sensations that allowed the child to feel strong and soft sensations that allowed him to feel soothed (Tustin, 1981). Since dependence on separate people was side-stepped, the child's internal personality structure was correspondingly rudimentary and impoverished. Because of this, she thought that narcissism was an inappropriate term to use in describing children with autism, because they did not possess a sense of self as this is usually understood (Tustin, 1986c). Meltzer and his colleagues (Meltzer et al, 1975) similarly emphasized the characteristic mindlessness of autistic states and the poverty of personality development: those children who had developed narcissistic structures, such as Isca Wittenberg's John (1975) did so after emerging from the autistic state proper. Such a deficit model sits well with both relational (Hobson, 2002) and cognitive theories of autism (e.g. Frith, 2004; Baron-Cohen, 1988), although, as Alvarez (1999) has recently pointed out, individual children with autism differ with regard to the balance in each case of issues of defence and of deficit.

Both the central motivations for narcissism—shoring up the sense of existing and the pull away from relationships—apply also to autism. The difference may be a matter of degree, in that the child with autism is concerned, as Tustin described, with shutting out anything that could impinge on the feeling of physically "going on being". Because the outside world can feel so dangerous, the child does not engage in the relationships that could allow his sense of self to develop. Instead, he relies on self-generated physical sensations rather than on defence mechanisms. A marked sensuality has often been noted in children with autism (Tustin, 1972; Meltzer, 1975); this bodily dimension constitutes an important distinction between them and others with whom they may share important patterns of motivation and behaviour. For example, I have described elsewhere (Rhode, 2004) two boys with autism who had each responded to trauma according to one of the alternatives—subjectivity and objectivity—delineated by Britton (1998) in relation to patients who felt in danger of being overwhelmed by what he called a "Chaos Monster" as a consequence of the closure of the Oedipal triangle. The difference was that the two autistic children experienced the threatened danger as a bodily mutilation, and responded on a physical level. One sought bodily fusion which was in danger of being cut into by an intrusive father element, while the other literally hardened himself against the threat of being physically engulfed.

Clinical illustrations

The three children I shall refer to in this chapter had all developed beyond the state of autism proper, though two of them, Anthony and Lina, continued to rely, to different degrees, on the physicality of autistic objects and autistic shapes. At this point, it becomes helpful to think in terms of narcissistic patterns. While a vignette (Shulman, 1998) concerning the first child, Andrew, illustrates how communication, particularly verbal communication, can be vetoed by a narcissistic gang leader, Anthony and Lina both turned to narcissistic withdrawal as a means of dealing with the lack of a cohesive sense of self and with their profound fears about the state of the mother figure. Lina, a nine-year-old with a diagnosis of Asperger's syndrome, managed to achieve an accommodation with an Oedipal couple who provided a framework within which her sense of identity could develop. In contrast, Anthony's experience of the Oedipal couple was one in which narcissistically-absorbed parents were seen as mirror images of each other who cruelly excluded him. His own narcissistic imperviousness seemed to involve identification with such a couple, in which I was to be the cruelly excluded child. In both children, the narcissistic part of their personality that led them away from human relationships turned out to be based on a frightening parental figure: a damaged, engulfing mother in Lina's case, and a sadistic father in Anthony's.

Andrew: Autistic withdrawal as dictated by the narcissistic gang leader

Before I go on to the second part of my title, which concerns the child's reflected image of himself, whether in the context of narcissism or of object relations, I would like give an example of the interplay between loving and narcissistic aspects of the child's personality and the therapist's countertransference response. This vignette also illustrates how the mutism that is typical of autistic states may be imposed by the leader of a narcissistic organization.

Andrew was a four-year-old boy with mild to moderate autism whom I assessed together with a colleague, Graham Shulman.[1] Andrew's disruptive behaviour meant that his parents could not take him anywhere; in addition, he insisted on sleeping in their bed, and they felt it would be cruel to stop him. On the positive side, he had begun to make more contact since his mother became pregnant, and he also made good contact with my colleague. I, on the other hand, found myself feeling a strong dislike. This was not because of the way he climbed over me as though I were a piece of furniture: that is more or less expectable in a child with autism. It was more because of an implacable, machine-like quality in his behaviour.

My colleague took Andrew on for intensive psychotherapy (Shulman, 1998), and he progressed to the extent of transferring to a mainstream school and of being able to sustain a warm and co-operative relationship with his therapist. However, he then noticeably reverted to playing and talking without allowing any real emotional contact. One day, after a conversation with his therapist, he turned to address a brick that lay on the floor among other scattered toys. "I'm sorry" said Andrew "that I spoke in words." It was a chilling illustration of his submission to an inhuman part of himself that forbade contact with other people and had presumably reasserted itself to cause Andrew's change of attitude. I suspect that, during the assessment, these two aspects of Andrew had produced a countertransference response that was split between my colleague and me, much as his refusal to sleep in his own bed split the parental couple, and that our separate responses taken together gave a good indication of how things were to go.

It was not until Andrew had been in treatment for four years and had improved greatly that his mother was able to talk about the terror that a violent uncle had inspired in her when she was a child. She had experienced Andrew's tantrums as though he were a reincarnation of this man: she could not stop him from coming between herself and her husband, who felt equally unable to assert himself. Many writers (e.g. Rosenfeld, 1971; Meltzer, 1973, 1992; O'Shaughnessy, 1981; Sohn, 1985; Steiner, 1982, 1987) have described the process by which parts of the self are located in various figures with which they are then identified—one reason for the resistance to change of the resulting narcissistic organization. In Andrew's case, there were additional transgenerational complications: his aggression had become confused with the aggression of one of his mother's internal figures. These circumstances must greatly have heightened Andrew's fear of the cold, destructive part of his personality, which no one seemed to be able to stand up to. Jackson (2004), writing about a child who was not on the autistic spectrum, has illustrated in detail how the absence of adequate boundaries can contribute to the growth of destructive narcissism.

This vignette illustrates the centrality of Andrew's revolt against Oedipal restrictions. It also illustrates how his ability to make contact increased through the realization that his attacks had not been successful: that he had not prevented the conception of the next baby. I would like to develop this line of thought by considering the importance of the balance between the place occupied by the developing child and the place he or she may imagine is occupied by central figures in the mother's mind. This balance, I believe, is crucial to the capacity to internalize experience, and therefore to the development of a sense of self that is based on relationships with others rather than on a narcissistic stance. I will illustrate this with material from work with Lina, a girl with a diagnosis of Asperger's syndrome who made extensive use of the mirror in the search for her own identity.

Lina: "I'm looking for myself"[2]

As Winnicott (1967) proposed in *The mirror role of mother and family in child development*, the baby derives its fundamental sense of existence and goodness from what it sees reflected in its mother's face: on that most basic of levels, we are what we see. If the mother's preoccupations intrude excessively for too much of the time, then these are what the baby will see in her face rather than himself. I shall suggest that this line of thought can usefully be combined with Melanie Klein's observation (1961) that small children tend to personify the mother's qualities. They think of these qualities as though they were literally people who lived inside the mother's body rather than more abstract properties of her mind and character. (For example, in *Narrative of a Child Analysis*, Klein's patient Richard wanted to turn off the glowing bar of an electric heater which had previously been understood in terms of the father's presence inside the mother. Once he had done so, the playroom felt dead to him (Klein 1961,

p. 46–49). The mother may be felt to contain a benign internal family that receives the child with love, or a hostile internal family that makes her into someone angry, or intrudes into his relationship with her and undermines his sense of self. This means that, if the mother is mentally preoccupied, the child can experience this as though she were physically occupied; if she is depressed, the child may feel that she is literally full of ghosts. This is of course unrealistic, and may sound like introducing unnecessary complications; but it is, as it were, the fairy-tale component of the way young children often interpret eye contact.

> Lina used a mirror very creatively to explore and communicate aspects of her sense of self. Since the mirror was an inanimate object that she could control, her reliance on it could in itself seem narcissistic. In fact, it served as a stepping-stone towards more direct contact, and allowed us to understand some of the reasons why this felt so dangerous to her. (While Winnicott [as well as Spitz (1955), Meltzer (1986), Haag (1985, 1991) and Wright (1991)] emphasized the developmental contribution of being seen by another, Lacan (1941) saw the mirror stage as the beginning of alienation. More recently, Britton (1998, p. 45) has quoted Sartre on the alienating gaze of the Other, and Steiner (2004) has described the destructive function of the gaze in relation to narcissism.) Sinason (1999) has described a similar useful function of the mirror with learning-disabled patients. Looking into a mirror need not be narcissistic, any more than was Narcissus's behaviour towards his own reflection. It is easy to forget that Narcissus pined away and died when his reflection did not respond to him; he declared his love to it as though it were another person, and as though he were a child who could not yet recognize his own reflection in the mirror. From this perspective, it is not so much that self-love made him turn away from other people as that his sense of identity was inadequately developed, leaving him without the necessary emotional equipment to sustain reciprocal relationships. Some 40 years ago, Lichtenstein (1964) pointed out the difference between being in love with oneself and being in love with one's reflection, and suggested that such a fascination with one's own mirror image was related to fundamental problems of identity. One need only

remember how Freud's grandson in *Beyond the Pleasure Principle* (Freud, 1920g) repeated his fort-da game with his own mirror reflection to realize that looking in the mirror can be object-related. Athanassiou (2006) has provided a fascinating discussion, from a psychoanalytic perspective, of the developmental studies on children's recognition of their mirror image, shadow and photographic image carried out by Fontaine (1992).

Lina had been echolalic and extremely withdrawn, but she improved to a gratifying extent during treatment. I began to work with her when she was six-and-a-half, following a family bereavement. Not surprisingly, she was inhibited by her confusion between growing by taking things in and by damaging other people. She maintained a narcissistic mode of relating in the sense that she usually ignored me. She either read for the whole 50 minutes unless I stopped her, or filled up the session by reproducing pictures she had seen in books or television programmes. Sometimes these were used communicatively, to help me to understand something about her; but often they were used as a means of feeling that she could be the source of everything she needed, and that it did not matter whether I was in the room or not.

Lina seemed quite clear that my qualities were a function of my internal occupants: she even brought along a plastic toy with a pregnant-looking stomach that could be rotated in order to change the expression in the eyes—from happy to sad to angry to surprised. In addition, she was preoccupied with the difference between the reflecting side of the mirror and its opaque wooden backing. She compared the wood to the door of the room which felt shut to her between appointments, and also to the wall, which she tried to run through with predictably painful results. In contrast, seeing herself reflected in the mirror seemed to feel like finding the doorway into my eyes and mind. She became capable of much more enduring eye contact, though she could still feel in danger of being engulfed, and habitually made rafts for the toy animals to save them from drowning in the sink and being eaten by the crocodile on the bottom.

I would read this as a vivid illustration of Lina's desperate, precariously balanced clinging to surfaces, and of her fear of dangerous depths in other people and in herself. However, she did manage to differentiate this version of a malign internal family from a helpful one that could provide support. This support was represented by the solid trunk of a pot plant on the draining board, on which the farm animals sought refuge so as not to drown. Lina tended to attack this plant, as though she felt it to be a rival that was always in my room; but gradually she began to want to look after it. It was as though she had come to value the enduring presence of an object that she had not been able to get rid of, and the solidity of which saved her from being engulfed, just as the presence of the father serves to regulate the distance between mother and child. She began to feel that it was possible to get through emotionally without destroying the solid paternal function and being sucked into the depths.

In parallel with these developments, Lina took courage to be naughty and rebellious, whereas previously she had had the fairy-like, somewhat unreal quality that is characteristic of some children on the autistic spectrum. She seemed initially to experience this unintegrated side of herself as though it were a double or alter ego, like Bion's (1950) imaginary twin. She had always been annoyed by the presence in a glass-fronted cupboard of some toys used by the colleague with whom I shared the room. She had similar toys of her own, but the fact that the ones in the cupboard were, as she put it, "not playable" understandably felt tantalizing and provocative, so that they became connected in her mind with my own supposed internal occupants. One day she took a mouthful of water after some play at the sink, and held it in her mouth without swallow-ing while she stood gazing into the cupboard. She swallowed, then became acutely distressed. She wailed, "My sister Flo—I'm look-ing for my sister Flo," and had to run to the lavatory. As I waited for her, it struck me that her panic had been triggered by the act of swallowing, as though she feared that it might have destructive consequences. She was still quite distraught when she emerged from the lavatory, and in the room went back to stand in front of the cupboard, talking about her sister Flo whom she could not see. I said to her that perhaps, when she felt annoyed about things in the cupboard or in me which she felt blocked her access, she might get muddled between the kind of taking in that she needed to do in order to grow, on the one hand; and, on the other, the effect of what she had previously called her angry "monster mouth". It might be hard then to feel that she had the right to keep the water inside her after swallowing, instead of letting everything "flow" (Flo) out of her. She calmed down, and went to look at herself in the mirror as though to reassure herself that she was still there. In the next session, she again swallowed a mouthful of water while standing in front of the cupboard, and I asked whether she was looking for her sister Flo. "No," she answered in an assured tone of voice, "I'm looking for myself." Addressing her hostile impulses towards my internal occupants allowed her to look for her own reflection without feeling that she had bitten them out of me (compare Tustin 1990a, p. 203). This meant that she could retain what she took in—the water, for example—and use it as a source of strength, instead of equating herself with me as someone that water "Flo'ed" out of.

Some weeks later, in a pivotal session, Lina developed the theme of her position relative to the mother's internal occupant:

Lina drew many little circles in different colours on the surface of the mirror. Previously, this had been in the context of wondering how babies were made: she had said that the circles were created by Mr. Green, Sir Blue, and so on. Now, she said, a bit defensively, "I'm only trying to make stained glass." I said that perhaps she thought stained glass looked lovely—all those colours with the light coming through—and that she was curious about how it was made, and would like to make some. In terms of her and me, this would be like feeling that it was she who elicited the expression—the colour—in my eyes when I looked at her—that it was important to feel that she could make something nice like that happen, instead of imagining that a baby inside me determined my expression, as seemed to be the case with her toy. She wiped the coloured circles off the mirror, and said, "It looks grey now," moving her hand furtively past her bottom as she threw the tissue in the bin. Wiping off the coloured circles, which did in fact get in the way of her own reflection, made her feel that my mirror-gaze was empty—depressed, grey, and messed up.

Now she drew a bull on the mirror, with angry-looking eyes, coloured in red as though it were bleeding, She turned the mirror over, and seemed to be trying to see herself in the wooden back. I commented that one couldn't see oneself in that side, but that perhaps she was also wondering whether that was where the picture of the bull came from. Then she held up the mirror at an angle to the window, and said, "Now the light is shining through." In fact, of course, it was not; but I said she was looking for a situation where the light could shine through, without being blocked by the picture: where there was room for life to go on behind my eyes in a way that encompassed her, and did not get in the way of room for her feelings.

Lina responded, "You can do something else, too." She took the mirror to the sink, and, balancing it carefully, filled it up to the rim of the frame with water, so that the picture of the bull was now beneath the surface. She bent over it, as though, again, she were looking for herself: this time, however, she said, "I can see myself." I agreed that the water was different from the mirror, because it had actual depth, so that the picture of the bull did not get in the way of her seeing herself reflected.

I would like to highlight two related issues: first, the position of the child in relation to the mother's internal occupant: second, the importance of depth within the mother which this occupant does not fill. (Early in treatment, Lina seemed to illustrate this when she meticulously arranged two calves face to face, one on a plate, one outside it, in such a way that they were equidistant from the rim.) Where this balance is right, the baby can bring his own qualities to engage with the mother's, as in developmental imitation (Rhode, 2005), without feeling either that his own vitality or aggression are causing damage (so that he is sucked into the depths where a crocodile waits for him), or that he will be crowded out or projected into by an internal occupant of the mother who lies, as it were, "too far forward". In a situation such as Lina managed to establish, the child's way in is not blocked: space is available for emotional containment, the light "shining through" makes the child feel that he can elicit a response, and, at the same time, the presence of the internal object means that the child is neither in danger of being engulfed nor of feeling responsible for an empty mother-figure. In other words, mother and child are both complete: they can evolve reciprocal interactions that the child can internalize. Because he has had the experience of not being crowded out of his mother's mind by her internal occupant, he can in turn take her in without feeling that doing so may crowd him out of his own mind; and in this way he can enrich his own personality in a way that is based on relationships instead of relying on a narcissistic stance.

Lina's ninth birthday, some weeks after this pivotal session, encouraged her to feel that she would one day be a woman who could herself have children, and to be more able to identify with me in that respect. In parallel with these developments, her hostility, including the anal attacks that had been hinted at in connection with the mirror's becoming grey, came more directly into her play and could be worked on. Equally, the fluctuations in her use of drawing, between narcissistic and communicative modes, became an explicit focus of the therapy and could be related meaningfully to breaks between sessions and during holidays.

This material suggests, I think, that Lina's narcissistic withdrawal and attempts at self-sufficiency had the aim of protecting her from the feared consequences of her own aggression, whether expressed as attacks against the "father" plant or as the angry devouring of a rival who was felt to inhabit me (her sister Flo) (These fears would of course have been aggravated by the family bereavement.) Along similar lines, Hamilton (1982) has suggested that the narcissistic adolescent has often lacked a strong father and therefore has difficulty in freeing himself from the way his doting mother perceives him.

After a session when she had been more than usually withdrawn following a break in treatment, she drew a fantasy creature with spirals in his eyes, whose name, she said, was Swirly. Looking straight at me, she said, "He hypnotizes people." I said that she needed to be sure that I would not hypnotize her, so that she lost a will of her own and was sucked into my eyes; and that, when she was frightened of this, she allowed herself instead to be hypnotized by a part of her own personality that lured her into the world of fantastical drawings and away from contact with me. In other words, the narcissistic part of her was based on the damaged mother figure by whom she was afraid of being engulfed.

Anthony: Identification with a narcissistic couple[3]

I would now like to discuss some material from the treatment of Anthony, a boy whose autistic spectrum disorder was much more severe and intractable than Lina's. Like her, Anthony was faced with loss he was unable to cope with. However, while she allowed herself to be hypnotized by a part of her personality modelled on an engulfing mother whose internal occupants had been eliminated, he was dominated by a cruel narcissistic part based on a sadistic fantastic father figure, which actively enjoyed killing off his own capacities.

Anthony was referred urgently at the age of six because he was attacking other children. He was described as intelligent, and he was capable of speaking emotionally, indeed poetically. Before the first Christmas break, he drew the curtains: "Dark," he said, "dark, dark, dark. No more lady, never, never, never." However, most of the time he was unreachably withdrawn, and produced mutilated bits of words and sentences in voices not his own; as though, like Andrew, he were truly not being allowed to "speak in words". The voices included that of the cruel Giant from *Jack and the Beanstalk*, who threatened to devour him; and also a caricatured version of a mother who seemed to be humouring him rather than taking him seriously—a voice that he called "cruel Mummy". He constantly repeated what seemed to be catastrophic birth sequences such as Winnicott (1949) and Tustin (1981a) have described, in which he let himself fall off the desk, struggling to reach the safety of a chair. As he did so, his mouth was twisted into a painful, lopsided shape, and he clutched the drawstring of his trousers as though he thought it could support him. He looked tortured, and in turn he inflicted tortures on the plastic toy animals, whose muzzles, hooves, ears and tails he cut off. Although they pleaded, "Please don't do this to me," he habitually continued until I stopped him. At such moments, his cruelty seemed to involve identification with two aggressors— a cruel Giant father who actively inflicted these torments, and an impervious mother who took no notice.

I should emphasize that these meaningful sequences occurred quite rarely: most of the time Anthony was unreachable. His preferred position was on a table, high above me, where he either muttered in the Giant's voice or reassured himself in the robotic voice of a computer: "Those-answers-are-all-correct. You-are-a-genius." At the same time, his balance was uncertain, and I had to take care to make sure that he did not fall. The gulf seemed unbridgeable between the helpless, traumatized infant and the sadistic, narcissistic bully.

Anthony appeared to share many of the catastrophic anxieties that Tustin (1972, 1986a,b) and others (e.g. Haag, 1985) have described in children with autism. These include falling, having a damaged mouth, and losing parts of the body. He behaved as though these anxieties had been caused by an actively cruel father and an impervious mother, whom he seemed to experience as though they were mirror images of each other and formed a narcissistic "unit" that had eyes for no-one else. For example, he tipped a toy cow forward so that it stood on its muzzle on the mirror, and, pointing to the reflection, he said, "Mummy and Daddy". When he ignored me, he seemed to be identified with this narcissistic parental unit; and indeed he would enact being his mother on the telephone— "Yes, all right, darling"—or a performer singing into a microphone that he held as though it were a mirror and he were receiving the adulation of an adoring public. Alternatively, as I have mentioned, he tormented the toy animals as though he were at the same time a cruel father and an impervious mother; or he tormented me by mutilating the dolls, arranged inside the shut dolls' house as though they were my family. He would follow this up by physically attacking his own head, as though demonstrating the equivalence between his own mental capacities and my supposed internal occupants. Similarly, he might play at setting fire to the house, gloating at the dolls' ineffectual struggles to escape, and then lurch about the room grimacing and laughing madly, muttering fragments of words as though his sanity and his capacity for thought and speech had been literally incinerated along with my family.

I hoped it might be possible to use the mirror as a third object that could reassure Anthony about making eye contact, so I tried to play at "finding" him by catching his eye in the mirror. Usually this did not work: it seemed that Anthony felt too insecure to tolerate my reflection in the mirror alongside his. It was as though he himself, together with his reflection, had to constitute the mutually-adoring, twin-like, mirror-image parental couple, whose preoccupation with each other left no room for my existence to be recognized. He may well have expected any intruding third person to be hostile and dangerous. However, one day when he was feeling more robust, he did allow my reflection in the mirror alongside his, so that I could catch his eye. Smiling with pleasure, he said, "Hullo mirror." Unlike Lina, he did not seem to think of me as a human mirror, someone who could reflect him and reflect on him: instead, I seemed to be in the role of a rival—like her sister Flo—competing with him for the mirror's reflecting surface, much as Britton (2003b) has recently described in *Narcissistic problems in sharing space*. But on this occasion, when he did feel able briefly to tolerate another face in the mirror, he appeared to be liberated for a moment from his imprisonment in sterile narcissism, and he found his voice to speak to the mirror as though it had human qualities. It is as though the narcissistic couple who were mirror-images of each other had become a couple that provided space for a child. Briefly, the growing part of Anthony escaped from its usual condition of mutilation, and so did the words he was able to produce.

Gradually, Anthony began to be able to use the mirror to fulfil its proper function—to provide information about himself rather than to confirm that he existed. One of the things that most held his attention was moving the mirror away from his face and back closer to it while making terrifying grimaces. He seemed to be experimenting with getting the right distance to a monstrous part of himself, and trying to establish where it was located. It was as though he were concerned with differentiating between his own active cruelty and the cruel Giant figure by whom he felt excluded and in danger of being mutilated. Like Lina when she referred to her monster mouth, Anthony seems to have felt responsible for the state of the mother figure he was so frightened of losing ("no more lady"). Again as with Lina, the narcissistic part that held Anthony in thrall was modelled on a figure of whom he was frightened. However, with Lina this was a damaged mother figure by whom she was frightened of being engulfed; with Anthony, it was the sadistic father figure who enjoyed inflicting tortures on him.

As I have suggested, the effect of these narcissistic devices on the countertransference can be complex, particularly where the child does not have the opportunity to divide the narcissistic and growing aspects of himself between two therapists as Andrew did during his assessment. I was often submerged in despair, particularly when I compared Anthony's habitual behaviour with what I knew him to be capable of; and it could be difficult to believe that this despair was a communication, not just an appropriate response to the realistic situation. I also came to realize how easily any step forward could disappear by the next session as though it had never been; and not only in Anthony's mind, but in mine as well. Partly, no doubt, this was Anthony's narcissistic organization reasserting itself after every break, no matter how minor; but partly I think it was also an indication of the degree to which I had actually become a "cruel Mummy"

THE LOST CHILD   35

who did not notice what was happening, whether it was a terrible event or an important development. This easily turned into a vicious circle in which hopelessness ground me down to such an extent that I became incapable of doing justice either to faint indications of promising developments or to the full degree of the cruel Giant's destructiveness. It was as though Anthony's narcissistic organization had hypnotized me as well as himself. This lack of energy in his therapist was bound to leave Anthony even more at the mercy of the narcissistic part of his personality.

The first step in breaking out of this vicious circle, not surprisingly, had to be made in terms of my own attitude, by "working through in the countertransference" (Brenman Pick, 1985). I realized that I was not obliged to continue indefinitely with a treatment that did not seem to be getting anywhere, and that I could consult with colleagues and with Anthony's school to make sure that, in the event of my stopping work with him, others would be alert to any indication of his becoming more of a danger to other children. In fact, as soon as I had come to this conclusion—as I thought later, as soon as I had freed myself somewhat from feeling hopelessly dominated by his destructive part and uniquely responsible for protecting his good self which was being held hostage—Anthony became far more communicative. He began to enact a conflict: both his burning feelings of aggression against any rivals, and also his attempts to keep these feelings from bursting out. Often he would fall asleep, as though, like Lina, he were being hypnotized to turn away from human contact; there seemed to be a sparing component in this sleeping, much like the sparing component of suicide as described by Klein (1935), since he resumed his aggressive activities as soon as he woke up. At the same time, he was fully aware of the destructive aspect of falling asleep, and several times said "I was dead" after being awakened. He was very obviously engaged in the therapy, and there could be no question of stopping at that point. Instead, I felt able to address his cruelty more firmly, and also to remind him of times in the past when he had shown me the other side of him.

Recently, after a cancelled session, he rushed to the therapy room, all the while growling loudly in the Giant's voice. I said that I thought he was really glad to be back and was in a hurry to get started, and that, at the same time, he was furious with me for having cancelled his appointment. Somewhat to my amazement, he answered, in an ordinary voice, "You're right." This did not prevent him from going to sleep quite soon afterwards; but he stirred spontaneously, without my having to wake him, and said, very softly, "I awake." I answered, equally softly, that he wanted to stay awake, and to talk to me, and felt perhaps that he had to tell me very quietly so that the Giant should not hear. On that occasion he succeeded in staying awake for the rest of the time. It remains to be seen how far it may be possible to encompass the good and the destructive parts of himself at the same time, as Lina is beginning to manage: how far there may be room in the mirror, as it were, for both Anthony's good and bad selves.

Concluding remarks

In summary, then, conflicts surrounding the Oedipal constellation—which Lina and Anthony seemed to hold responsible for their own sense of endangered existence—appeared to be central to all three children's narcissistic retreats. While all were trying to circumvent the fear of having irreparably damaged a mother figure, sadistic enjoyment was more prominent in Andrew and Anthony than in Lina. Andrew's case provides an illustration of a narcissistic gang leader who imposes autistic mutism as part of withdrawal from relationships; Anthony, who started from a position of seeking to protect himself against an experience of trauma, appeared to relish the cruelty he enacted, and this aggressive narcissism made it difficult to sustain progress. Interestingly, the idea that extreme distress and helplessness are associated with thin-skinned rather than with thick-skinned narcissism does not seem to be borne out in Anthony's case: what is striking with him is the extreme contrast between the helpless baby and the narcissistic bully. This degree of unintegration is, in my experience, often seen in children with autism, perhaps more so than in those narcissistic patients who do not have a diagnosis of autistic spectrum disorder.

Both Lina and Anthony were in thrall to a narcissistic part of their personality that appeared to be modelled on what they most feared—a damaged, hollow, engulfing mother in Lina's case, and a sadistic, traumatizing father in Anthony's. Anthony experienced the parental couple as sterile, narcissistic mirror images of each other who left no room for the child, and in turn he identified with them, leaving no room either for me or for the growing part of his own personality. In contrast, Lina increasingly became able to establish the right distance vis-à-vis the mother's internal object, so that she could internalize it without feeling crowded out of her own mind. In this way it became more possible for her to relinquish a narcissistic stance in favour of basing her development on relationships with others, and to identify with me as a woman who could have children.

Notes

1. I am grateful to Graham Shulman for permission to refer to his clinical material.
2. Some of the material in this section has previously been discussed in a different theoretical context (Rhode, 2005, 2008, and is reproduced by kind permission of the *Journal of Child Psychotherapy* and Taylor & Francis, and of Kate Barrows and Karnac Books.
3. Some of the material in this section was previously published elsewhere (Rhode 1999, 2001) and is reproduced by kind permission of Brunner Routledge.

References

Abraham, K. (1919). A particular form of neurotic resistance against the psychoanalytic method. In: D. Bryan & A. Strachey (Trans.), *Selected Papers of Karl Abraham*. London: Hogarth, 1973.

Alvarez, A. (1999). Addressing the deficit: developmentally informed psychotherapy with passive, "undrawn" children. In: A. Alvarez. & S. Reid (Eds.), *Autism and Personality*. London: Routledge.

Athanassiou, C. (2006). *Représentation et Miroir*. Paris: Popesco.

Balint, M. (1968). Freud's three theories. In: *The Basic Fault: Therapeutic Aspects of Regression*. London: Tavistock.

Baron-Cohen, S. (1988). Social and pragmatic deficits in autism: cognitive or affective? *Journal of Autism and Developmental Disorders, 18*: 3.

Bick, E. (1964). Notes on infant observation in psychoanalytic training. In: A. Briggs (Ed.), *Surviving Space: Papers on Infant Observation*. London: Karnac, 2002.

Bion, W.R. (1950). The imaginary twin. In: *Second Thoughts*. London: Heinemann, 1967.

Brenman Pick, I. (1985). Working through in the counter-transference. In: Spillius, E.B. (Ed.), *Melanie Klein Today: 2: Mainly Practice*. London: Routledge, 1988.

Britton, R. (1998). Subjectivity, objectivity and triangular space. In: *Belief and Imagination*. London: Routledge.

Britton, R. (2003a). Narcissism and narcissistic disorders. In: *Sex, Death and the Superego*. London: Karnac.

Britton, R. (2003b). Narcissistic problems in sharing space. In *Sex, Death and the Superego*. London: Karnac.

Fontaine, A.M. (1992). *L'Enfant et son Image*. Paris: Nathan.

Freud, S. (1905d). *Three Essays on the Theory of Sexuality*. S.E., 7. London: Hogarth.

Freud, S. (1914c). On narcissism: an introduction. S.E., 14. London: Hogarth.

Freud, S. (1920g). *Beyond the Pleasure Principle*. S.E., 18. London: Hogarth.

Frith, U. (2004). Confusions and controversies about Asperger's Syndrome. *Journal of Child Psychology and Psychiatry*, 45: 672–86.

Haag, G. (1985). La mère et le bébé dans les deux moitiés du corps. *Neuropsychiatrie de l'Enfance*, 33: 107–14.

Haag, G. (1991). Nature de quelques identifications dans l'image du corps (hypothèses). *Journal de la Psychanalyse de l'Enfant*, 4: 73–92.

Hamilton, V. (1982). *Narcissus and Oedipus: The Children of Psychoanalysis*. London: Routledge & Kegan Paul. Second edition, London: Karnac, 1993.

Hobson, P. (2002). *The Cradle of Thought*. Basingstoke: Macmillan.

Jackson, J. (2004). The indulged child. Paper presented as part of the lecture series on *Narcissism Throughout the Life Cycle*, Institute of Psychoanalysis, London, 4 December.

Klein, M. (1930). The importance of symbol formation in the development of the ego. In: *The Writings of Melanie Klein, 1*. London: Hogarth, 1975.

Klein, M. (1935). A contribution to the psychogenesis of manic-depressive states. In: *The Writings of Melanie Klein, 1*. London: Hogarth, 1975.

Klein, M. (1961). *Narrative of a Child Analysis*. In: *The Writings of Melanie Klein, 4*. London: Hogarth, 1975.

Kohut, H. (1971). *The Analysis of the Self*. New York: International Universities Press.

Kohut, H. (1977). *The Restoration of the Self*. New York: International Universities Press.

Lacan, J. (1949). Le stade du miroir comme formateur de la fonction du Je. In: *Écrits*. Paris: Éditions du Seuil, 1966.

Lichtenstein, H. (1964). The role of narcissism in the emergence and maintenance of a primary identity. *International Journal of Psychoanalysis*, 45: 49–56.

Mahler, M. (1961). On sadness and grief in infancy and childhood: loss and restoration of the symbiotic love object. *Psychoanalytic Study of the Child*, 16.

Meltzer, D. (1973). *Sexual States of Mind*. Strathtay, Perthshire: Clunie.

Meltzer, D. (1975). The psychology of autistic states and post-autistic mentality. In: Meltzer, D., Bremner, J., Hoxter, S., Weddell, D. & Wittenberg, I., *Explorations in Autism*. Strathtay, Perthshire: Clunie.

Meltzer, D. (1986). On the perception of one's own attributes. In: *Studies in Extended Metapsychology*. Strathtay, Perthshire: Clunie.

Meltzer, D. (1992). *The Claustrum*. Strathtay, Perthshire: Clunie.

Meltzer, D., Bremner, J., Hoxter, S., Weddell, D. & Wittenberg, I. (1975). *Explorations in Autism*. Strathtay, Perthshire: Clunie.

O'Shaughnessy, E. (1981). A clinical study of a defensive organization. *International Journal of Psychoanalysis*, 62: 359–369. Also in E.B. Spillius (Ed.), *Melanie Klein Today, 1: Mainly Theory*. London: Routledge, 1988.

Rhode, M. (1999). Echo or answer? Towards the development of ordinary speech in three children with autistic spectrum disorder. In: A. Alvarez & S. Reid (Eds.), *Autism and Personality*. London: Routledge.

Rhode, M. (2001). The sense of abundance in relation to technique. In: J. Edwards (Ed.), *Being Alive: Building on the Work of Anne Alvarez*. London: Brunner Routledge.

Rhode, M. (2004). Different responses to trauma in two children with autistic spectrum disorder: the mouth as crossroads for the sense of self. *Journal of Child Psychotherapy*, 30: 3–20.

Rhode, M. (2005). Mirroring, imitation, identification: the sense of self in relation to the mother's internal world. *Journal of Child Psychotherapy*, 31: 52–71.

Rhode, M. (2008). Joining the human family. In: K. Barrows (Ed.), *Autism in Childhood and Autistic Features in Adults*. Psychoanalytic Ideas Series. London: Karnac.

Rosenfeld, H. (1971). A clinical approach to the psychoanalytic theory of the life and death instincts: an investigation into the aggressive aspects of narcissism. *International Journal of Psychanalysis, 52*: 169–178. Also in E.B. Spillius (Ed.), *Melanie Klein Today, 1: Mainly Theory.* London: Routledge, 1988.

Rosenfeld, H. (1987). Afterthought. In: *Impasse and Interpretation.* London: Tavistock.

Shulman, G. (1998). Andrew: psychoanalytic psychotherapy with an autistic child. In: D. Syder (Ed.), *'Wanting to Talk': Counselling Case Histories in Communication Disorders.* London: Whurr.

Sinason, V. (1999). Psychoanalysis and mental handicap: experience from the Tavistock Clinic. In: J. DeGroef & E. Heinemann (Eds.), *Psychoanalysis and Mental Handicap.* London: Free Association.

Sohn, L. (1985). Narcissistic organization, projective identification, and the formation of the identificate. *International Journal of Psychoanalysis, 66*: 201–213. Also in E.B. Spillius (Ed.), *Melanie Klein Today. 1: Mainly Theory.* London: Routledge, 1988.

Spitz, R. (1955). The primal cavity. *Psychoanalytic Study of the Child, 10*: 215–240.

Steiner, J. (1982). Perverse relationships between parts of the self: a clinical illustration. *International Journal of Psychoanalysis, 63*: 241–251. Also in: *Psychic Retreats* (Chapter 9). London: Routledge, 1993.

Steiner, J. (1987). The interplay between pathological organizations and the paranoid-schizoid and depressive positions. *International Journal of Psychoanalysis, 68*: 69–80. Also in E.B. Spillius (Ed.), *Melanie Klein Today, 1: Mainly Theory.* London: Routledge, 1988.

Steiner, J. (2004). Gaze, dominance and humiliation in the Schreber case. *International Journal of Psychoanalysis, 85*: 269–84.

Stern, D. (1985). *The Interpersonal World of the Infant.* New York: Basic.

Stolorow, D. & Lachman, F.M. (1986). A functional definition of narcissism. In: *Psychoanalysis of Developmental Arrests: Theory and Treatment.* New York: International Universities Press.

Trevarthen, C. (2001). Intrinsic motives for companionship in understanding: their origin, development, and significance for infant mental health. *Infant Mental Health Journal, 22*: 95–131.

Tustin, F. (1972). *Autism and Childhood Psychosis.* London: Hogarth.

Tustin, F. (1981). *Autistic States in Children,* London: Routledge [Second revised edition, 1992].

Tustin, F. (1981a). Psychological birth and psychological catastrophe. In: *Autistic States in Children.* London: Routledge [Second revised edition, 1992]. Also in: J.S. Grotstein (Ed.), *Do I Dare Disturb the Universe?* Beverly Hills: Caesura Press, 1981.

Tustin, F. (1986a). Falling. In: *Autistic Barriers in Neurotic Patients.* London: Karnac [Second revised edition, 1994].

Tustin, F. (1986b). Spilling and dissolving. In: *Autistic Barriers in Neurotic Patients.* London: Karnac [Second revised edition, 1994].

Tustin, F. (1986c). The growth of understanding. In: *Autistic Barriers in Neurotic Patients.* London: Karnac [Second revised edition, 1994].

Tustin, F. (1990). *The Protective Shell in Children and Adults.* London: Karnac.

Tustin, F. (1990a). Being born from the autistic shell: becoming part of a group. In: *The Protective Shell in Children and Adults.* London: Karnac.

Winnicott, D.W. (1949). Birth memories, birth trauma and anxiety. In: *Through Paediatrics to Psycho-Analysis.* London: Hogarth, 1958.

Winnicott, D.W. (1967). The mirror role of mother and family in child development. In: *Playing and Reality.* London: Tavistock, 1971.

Wittenberg, I. (1975). Primal depression in autism—John. In: Meltzer, D., Bremner, J., Hoxter, S., Weddell, D. & Wittenberg, I., *Explorations in Autism.* Strathtay, Perthshire: Clunie.

Wright, K. (1991). *Vision and Separation: Between Mother and Baby.* London: Free Association.

PART II

ADOLESCENCE

CHAPTER THREE

Dying to live: Mourning, melancholia and the adolescent process

Caroline Polmear

Introduction

In this paper I will explore the idea that adolescent development in the "normal" young person involves successful mourning, while disturbed, or failed, adolescent development more closely resembles the process of melancholia. In the two troubled adolescents I will describe, the adolescent process has produced a "diseased" superego (Freud, 1917) and crippling psychiatric compromises. In both cases the young person has failed, at the point of beginning treatment, to give up and mourn the parental attachments of childhood and has instead incorporated them into his and her final sexual organisation, or adult sexual identity.

Freud's paper *Mourning and Melancholia* has a poignant history very relevant to my theme. Before and during the First World War he was excitedly involved in writing a new book on metapsychology, some ten to 12 chapters long. In his letters he speaks of it with conviction, aware of its importance. Gay (1988) reports that in June 1915 Freud wrote to Ferenczi: "True, I am working morosely, yet steadily. Ten of the 12 articles are ready. Two of them, however in need of revision." The following month he wrote to Lou Andreas-Salomé that the "fruit" of these months would "probably be a book consisting of 12 essays, introduced by a chapter on drives and their fortunes". He added that "it has just been finished except for the necessary reworking". A year passed and references to it show some doubts. He suggests that the war is not the time to publish. To publish what? Something dealing so frankly with man's destructiveness, with the death instinct? We can only speculate. Or was the hesitation due to the beginnings of doubt and unease about his theory of drives? What we do know is that after the war Freud destroyed at least seven of the chapters. The book was never published. In 1923 *The Ego and the Id* set out a whole new theory of the mind. One of the surviving chapters of the original metapsychology book was published in 1917 as the paper *Mourning and Melancholia*. It seems that with a struggle, Freud had managed to detach himself from an old identity, an old beloved theory, and move on to something new. He had been able to leave behind a part of himself in which he had had a great investment, and had survived, moving forward with creativity and hope through uncertainty towards a new and greater synthesis.

Rather than give a full review of the paper *Mourning and Melancholia*, I would like to highlight some of the points Freud makes in it which I think are particularly salient when we are thinking about adolescence. There are some important new ideas in this paper all of which are relevant to understanding the adolescent process.

Freud gives us a beautiful and enduring description of the mourning process. The person who has lost a loved one revisits each aspect of their relationship with that person, reliving in memory and feeling their love for that particular feature of them or that special time with them. By revisiting each aspect of the relationship with the lost object, painfully, bit by bit, the object is relinquished, given up.

A comparison between mourning and melancholia reveals that melancholia resembles mourning symptomatically, in being marked by loss of interest in the outside world, persistent low spirits and indifference to work and love. But beyond that similarity the melancholic suffers from continual self-reproach, low-self esteem, and in a delusional way anticipates some sort of punishment. The melancholic endlessly and loudly describes himself as morally reprehensible. Thus while his symptoms resemble the symptoms of mourning, there are differences. He has lost an object to which he remains attached by being in identification with that object. On closer examination, we discover that the object was not only loved by the melancholic, but was also hated by him. In taking the lost object into himself by identification, he begins to hate and rage against a part of his own ego, that part identified with the lost object. So one part of the ego sets itself up in judgement and hatred of another part, which results in self-hatred and self-torment. Instead of railing against the object, he rails against himself; instead of separating from and giving up the object of his ambivalent feelings, the melancholic has remained attached by becoming the object himself. That way, as Freud so poetically put it, "love escapes extinction".

Four important new theoretical and clinical developments arise from this comparison between mourning and melancholia. First, he introduces the idea of a separate part of the ego, split off and judging. At this stage he has no special name for it, but likens it to what people call conscience. It is to become the superego in later writing. He speaks about ways in which the superego can be "diseased" (Freud, 1917: p. 247). As I will describe below, the role of the superego is particularly important in adolescent development.

Secondly, Freud begins to focus more than ever before on the destructive power of aggression. Of particular interest and importance is his account of suicide as a supremely aggressive object-related act. As we know, in later work Freud elevates aggression into a drive ranking with libido. It is in this paper that we begin to see that shift in his thinking. His observation that it is the strength of the aggression towards the object that determines the melancholic reaction is brilliantly insightful.

Thirdly, he examines the nature of identification as a preliminary stage of object choice, in which the ego incorporates the object into itself. In a particular way the person becomes like the lost object. In this paper he describes the way in which an object cathexis, or an attachment to someone, is replaced by an identification. Later, in 'The Ego and the Id', he extends this idea beyond melancholia and describes it as a common process which goes to make up a person's character. Identification is a valuable keystone in understanding character at all stages of development, but has special significance when thinking about adolescence, as I will describe later.

Finally, he helps us to think about the difference between hysteria and melancholia. Although he only devotes a few lines to it in this paper, we see the beginning of a distinction which is vital clinically;

this was certainly important in helping me to understand the second patient I will describe.

The developmental tasks of adolescence

Adolescence begins at puberty. With the maturing of his or her body, every young person faces an enormous psychological task. By the end of adolescence, one could say that a young man or woman has moved from living in a child's body to living in an adult's body, now sexually mature and physically as strong as his parents. The psychological adjustment is complex and we know a lot about it because it so often goes wrong (Laufer & Laufer, 1984).

As a child the boy or girl is dependent, essentially passive in relation to the parents' care and wishes. During adolescence the young person has to achieve an active position, responsible for his or her own care and management. The young person must become active in relation to their family, friends and the wider community. They must feel independent and responsible without being overwhelmed by anxiety.

At the same time as moving from passive to active, they have to integrate the upsurge of genital sexual and adult aggressive impulses that come with the changes of puberty. As children, their loving and hating feelings are felt mostly in relation to parents and siblings. During adolescence they need to detach themselves from family as love objects and look outwards towards people outside the family. Failure to do any or all of these tasks is at the heart of adolescent breakdown.

The role of the superego in adolescent development is crucial. With the onset of puberty and increase in sexual and aggressive wishes, the young person is faced with the impossibility of being primarily attached to parents and siblings and of living up to parental ideals. The loving and hating attachments to their family were normal and acceptable as children, but now that they are sexually mature they must cause a conflict or incestuous relationships would result. The adolescent is impelled to turn away from the parents and siblings and look outside to find new objects of their affections. This is where peer groups become so essentially important. Yet, in turning away from the parents' ideals and adopting those of their peer group—an essential step in the process—young people can feel that they are attacking their parents and that they may lose their parents' love.

Not only do young people have to detach from parents as love objects, they also have to detach themselves internally from the parents' ideals, now firmly established as their own childhood ideals in the form of the superego. In early adolescence we see a succession of ideal loves come and go—pop stars, footballers, film stars—and a parallel succession of ideological positions, philosophies and ideals that are passionately held. The exaggerated attractiveness of the stars can rival the regressive pull back to the old incestuous love objects, holding the young person's libidinal attention safely outside the family and helping them in their move forward towards independence. The passionately held ideas seem to be part of the attempt to detach from the internalized parental ideals and find a temporary alternative by which young people can judge themselves. Although in the longer term the content of the superego does not change very much from that formed during the resolution of the Oedipus Complex in childhood, over time it does become more general and less personal. From the young person's point of view it is no longer simply a matter of "what Mummy and Daddy want me to do and be", but rather "my own standards of behaviour".

During adolescence the childhood superego needs to be temporarily suspended or rivalled in order that the young person may turn away from parents towards the external world. Moses Laufer (1964) suggests that in adolescence the ego ideal plays a particularly significant part in this process. So what is the ego ideal in adolescence? Temporary identifications derived from living up to the expectations of one's peers are felt to be equivalent to internal superego expectations and demands. It is for this reason that friends become so vitally important during adolescence. Being accepted as normal and part of a peer group, sharing the same views and beliefs and having the same tastes, lends the adolescent a temporary ego ideal which can help maintain equilibrium and feeling well enough loved while shifting allegiance away from parents to those outside the family.

The struggles and fights with parents of the ordinarily progressing adolescent will be a sign of the process of giving up the oedipal and pre-oedipal parents or, to put it another way, the parents of their childhood. Fights about who controls the young person's body, what time they should come home and who they should spend their time with, represent the need to take control of themselves and to not give in to their own wish to submit passively to their parents. The fight against parents may well be a fight against the young person's own wish to regress rather than go forward. Rows which suggest that the young person is really shouting at the parent of themselves at two, rather than at the parent of a 14-year-old trying to keep up, keep them safe and do their best for their child, are common. It seems that the young person is successfully mourning, as Freud so beautifully describes in the paper, by singling out each aspect of the object, revisiting it, then letting it go. The relationship with the mother of the two-year-old self must be revisited and given up if the young adult is to be able to move to a new relationship with the mother of the present.

In this way adolescence is characterized by a forward and backward struggle. The push forward comes from the need to detach oneself from the potentially incestuous love and hate objects now that the young person has a physically fully mature body capable of sexual intercourse and violent aggression which could kill or damage another. The terror of incest or patricide serves as a healthy push forward. Regressive pulls, on the other hand, come from the need to mourn and give up the childhood love objects by revisiting them and letting them go. So a young person who one moment is surprisingly babyish, resorting to their favourite teddy, and the next moment is slamming doors in objection to restrictions placed on them by their parents, is probably doing quite well.

In early and mid-adolescence young people most fear not being able to make the necessary moves forward and getting stuck in a state of regression, and thereby remaining passive in relation to parents and others. The adolescent ego ideal is important here; it sets the standard by which the young person judges the normality of his progress. The standards set are those of the peer group with which the young person identifies, and in this way he or she detaches and distances their self from the parents and their standards as laid down in the superego.

I think it is relevant to mention bullying here. Bullying is a process by which we find in someone else the very thing we are anxious about in ourselves. In the other we hate it and try to eradicate it. In a boys' secondary school, for example, the bullied one might be accused of babyishness and dependence on mother, or of having feminine characteristics, such as being fat. They might be accused of being literally "mother-fuckers", expressing very directly the fear of incest. The bullied boy may be a passive type who represents the feared and not yet relinquished passivity of childhood. He may be accused of being gay, representing the bully's own fears of his gay feelings and anxiety that in him things are not developing as he would like. And so on. It seems that the adolescent peer group, so vital to normal development, can easily resort to this form of getting rid of anxiety, particularly within institutions where there is a hidden culture of bullying to enforce rules.

So far I have been talking about the normal development of the adolescent, the need to detach oneself from both parents as love objects and from the superego of one's childhood self which represents parental standards and demands and feels like an internal embodiment of the parents. It goes without saying that the adolescent who has failed at the oedipal stage to give up their idealized position in relation to the parental couple will have more difficulty during adolescence. I hope it is clear that a capacity to mourn, in the sense of re-cathecting and then relinquishing early childhood objects, is crucial to successful progress through this eventful stage of development. We know from our work with adults that failure during adolescence to separate internally from the parents of our childhood results in permanent emotional difficulties in adult relationships.

I will turn to the difficulties encountered when a young person either loses the struggle to move forward healthily or is forced to make compromises which prove emotionally disabling in adulthood. I will be likening these failures in development to Freud's notion of melancholia in the sense that rather than give up the loved and hated object of one's childhood affection, a compromise is found whereby the oedipal or pre-oedipal parents retain their internal position and become incorporated into the young person's adult sexual identity and sexual life. Freud's observation that the strength of the hatred is what makes it difficult to give up the infantile objects is a crucial clinical observation.

Clinical illustration: Gavin

The clinical case that follows is one that I supervised. Gavin sought help from the Student Counselling Unit at the university where he was studying for a PhD in Social Psychology. At 27 he was unable to finish his thesis despite being told that it was good enough and only needed tidying up. This situation had gone on for nearly 18 months. He also reported an uneasy feeling that he had always made up stories about himself and his life, and that he no longer thought they were true. He experienced a lack of authentic feelings and felt he was living life at second hand. He appeared to be a calm, well adjusted young man, every inch the aesthetic academic dressed in cord trousers and a check shirt. His counsellor found herself noticing that he wore heavy black boots which seemed out of keeping with his mild manners and unremarkable regulation academic dress. In describing him the word "harmless" came to mind.

In his sessions he found himself going back, time and again, to his experiences at secondary school and he wondered why he was talking about it so much. A picture of an unresolved adolescent struggle began to emerge.

Soon after puberty Gavin's sexual feelings towards men convinced him that he was "gay". Fearful of acting on his realization and despising himself as a result, he did nothing. However in his reports of life at school, he spoke of various boys who fancied *him*. He particularly dwelt on the fact that one especially popular and macho senior boy, Simon, became obsessed with him, wanting to sleep with him. He maintained a fiction conforming to the mores of his peer group that he was heterosexual but simply had not got as far as the other boys who bragged about their adventures with girls. A crisis came however during his first year at university. He bumped into an old school friend quite by chance. Over a beer, this young man told him of all the things he was doing and came to the point where he announced that he had his first girlfriend and was now no longer a virgin. Gavin felt himself panic inside but dealt with his crisis by swapping fictitious girlfriend stories, which he told so amusingly and elaborately that he even began to believe them himself.

Gavin buried himself in his work and went on to a higher degree. His studies took him abroad to South America where he had his first sexual encounter. He got very drunk in a bar and left with a man he had become friendly with during the evening. In a drunken state he allowed this man, who turned out to be an undercover secret policeman, to have sex with him. His phrase was "I allowed sex to be performed on me". After this it seems that the flood gates opened on his sexuality and he became highly promiscuous, often with friends of the original policeman who were also members of the secret police. A year later he was thrown out of the country. At first he maintained that he did not know why he had been thrown out, assuming that it was for political reasons, a fiction which made his father rather proud of him. However it gradually became clear to him during counselling that it was actually brought about by these dangerous undercover sexual activities. Gavin in effect got himself thrown out of the country because of his gay activities with policemen while persuading himself that it was because of his politics.

Discussion

How can we understand Gavin's difficulties and the solutions he found? Adolescence confronted him with a situation which made him unacceptable to his own superego and unlovable to his conventional parents. He was "gay". His own survival now became paramount. Pressure to be like his peers required him to be heterosexual. He created a pseudo ego ideal to offer to the superego instead of showing his real self or committing suicide. He created a narrative of his life as if he were the ideal that his father would have wanted him to be, thus staying attached and submissive towards a hated father. To maintain this fiction he had to project all his sexual and aggressive wishes out into others. He remembered his school experience as horrible, and to explain this horribleness he relied on descriptions of all those macho boys who fancied him. His ego ideal said: "Look at those apparently normal young men with this surprising flaw—they are gay and they fancy me." He had safely evacuated the damaging information about his own desires into those who fancied him. However, a breakthrough of anxiety came at night in a recurring dream. Gavin regularly dreamt of himself as a zombie, trapped in a house with other zombies, terrified to go outside for fear of nameless bad and frightening things out there. Having projected his sexual and aggressive wishes outside he was empty and "zombiefied while the world of those holding his projections had become too frightening to venture into. Real contact with other young people became more and more impossible in case they recognised that they were relating to a fictional character.

As Gavin entered young adulthood he was unable to resist his sexual wishes and found an ingenious solution by which he tried to continue to cheat his superego. He offered himself for sexual inter-course to a man who in a way represented a superego, a policeman, and through the promiscuous behaviour which followed he ensured a punishment by the now externalised superego in the form of being thrown out of the country while at the same time satisfying his libid-inal demands.

It seems to me that Gavin found himself unable to give up his attachment to the parents of his childhood, while at the same time he was unable to be what he felt he must be in order to secure their love. He submitted to the father in his mind in the sexual act, thus holding on to his incestuous wishes.

It is common to find that those who cannot move on to adulthood—like Gavin who remained a student unable to take on adult responsibility—feel they are irrevocably stuck in deadlock. They may appear to have made the step from child to adult but inside they feel fraudulent.

Anyone who works in schools will recognize the "too good" adolescent—a young person who chooses the path of going on try-ing to please his parents. Too frightened to establish his or her own independent thoughts and identity, they retain a dependent rela-tionship to their parents. It may not show as babyish behaviour, or obvious dependence, but may appear as an excessive maturity. I sometimes refer to this as "the head boy syndrome". Sometimes these young people are chosen to be head boys and girls because they appear unusually mature. But in fact it is a borrowed iden-tity from parents—assumed rather than acquired through real and conflictual development. Gavin's cord trousers and check shirt, the academic garb, suggest this same borrowed fake identity; only the boots gave a clue to his conflict.

Case illustration: Bella

I will turn now to my second case example. Bella, a 17-year-old young woman whose family originally came from Portugal, was brought to the Brent Adolescent Centre (now the Brent Centre for Young People) by her mother and father. Following panic attacks during her GCSE exams the previous summer, she had dropped out of school and was doing nothing at home. She was too frightened to go out in case she was "sick". It was hard to establish what she meant by this, and despite being an intelligent young woman she sounded very inarticulate on the subject of what she feared might happen. Her discourse consisted of rather opaque phrases like "an' stuff ...", "Yeah, like sick an' stuff" and "I dunno". It gradually became clear that "sick" was a general purpose idea which covered any feeling which could overwhelm her. At the same time, "sick" was also literally a fear of being sick in public and people seeing her moving or shaking or falling to the ground.

Bella referred to her mother as "sick" too. This description meant different things at different times. Sometimes it was used to mean "mad", at others to mean "incapacitated and lying in bed" and at others to mean "she has cancer". Over time, I learned that her mother had had an adolescent breakdown and had herself led a restricted life. Her father had been brought up by a neighbouring family in the village instead of by his own family, and he carried with him a terrible fear of abandonment. Bella had one sibling, a sister who was six years older, working but still living at home having dropped out of university after just a few weeks there.

When Bella was five, the family was on holiday in Portugal. Her parents took her to a doctor about her pigeon toes. She recalled that while her parents were outside the doctor's consulting room looking at the view over the city, the doctor touched her vagina inappropriately. She was unable to get their attention although she could see them behind the glass which separated them. When they came back in she cried and told them what was wrong. It seems the family picked her up and ran away from the hospital. Bella was nine when her mother developed cancer. Although it was treated, from then on mother lived as if she were still very ill and, I think, with the air of one who is dying. During her therapy, and after Bella had made some progress, her mother was diagnosed with a further cancer and received further treatment.

In her sessions, Bella presented as someone who was deeply depressed and unable to move forward in her development. She had no interest in boyfriends and found everything she managed to do outside the house an exhausting demand from which she would have to recover by staying at home doing nothing for at least a day. Her sessions were heavy and despairing. In Bella's manner and exhaustion she communicated to me that coming alive in adolescence felt to her more like dying than living. Unconsciously she seemed to be guilty about being well and about wanting to separate from her parents by having friends and a life of her own. She seemed to fear her potentially aggressive attack on her mother implied in her wishes. She also felt angry with her father for not being able to support her mother and come between them in a way that would have allowed Bella some freedom to go forward. Instead she experienced him as yet another collapsed figure.

Every step forward was soon followed by a period of "sickness" and depression which suggested that she felt unable to progress for fear that in doing so she attacked her parents. Instead she launched, unconsciously, a vicious attack upon herself.

I will describe a period in her treatment which demonstrates the difficulties she and I faced.

It was in June, and Bella, now at university in London, had just finished her end of year exams. In the run-up to the exams she had cried continually in sessions about how hard she had to work and how frightened she was of the exams. She showed me in graphic detail how she suffered all the time. In the event, she had done all the exams without undue difficulty except the last one. She had panicked before that exam, fearing she would be sick, and had rung her mother to tell her that she was panicking and could not do it. However, somewhere inside—she acknowledged to me later—she knew that she could do it and that after she put the phone down she would go into the room and sit the exam.

The exams came to an end and being with Bella felt like being with someone in the depths of mourning. She wept silently and inconsolably, yet was unable to tell me what made her so sad. After a couple of weeks of this, I pointed out to her that since her exams had finished she had been plunged into despair. I told her that I had a hunch that she thought she had done rather well and that this was depressing her and making her feel that all she could do was to cry and live the life of one who was waiting to die. She looked mildly interested and said that she had completed a questionnaire in the paper about how old you really are. She had a score that correlated with someone who was retired!

I said that I thought she felt some relief at that! Somewhere she knew that she was young and capable, that she could do well at university and make her way in life. But she kept that part of her secret from me, her mother, and the fearful part of herself, trying to persuade us all that she was incapable of coping in the world and was ready to die.

She said that she thought she forgot things. This promising opening thought lapsed for some time into "and stuff … Dunno … well … Kinda … yeah … Like … and stuff". Gradually, she allowed herself to express an idea, bit by bit, over about 20 minutes, unconsciously hoping, and fearing at the same time, that I would not be able to keep the bits together in my mind long enough to make sense of it all. She let me know that she could not remember being the person who went to university last term, who managed last year to go abroad for a holiday and who went to a pop concert and enjoyed it.

It began to emerge that she recognized that there was a capable her, one who did age appropriate things. In those moments she felt like other young people of her age. But then she would forget that she had done such things, she would feel utterly defeated and despairing and thought she would have to start all over again, in terror of going out or of being "sick" next time she tried anything new. In experiencing the laborious process of Bella describing the way she had to start all over again each time, I recognized in my own feelings a flash of annoyance that all the painstaking slow work of the last two years ended up being wiped out every time we got anywhere. "Why bother?!" I complained to myself ungenerously. Noticing this, I thought how easy it would be for both Bella and me to give up on this apparently hopeless task we were engaged upon. I could end the session and hope that the next patient would be more rewarding, and she could submit to the terrible superego restrictions which told her that she must attack herself as incompetent and unable to manage herself in the world.

I put to her that she was able to show me that I was useless in helping her because whatever we understood and however she learnt to think about her difficulty it really did not help her deal any better with the world, that she was as despairing and unhappy now as when she first came to see me. I spoke of how I thought she felt I was incompetent, and that she was furious with me for this. But it also seemed to me that when she felt like that, she then worried that I might not bother any more, and that I might give up and die on her, just as she worried about her mum all the time; therefore, instead of feeling furious with me, she attacked herself and convinced herself that she was the useless one, the one who was incompetent and who could not help her survive in the world and protect her from dangers. I suggested that having convinced herself of her incompetence she had to stay at home and forget what she can do. In that way, the capable her was subdued and kept secret and she persuaded herself that she did not hate me or her parents for being incapable of helping her, but hated herself instead.

When she came back to her next session she was looking a little brighter and announced in a flat tone and with a shrug that her sister had booked for them both to go on holiday. In this statement I recognized that she must have felt helped last session and had allowed herself to plan a holiday, but that she had not been able to take responsibility for this act. Instead she was suggesting to me that she was only going along passively with her sister's demands and could not be held responsible for deciding to go herself. It had an "It wasn't me guv!" quality about it.

Discussion

Using the tools that Freud gives us in *Mourning and Melancholia*, how did I understand Bella's awful predicament? Bella's hidden complaint against her parents was that they were and are incapable of looking after her. They took her to an incompetent doctor at five for a complaint that she maintains needed no medical attention in the first place, and they were unavailable to protect her when he touched her vagina. After this event she became angry and difficult to control. But her mother's illness and her father's constant fear of loss and abandonment made it doubly hard for Bella to be angry with them. When Bella reached puberty her mother seemed to become sicker and more helpless, possibly because of organic reasons, possibly because of her own conflicts in adolescence which had resulted in her breakdown being stirred up as her daughter reached the same age. Bella was in an impossible predicament. She was angry and hating towards her parents who she felt had not protected her, and at the same time she needed to turn away from them towards her peers. To Bella, her mother seemed frighteningly fragile and Bella's aggression must have felt unmanageable. How could she turn away from a "sick" mother who was threatening to die and a father who interpreted any outside interest in his girls as a sign of their abandonment of him? Perhaps her compromise was to replace what Freud called her object cathexis, or what we would call her ambivalent attachment to her mother, with an identification with a sick mother. In that way she could strike a deal with her super-ego. She could allow herself to move into adolescence as long as she maintained an identity with a sick and dying mother. Freud (1917: p. 249) puts it poetically in the paper: "Thus the shadow of the object fell upon the ego, and the latter could henceforth be judged by a special agency, as though it were an object, the forsaken object."

I do not wish to oversimplify Bella's internal situation. One may recognize certain hysterical features in my description of her: for example, in her attack on thinking, her negation of the truth about her capacities and her real age, the threat of catastrophe never far away, her difficulty identifying feelings one from another, her phobic reaction to her sexual life and to life in general. One may also recognize in her mother a hysterogenic mother (Brenman, 1985) who responds confusingly to her daughter's needs and instils in her a fear of the outside world, unable to say "we'll sort it out, it will be OK". I suspect that alongside the identification with a sick mother which Bella adopted—the melancholic identification—the fear of being "sick" when she went out also had hysterical overtones; perhaps in some way the fear of being seen shaking and falling down in the street captured her sexual desire in an image against which she could defend herself. Perhaps in her mind her mother's adolescent breakdown represented the outcome of her mother becoming a sexual woman. Bella might therefore have needed to defend herself from any idea that she would become sexual herself. The hysterical symptom would then contain all the sexual desire and the defence against it: it puts a stop to ordinary sexual development. In her internal compromise she had to silence a mother in her mind who says to her: "You will fail as a sexual and active woman out in the world like I did." When she found herself succeeding through her own enormous and exhausting ambition and effort, she feared that she was attacking her mother, triumphing over her with hatred. In her mind this fragile mother would attack her back by dying and deserting her or by making her "sick" too.

I am suggesting, then, that Bella showed both melancholic and hysterical types of identification. A distinction between the two might be simply expressed in the following way: melancholic identification involves becoming the lost hated and loved object, whereas hysteria involves assuming that one has become sick as a result of retribution by the attacked hated and loved object who has made one sick as a punishment for being made sick themselves. Bella's melancholic type of identification involved her becoming the sick mother rather than lose her mother's love or feel that she might kill her. By becoming the sick mother she also felt that she held her father's love. At other times I thought Bella felt she was sick and dying as a punishment or retaliation by the internal mother who she wished to attack with her ambition and desire for life.

The compromise Bella made was to submit to her internal mother in obvious ways—through her identification with her, through her helplessness in the face of her wish for an independent life hile keeping alive a secret capacity to do well and to go out with friends like an ordinary young person. The secret capacities and activities surfaced from time to time. It is perhaps not surprising that in the exams which Bella took that June, she achieved a first!

Bella was unable to separate during adolescence from a sick, possibly dying mother, and when she came for therapy she was in the dangerous process of forfeiting her own sexual development into adulthood in a vain attempt to avoid fatally attacking the mother for whom she had an ambivalent attachment that was in fact full of hate.

Conclusion

Mourning and Melancholia is a paper written on the cusp of Freud's theoretical development from the Topographical to the Structural model of the mind. In it he introduces some important concepts which were destined to become keystones in psychoanalytic theory, notably the concept of the superego, an understanding of the importance and role of aggression, and the central developmental concept of identification. In the paper he also gives us a description of the process of mourning, one which has stood the test of time, remaining as it has at the heart of the way we understand it.

In relation to adolescence I hope to have shown that the healthy adolescent demonstrates a capacity to mourn, and armed with this capacity she or he can move away from the dependent attachment to parental figures to independence and their own adult sexual identity and relationships. For complex reasons particular to each individual's case, less fortunate adolescents are unable to mourn the loss of their childhood relationships to their parents. The ambivalent nature of those relationships is one important factor in their difficulties. They tend to cling in binding hatred to their internal parents. In the two cases which I have briefly described, the adolescent remained attached by identification with their hated and loved childhood parental figures, much as Freud describes in the process of melancholia.

References

Brenman, E. (1985). Hysteria. *International Journal of Psycho-Analysis*, 66: 423–432.

Freud, S. (1917e). Mourning and Melancholia. S.E., 19: 237–260. London: Hogarth.

Freud, S. (1923). The Ego and the Id. S.E., 14: 12–66. London: Hogarth.

Gay, P. (1988). *Freud: A Life for our Time*. London: Dent.

Laufer, M. (1964). Ego Ideal and pseudo Ego Ideal in adolescence. *Psychoanalytic Study of the Child*, 19: 196–221.

Laufer, M. & Laufer, M.E. (1984). *Adolescence and Developmental Breakdown*. New Haven, CT: Yale University Press.

CHAPTER FOUR

Narcissism—an adolescent disorder?

Margot Waddell

In the *Three Essays on Sexuality*, Freud (1905) nominates adolescence as one of the crucial developmental phases in the human life cycle. Yet, 52 years later, his daughter Anna was to refer to it as a "neglected period", "a step-child where analytical thinking is concerned" (1958, p. 255). Her own suggestion as to why this should be so was that after her father's "discovery" of infantile sexuality, adolescence was, in a sense, demoted. In the *Three Essays* it is described as the time when changes set in which give infantile sexual life its final, normal shape. The tripartite achievement of this final shape was the crystallization of sexual identity; the finding of a sexual object, and the bringing together of the two main stems of sexuality—the sensual and the tender. There was nothing of the contemporary sense of adolescence as performing a major developmental task: that of providing a crucial period for the restructuring organization of the personality. My own sense is that despite the impact of the developmentally orientated thinking of, in particular, those working with children since the 1920s, most notably Anna Freud and Melanie Klein, adolescence is still seldom focused on as a source of interest or enlightenment about the evolution of psychoanalytic concepts as such. Nowhere is this more definitively so than in the complex and theoretically contentious area of narcissism.

Prima facie, the multifarious presentations of the characteristically self-orientated and self-preoccupied adolescent attitude and behaviour could hardly be more "narcissistic" in flavour and tone, nor, indeed, in the flagrancy of exhibitionistic and selfish activities and affect, whether manic, destructive, depressed, obsessive, perfectionist and so forth. In less superficial ways, it could also be argued that the classic manifestations of adolescent angst and disturbance correspond, in quite detailed and specific terms, as we shall see, to some of the unconscious mechanisms and modes of defence that are, with respect to narcissism, central to the classic psychoanalytic descriptive canon. And yet, in what I shall be describing as the specificity of adolescent states of mind, we have to be asking whether these mechanisms and modes of defence are really so pathological. Could it be that where the adolescent process is concerned, we may need to focus, perhaps surprisingly, on characteristics which could, at a stretch, be regarded as developmental and not, more obviously, as anti-developmental—the line between the two always being hard to draw with any confidence.

I shall concentrate on what I shall be calling the "adolescent organisation", its composition and expression, both in the internal structuring of the mind and in the external groupings and "gangings" typical of the teenage world. The place of narcissism in adolescence can be better understood precisely by examining not just its presentation, but its purpose and function in the adolescent mind—a mind which is at once fluctuating, concrete, self-deceiving and, above all, turbulent in ways which, at other stages of life, would be straightforwardly recognizable as clinically disturbed. To some extent, they *are* recognizable and describable as so being, and yet the similarities are also, in some quite elusive sense, virtual. For the "agitation of inexperience" (Pushkin, 1831) of this age group inevitably locates its inhabitants somewhere between their infantile past and the possibility of a mature adult future. More specifically, they are caught, uncomfortably, "betwixt the unsettling of their latency period and their settling into adult life" Meltzer (1973, p. 51). Being caught in this way leaves most of them, in one way or another, temporarily stranded, as if perched on some kind of raft in the tempestuous waters of unfulfilled need, unfamiliar sexual desire, unwarranted aggression and felt deprivation, in a sea of what seems like unrealizable aspirations and, most significantly, all too real relinquishments and losses—losses, for example, of the known childhood-self with its known family structures. Yet in most, too, there remains, underneath all this, a striving towards independence, growth and development, towards intimacy and the potential satisfactions of maturity. As Irma Brenman Pick (1988) so rightly puts it, "The powerful forces and pervasive defences of adolescence may disturb or interfere with further growth; [but] they are also forces which make for the charm, vitality, enthusiasm and development of adolescents" (p. 193).

It is thus an age group, especially where narcissism is concerned, which needs to be accorded its own particularity of reference and detail in order properly to trace and understand how the "classic" narcissistic mechanisms, whether thought to be primary or defensive, may, in any one case, be being deployed and exhibited to the detriment of the personality, and where, by contrast, what looks like the pure culture of narcissistic splitting and projection is actually a form of exploration, of temporizing and of discovery—and thus much more in the service of development than it may appear to be.

In significant ways, the predicament of the adolescent state perfectly accords with post-Kleinian theory of what constitutes narcissistic pathology. It has all the characteristics of the adult "narcissistic" or pathological organizations described by Rosenfeld, Steiner, O'Shaughnessy, Sohn, Rey and others. Yet its essential fluidity, its culture of experiment and self-exploration, its rootedness in transition and, despite all the usually glaring and obvious signs to the contrary, its developmental potential, tell a different story. For these characteristics mark it out as a period which can eventuate, as Freud suggested, in the emergence of a sense of sexual identity and the bringing together of the sensual and the tender in a hard-won relationship that can eventually bear the otherness of the other.

The point is that that emergence is predicated on the capacity for separateness and individuation which is, in turn, dependent on the necessary and successful working through of narcissistically structured relationships, both within the self and in relation to the outside world. When this fundamental developmental shift cannot, for whatever reason, be made, the potential richness and creativity of the personality will be arrested, leaving it prey to the more established pathology we encounter in adult clinical practice. Few have stated this shift more evocatively than George Eliot in her novel,

Middlemarch. She described the painful recognition on the part of one of the central characters, Dorothea, of the contrast between those who take "the world as an udder to feed their supreme selves", and those who can recognize that others have "an equivalent centre of self, whence the lights and shadows must always fall with a certain difference" (p. 243). When the adolescent process runs reasonably smoothly and a degree of maturity is achieved, there is usually a shift from the first outlook to the second, from selfishness and self-regard to generosity, responsibility, and the capacity to think for oneself, and to be aware of the needs of others, genuinely as others. The world is taken as an "udder" to feed the supreme and over-valued self because this illusion is less intrinsically painful than suffering the necessary relinquishments and manifold losses that attend these years; than having to recognize the implicit loneliness and pain of struggling with the otherness of the other; and than bearing separateness and the fear of feeling alone, despite being apparently surrounded by others. The ability to make such a shift and the failure to do so are highly contingent on the kinds of internal and external factors that I am about to describe. Perhaps I should qualify the notion of failure here. For one very recognizable characteristic of the adolescent organization, and certainly so in the case of Susan whom I shall be discussing, is the swiftness with which what seem to be deeply entrenched narcissistic structures may be modified or modulated in response to even quite small internal or external changes. So, too, what may seem like quite small external changes or, say, minor illnesses or losses, may swiftly propel an adolescent into narcissistic states near psychotic in their intensity.

Why this should be so for some and not for others carries no ready explanation, although, as I shall be arguing, the roots in infancy can make for a good foundation. So, while in obvious ways, the mental mechanisms characterizing the paranoid-schizoid position—those of splitting, projection, omnipotence, and denial—could be said to be intrinsic to the adolescent organization, yet the organization's very fluidity suggests that if such internally or externally generated forces are engageable with, and even assimilable into the personality, they can be the prelude to insight, self-knowledge and the capacity to bear the daily humiliations and sensed inadequacies that shadow these difficult years; to bear them without excessive denial, retreat, flight, or defensive manoeuvre. What looks like a narcissistic disorder may be nearer to a defensive/self-protective, two-stage process of the projection of unfamiliar, unwanted or unmanageable parts of the self, or, indeed, cherished and loving parts, to be followed, in time, and perhaps with help, by a painful re-owning of those projections—an intrinsic aspect of a personality-in-the-making, to be traced later in this paper in the characterization of Dorothea.

This kind of developmental picture moves us a long way from the traditional economic concept of narcissism as a libidinal investment in the self, and towards a position, especially important in adolescence, which is more to do with understanding the role, or purpose, of the narcissistic mechanisms and presentations and what has made them necessary (Lichtenstein, 1964, p. 25–26). "Selfish, self-engrossed, and self-indulgent" may be a superficially accurate descriptive set of terms for many adolescent characteristics, but its judgmentalism may miss the point, or certainly a point. For just as the Narcissus story can represent a young male figure, who has rejected Echo, as pining away for love of his own reflection, we might also construe it, as have others, as Narcissus needing to bolster his self-esteem by seeking a relationship with someone who looks like himself. Could this not be with a mirror image which might restore a fragile self-conception, a kind of intensely experienced twinning relationship, serving as a defence against feelings of isolation and possibly of smallness and humiliation?

Just such a vulnerability clearly plays a central role in, for example, the characteristic adolescent dress code. Similarity is all-important, difference poses a serious threat. Freud's notion of the "narcissism of small differences" is relevant here. Nowhere is the clannish or tribal imperative, to establish a sense of cohering identity in the face of intolerable uncertainties and fears of being left out, more evident than in the rivalry, even enmity, that can be stirred up among, and between, adolescent groupings. Here the small differences of, for example, the lacing of trainers or the cut of hair or jeans can become emblems of allegiance, or the basis for fundamental hostilities, determining inclusion or exclusion and even, at its most extreme, life and death.

Pausanias actually did give an account of Narcissus as having lost his twin and as refinding her in his own reflection in the pool. As Maria Rhode (2004) puts it, "Narcissus pined away and died when his reflection did not respond to him; he declared his love to it as if it were another person, and as though he were a child who could not yet recognize his own reflection in the mirror. From this perspective, it is not so much that self-love made him turn away from other people, as that his sense of identity was inadequately developed, leaving him without the necessary emotional equipment to sustain reciprocal relationships." How true this is of adolescents generally and how clearly stated in Shakespeare's extraordinary poem *Venus and Adonis*. In the face of Venus's intense erotic longing and protracted attempts at impassioned seduction, the beautiful youth, Adonis, protests his unreadiness to enter upon a mature sexual relationship. He wants to be hunting with the lads, he is still a group boy, running with the pack. He defends his lack of responsiveness as follows:

> "Fair Queen," quoth he "if any love you owe me,
> Measure my strangeness with my unripe years;
> Before I know myself seek not to know me;
> No fisher but the ungrown fry forbears;
> The mellow plum doth fall, the green sticks fast,
> Or being early pluck'd is sour to taste" (II, 523–528).

The capacity to tolerate two of the central tasks of adolescence, those of separating and of managing difference without flight into narcissistic states of delusional sameness, is rooted in, though by no means determined by, the earliest possible exchanges between the baby and the primary caretaker—usually the mother. Disturbances, of whatever kind, in early object relationships—whether because of inconsistency of care on the mother's part or, as Bion (1962) stresses, intolerance of frustration on the baby's—almost inevitably lead to emotional disturbance, and especially to fears about separateness, and a tendency for those fears to be defended against through various psychic mechanisms. Thus a narcissistic object choice, that is, one based on maintaining, through projective identifications, a link with those aspects of the self that have been lodged in the other, can function as a means of controlling that other, in order not to feel cut off from, or abandoned by it, nor to feel excessively envious of it. Not only does such an object choice affect relationships in the external world, it also links with internal structures, in that the reinternalization of the projectively possessed object has an impact on the structure of the ego and superego (Segal, 1964, p. 269). The following brief example may clarify some of the foregoing:

Susan, aged 18, was originally referred for three times weekly therapy because of her generally oppositional behaviour, towards her parents and teachers in particular; for her extreme envy of, and hostility to, her younger sister; for her feelings of intense self-hatred and her "black" moods, alternating anger with despair. She was not only a trouble to others, she had become deeply troubled about herself.

These emotional difficulties manifested themselves in a "wilful" refusal to study; in bouts of self-harm—mainly superficial cutting and scratching on her arms and thighs—and also, latterly, in her increasing obsession with the spots on her face. These so-called spots were imperceptible to all but herself. Yet her intense suffering over how disgusting she looked, kept her at times house-bound for many days. She was described as being "hell–bent" on failing her exams—a characteristic which drew little sympathy and was regarded, rather, as yet another example of her generally self-destructive behaviour. She described herself as feeling miserable, constantly aggrieved, envious, and furious with everyone: the world was against her, full of critical people who despised her, and so on. She feared and resented what she took to be her parents' judgmental attitude and unfairness, while, according to them, behaving in ways exquisitely honed to provoke them.

It could well have been, as so often, that in Susan's family—second generation immigrants from a persecutory regime—there was an especially strong commitment to the children's academic and social success. The family culture was one in which the father was necessarily absent for purposes of work and the mother tended to invest her own disappointed aspirations in her daughters, leaving them confused as to whose ambitions belonged to whom. I cite these details as possible factors in the situation, not as explanations.

A year into her treatment, Susan recounted the following dream, one which seemed to describe the internal predicament very precisely.

"I found myself in a forest near a little wooden house. I was feeling sick and lying on the ground. Three revolting-looking, green-eyed witches appeared and I was convinced that they were going to hurt me. I lay very still, hoping that they wouldn't see me. They came right up to me. I was terrified, but, instead of doing something cruel, they seemed sympathetic to my being so ill and weak. They carried me inside the little house and put me to bed. They tucked me up and gently looked after me. I was amazed. They were *so* kind, more like fairy godmothers really. Witches aren't supposed to be like that. At one point I started to feel too warm and threw back the covers, partly to cool myself but mainly, to be honest, because I wanted to have the experience of the witches covering me up again. This happened many times."

Reflecting on the dream, Susan at first associated the witches with her three close friends, in relation to whom she felt, by turn, competitive, excluded, and often both envious and jealous. She was constantly (and usually groundlessly) worried that they would leave her out, make her feel inadequate, or humiliate her. It would seem that her envious attacks on the three friends' caring capacities (standing, perhaps, for both her mother's care and for her three sessions) constantly turned her good figures into bad ones. She then re-internalized persecutory versions of these figures who became components of the sort of ego-destructive superego described by Bion (1962), Britton (2003), and O'Shaughnessy (1999). As a consequence, she felt not only threatened by the bad, afraid that it, or they, would attack her in return, but also left with very little sense of the support and internal resources of a more hopeful, valued, and aspiring part of herself. (It is not unusual for the representation of goodness to be broken up into pieces in a patient's mind, that is, into more than one aspect—often signifying the hostile tearing up, or breaking up, that has been going on in infantile unconscious fantasy.) Her therapist, whether as "witch" or "friend", suffered repeated attacks on any emergent links or potential understanding between them. So, too, her relatively coherent and well-intentioned group of friends were, at times, subjected to the virulence of Susan's verbal, and sometimes physical, assaults. Such assaults had been playing an increasingly regressive role in her life, the more so, it appeared, as actual separation from school and family increasingly shadowed her horizon. As so often, a fear of being outside and on her own had instituted a lurch backwards at the point when leaving suddenly felt all too imminent.

In Susan's dream we also find an explicit allusion to the witches of myths and fairy tales, suggesting that something primitively evil is afoot and, quite specifically, in this case, to the three witches in *Macbeth* and their associations with murder and guilt. Susan made this association herself, commenting that she was studying *Macbeth* for A level. It may be remembered that the witches' cauldron contains a ghastly recipe—part-objects, in psychoanalytic terms, of an especially nasty kind, epitomizing the killing of infantile possibility rather than the fostering of it.

> *"Pour in sow's blood that has eaten*
> *Her nine farrow; grease that's sweaten*
> *From the murderer's gibbet ..."* (Act IV, scene i, 64–66)

and

> *"Finger of birth-strangled babe*
> *Ditch-delivered by a drab"* (Act IV, scene i: 30–31).

Although, consciously, Susan felt almost continuously persecuted by the outside world, the dream suggests that, unconsciously, she was beginning to be able to render in symbolic form some insight into her predicament: that the problem was not so much that she was being attacked by hostile figures of mean intent, but that those she cared about became transformed into something bad by her *own* persecutory anxiety and her own destructive impulses, and took up residence in her internal world where they maintained an ego-destructive hold over her. The witches in the dream, however, were not malign as she had feared. On the contrary, they actually had her good at heart, to the point that, in Susan's mind, they became idealized "fairy godmothers", whose good offices she wanted repeated over and over again. This last is an interesting detail, for it suggests something of the emotional bankruptcy of the idealized, as opposed to the good, object. Such an object offers less the kind of strength that can be introjected and identified with internally (thus modifying the "frightful fiend" within), than a more superficial form of reassurance, one constantly having to be repeated and renewed. As long as this is the case, the internal structure remains unmodified and little genuine development can take place.

Moreover, the mythic fairy tale setting suggests how basic and polarized, all good or all bad, are the feelings to be found there. They belong to primitive psychic processes of splitting and projection in which, under the sway of "green-eyed" destructive envy, a perverse transformation takes place in which fair becomes foul and foul fair (to pick up the witches' deadly chant). The baby self is then left bereft of friendly objects and in thrall to persecutory ones.

In her own view, Susan's difficulties were compounded by the fact that, at 18, she had begun to develop some slight traces of acne on her face and back, about which she was desperately self-conscious. She took aggressive medication to cure what was, in fact, a simple outbreak of scarcely perceptible, age-related spots. The medication, however, dried up the moisture and mucus in her system. Her skin became parched, cracked and ultra sensitive to light. She had to wear intensive sun-block—factor 40—of the kind more appropriate to babies and young children, before she could even leave the house, let alone go into the sunshine. Her mother was enlisted in the application of the various emoluments, Susan thus reclaiming her position as the baby of the family, her infantile needs being attended to with the soothing, creaming, protective measures appropriate to an actual baby rather than to an actual adolescent. The aggrieved and rejecting fireball, who would dismiss her mother in contemptuous and denigrating terms—"You know nothing", "You haven't the faintest idea what you are talking about"-, would, all too easily, herself collapse into an infantile state, needing physically to be calmed and contained. As with the repeated coverings-up in the dream, the mother's regular application of cream to her daughter's skin, "over and over again", would seem to offer reassurance to Susan that her destructiveness had not definitively turned things bad. The external repetition would go on being required until, internally, the ferocity of her superego could be modified and yield to objects that were less harsh and more containing.

> It is hard to know, with any precision, the source of this fairly characteristic picture of adolescent narcissistic difficulties. At 18, they may, in part, relate to an intensification of anxiety about the oncoming necessity for actual separation and individuation: academic failure betokening an unreadiness to move into the external world. In some of the extreme narcissistic pictures one encounters, in eating disorders, for example, and in the kinds of body dysmorphic disorder suffered by Susan, one becomes especially aware of the developmental stage that is being struggled through at the time—in this case, the threat of having to

leave the relative safety, turbulence notwithstanding, of the family and to emerge into the external world where she would have to be "seen" as some version of "herself", and not simply as the daughter of her parents. As John Steiner pointed out in a recent paper, "Seeing and being seen are important aspects of narcissism, where self-consciousness is always a feature and one which becomes acute when a patient begins to tolerate a degree of separateness and becomes sensitive to being observed (2006, p. 1).

With adolescence, it seems to be more the fear of imminent separateness that propels many back into a strengthening of narcissistic structures which, although part of their ordinary development, can become seriously destructive at points of external transition. This often precipitates breakdown in the face of apparent success, quite as often as in failure. Susan did not break down. As her therapy progressed, the more hopeful elements indicated in the dream consolidated into a greater capacity to tolerate envy, frustration and separation. What had looked like a particularly worrying adolescent organization loosened its hold on her. Her gratitude to her therapist increased, and two years later she managed to leave home and go to university. Had she been 28 and not 18, I suspect there would have been a very different picture and outcome.

Susan's adolescent predicament made clear the immediacy of infantile states in the adolescent, and the recapitulation, as Ernest Jones (1922) put it, "In the second decennium of life [of] the development he passed through in the first five years" (p. 39–40). In the literature on narcissism, it is this link between narcissistic disorders and the nature and quality of early infant and young child experience, especially in the area of containment and of the development of the superego, that has been particularly emphasized more recently (see, for example, especially Britton, 2003). Though not talking specifically about adolescence, Freud himself made a clear link between early experiences and later developmental difficulties:

"If we throw a crystal to the ground, it breaks; but not into haphazard pieces. It comes apart along its lines of cleavage into fragments whose boundaries, though they were invisible, were predetermined by the crystal's structure (1933, p. 59).

The notion of planes of cleavage affords a way of thinking about the underlying operation of forces which often only become apparent in the age group we are discussing when the stress of the undertaking reveals cracks and fissures, vulnerabilities and weaknesses, which, though they may have long been present, have not been manifest hitherto. The nature of these underlying forces predominantly relates to the baby's early experience, particularly to the extent to which mental and emotional states were held and understood.

This relationship between the containing function and resilience of the parent, and later of the family, and the manner and intensity of the baby's projections, continues to be important throughout life—but at no time more significantly than during the teenage years. For the particular stresses of puberty and the revival of Oedipal conflicts test anew the emotional gains and losses of the early years as never before, early trauma or deprivation often stirring teenage angst, thus strengthening the narcissistic defences.

By contrast, those who have experienced their parents as able to be continent and cognizant of their own infantile needs, and to relate to their children as "other" rather than as narcissistic versions of themselves, will be likely to fare much better. A passage from A.S. Byatt's novel *Still Life*, quoted by Gregorio Kohon (2005) in his recent book, *Love and its Vicissitudes*, beautifully evokes a mother's capacity to engage with her newborn son, not as an extension of herself, weighed down with preconceptions and expectations but, rather, as a separate human being whom she must slowly find a way to get to know:

> "She had not expected ecstasy. She noted that he was both much more solid, and, in the feebleness of his fluttering movements of lip and cheek muscle, the dangerous lolling of his uncontrolled head, more fragile, than she had expected. ... She put out a finger and touched [his] fist; he obeyed a primitive instinct and curled the tiny fingers round her own, where they clutched, loosened, tightened again. "There," she said to him, and he looked, and the light poured through the window, brighter and brighter, and his eyes saw it, and hers, and she was aware of bliss, a word she didn't like, the only one. There was her body, quiet, used, resting; there was her mind, free, clear, shining; there was the boy and his eyes, seeing what? And ecstasy. Things would hurt when this light dimmed. The boy would change. But now in the

sun she recognized him, and recognized that she did not know, and had never seen him, and loved him, in the bright new air with a simplicity she had never expected to know. "You," she said to him, skin for the first time on skin in the outside air, which was warm and shining, "You" (Byatt, 1985, p. 100–101).

This whole passage is touchingly suffused with a mother's capacity to allow her infant to emerge as his own personality, not to project onto him her own hopes and fears, but simply to be ready to engage in the reciprocal emotional complexities of their mutual development. As Kohon says, "It is these words, 'There', 'You', as we imagine them being spoken with love by the mother, which makes the subjectivity of the baby possible. 'You', she says, the giver of meaning, provider of goodness, source of contentment." Kohon goes on, "How does the baby interpret this declaration of love? The word of the mother [and, we might say, the look or gaze of the mother], if spoken [or offered] with pleasure, will create pleasure. If uttered with love, it will … generate love. But if the word [or loving look] is not there, or the voice [or glance] is hateful, uncertain or troubled by too much ambivalence, if [either] is misleading or deceitful, then the baby responds with confusion, insecurity and a sense of loss." And there is likely to be the concomitant difficulty of managing to retain some secure emotional hold on the object even in its absence. "Pleasure will be replaced" as Kohon suggests, "by uncertainty; love, substituted by fear" (2005, p. 66–67). Whatever the baby's natural disposition, it will always be trying to interact with these potentially traumatic impositions from the outside, in terms of the state of the mother's mind and of her internal objects, which have so profound an effect on an infant and young child, and, in these terms, on the adolescent's capacity to manage the fundamental polarities of love and loss.

Steiner's recent work (2006) on gaze and seeing and being seen seems especially relevant to adolescent narcissistic structures, as we saw with Susan. How different might the development be of a baby whose experience of word and look had the quality of the foregoing description. Britton (2003) draws attention to a lack of containment in infancy and early childhood as characteristic in cases of narcissistic personality disorder and, inseparably related to that, to evidence of an "ego-destructive superego" which powerfully works against the development of the personality and, along with envy, is defended against by narcissistic character traits in particular. As has also been well documented, clinically one frequently detects the operation of this kind of internal juggernaut, especially at moments of the emergence of insight or meaning between patient and therapist. Burgeoning possibilities of mutual understanding are immediately crushed by the force and weight of a superego which disarticulates any links of relatedness and relegates the individual back to the defensive locations in which he or she has been seeking uneasy retreat or refuge.

For adolescents, one such refuge is the characteristic flight into an intense involvement in group life. This kind of passionate group involvement may represent a kind of ganging-up of the more perverse and destructive parts of the personality, whether located in actual external figures or in the kind of internal gang of witches revealed in Susan's dream. Or it may represent a denial of aspects of the self, thus diminishing the ego and draining it of its vitality. But it may, equally, indicate a healthy capacity to deal with a sense of internal fragility, even fragmentation, thus providing a constructive function, albeit narcissistic in essence.

By splitting off aspects of the self and locating them variously in different members of the group, it becomes possible to remain in touch with these parts without having to suffer them with too much immediacy. In this kind of group organization, as David Armstrong points out (2005, p. 55), the projected parts of the personality can be reassembled in a way that simulates the function of a containing object.

Such seemed to be the case for young Andrew who suffered a major breakdown at 14. Andrew described how little he could remember of his childhood, except the family house, the loss of which he had felt very keenly when his father sold it a few years after his wife had left him for another man. Andrew had no recollection of his parents being in any sense together in that house, only that the house itself provided what little feeling of "home" he had.

One particularly vivid recollection he did have, however, was of his own realization, at the same time as the house sale, that he was not "the same" as his older brother. He revealed that he had always felt identical, to the point that he was convinced that the two of them even shared each other's thoughts. He had, in other words, taken shelter from a sense of emptiness, loss, and abandonment in this close identification, oblivious of the brother's otherwise distinctive characteristics. This realization left him feeling very little and humiliated. He began to throw himself into group life, thereby constructing for himself a sort of alternative container. It was as if he adopted group life as a way of "tiding him over" until he hit puberty. But with the added stresses of pubertal change and the dispersal of the friendship group into other classes, he felt wholly alone and he completely broke down. In the face of what seemed a comparatively minor problem as to who was in what class, the narcissistic bonding which had, for a time, maintained an uneasy psychic equilibrium unravelled and left him without any internal resource.

This kind of grouping together can be thought of as a sort of safety-net measure which, developmentally, could support or obstruct, depending on the resilience of the internal structuring and on the nature of the external circumstances. As clinicians, we tend to encounter the situation where things have gone wrong. Seeking an example of the adolescent organization as temporizing, that is, holding things together while internal growth continues, I found myself turning to literature. For here, especially in the great 19th century novels, one can appreciate the broad developmental sweep which embraces the minutiae of internal and external experience, often describing what we would think of in terms of narcissistic mechanisms as providing a kind of in-between phase which allows things to develop. Two outstanding examples of this are the characterizations respectively of Jane Austen's Emma Woodhouse in *Emma,* and George Eliot's Dorothea Brooke in *Middlemarch.*

Two of the central protagonists in *Middlemarch,* Rosamond and Dorothea, offer utterly contrasting studies of narcissism that are, in a sense, the pure culture of the kinds of distinction I have been making. There is only space here to describe one of these young women in any detail and that is Dorothea. But Rosamond must get a brief mention as a brilliant delineation of a pretty, vain and self-regarding adolescent—"a nymph caught young and educated at Mrs Lemon's", as George Eliot puts it, whose ceaseless quest for admiration and social betterment brings disaster, or near disaster, on her marriage, herself and those around her. "She was" we are told, "little used to imagining other people's states of mind except as a material cut into shape by her own wishes" (p. 834). The anti-developmental picture is exquisitely drawn.

In Dorothea's case, the odyssey looks quite different: she grows up in the course of the novel, moving away from her metaphorically and literally short-sighted view of the world, one rooted in the projection into others of her own ideals, to a much more mature position.

Middlemarch begins and ends with her marriages—the contrast between the two measuring her development over time. The first marriage is to the desiccated pedant, Casaubon. At this point, Dorothea is described as wholly caught up in her own youthful ideas. She is "imbued with a soul hunger to escape from her girlish subjection to her own ignorance and the intolerable narrowness and purblind conscience of the society around her" (p. 60). This is a wonderful evocation of the adolescent's omnipotent wish to bypass the pains of ignorance and inadequacy, and of the defensive intolerance, superiority, and slightly prudish judgementalism which so often characterize an attitude to the rest of the world—to a society which is felt to be so woefully wanting.

Dorothea's response to Casaubon's proposal, we are told, is that of one whose soul is possessed by the fact that a fuller life is opening before her. "She was a neophyte, about to enter on a higher grade of initiation" (p. 67). Infused with adolescent idealistic fervour, Dorothea seeks to render her life complete by union to one whose mind, as she subsequently discovers, reflects "in a vague labyrinthine extension every quality she herself brought" (p. 46)—a wonderful description of projective identification. She is impressed "by the scope of his great work, also of attractively labyrinthine extension" (p. 46). She has, in other words, fallen victim to her own projections, to the idealization of a much older and, she believes, wiser man. She was "altogether captivated" by one who, to her mind, "would reconcile complete knowledge with devoted piety. Here was a modern Augustine who united the glories of doctor and saint" (p. 47).

Early on, Dorothea, like Casaubon, suffers from the delusion that to know about things, to accumulate sufficient "learning" or information, would provide "the key to all mythologies"—a key which would bring about a solution to life (again expressing the adolescent delusion that there could be such a thing), a flight, in other words, into certainty at the expense of a sense of reality. As Bion put it, she "could not see the wisdom for the knowledge" (Tavistock

Lecture, 1979, unpubl.). Dorothea's slow and painful disillusionment challenges to the uttermost her capacity to learn from experience. It initiates in her a state of mind in which, as admiration for erudition yields to appreciation of wisdom, and as narcissistic relations yield to more object related ones, she can begin to envisage a very different kind of relationship, one which also brings together "the sensual and the tender".

In the course of the novel, Dorothea loses those infantile dreams, she relinquishes her projective fantasies, and, in the ghastly loneliness of her honeymoon in Rome, she discovers the difference, noted earlier, between a narcissistic orientation to the world—as "an udder to feed our supreme selves", and an attitude of mind which can recognize "an equivalent centre of self whence the lights and shadows must always fall with a certain difference" (p. 243).

The working through of the adolescent's narcissistic orientation to the world is intrinsic to being able to tolerate the loss of a sense of one's own centrality in it. In her first marriage, Dorothea suffers the loneliness of disillusionment and separation, but also begins to recognize the significance of separateness. With Casaubon's sudden death, she lets go of her omnipotent adolescent ideals in favour of the more painful reality of frustration, disappointment, and a circumscribed life, her husband's will penalizing marriage to Ladislaw. During that first marriage, Dorothea discovers the emptiness and mistakenness of her choice: "that new real future which was replacing the imaginary drew its material from the endless minutiae by which her view of Mr. Casaubon and her wifely relation, now that she was married to him, was gradually changing with the secret motion of a watch hand, from what it had been in her maiden dream" (p. 226). When she believes, wrongly, that her new love, Will Ladislaw, has betrayed her in favour of Rosamond, she is wracked with inescapable anguish as "the limit of her existence was reached". Yet, unlike her former self, she is now able to draw on capabilities which she has "acquired" over time, as she begins to learn from her own real experience, relinquishing the "learning about" side of her and the "unselfish", narcissistic "under-labourer", or "too good to be true" versions of herself.

The inner reality and meaning of this momentous expression of the thrust towards development is beautifully described in external terms—a kind of "objective correlative" for internal processes.

"She opened her curtains and looked out towards the bit of road that lay in view, and fields beyond, outside the entrance-gates. On the road there was a man with a bundle on his back and a woman carrying her baby; in the field she could see figures moving, perhaps the shepherd with his dog. Far off in the bending sky was the pearly light; and she felt the largeness of the world and the manifold wakings of men to labour and endurance. She was a part of that involuntary, palpitating life, and could neither look out on it from her luxurious shelter as a mere spectator, nor hide her eyes in selfish complaining" (p. 846).

This is not only a movingly understated description of the generosity of a mature mind, it is also a marvellous evocation of introjective identification having been taking place over time. In the face of Dorothea's conviction that the external object has been lost, the internal object holds. It does not vanish or collapse because the external representation has gone. Unlike Rosamond, Dorothea is able to look outside the "entrance-gates" of her own mind to the existence of others' lives, "whence the lights and shadows must always fall with a certain difference".

In conclusion, the term "adolescent organization" designates not just narcissistic states of mind and behaviour which are actively anti-developmental butones that can have a developmental function too. In other words, narcissism can be designated an "adolescent disorder" but that would be to oversimplify the situation. For, as we have seen, the pathological impasse of 18-year-old Susan was already, at 19, yielding to a capacity to make more helpful internal alliances of a kind which permitted a degree of growth and change. The dream described is suggestive of an emergent self that is distinctly different from her early years. Andrew, too, began to recognize the dearth of any early experience to which he could attach any meaning and the catastrophic impact on him of the collapse of his substitute containing structures. Yet in families where periods of emotional drought have not been as extensive as in Susan's or Andrew's, or where the underlying foundations are strong, the positive function of the narcissistic *modus operandi* can be more evident, as seems to be the case with Dorothea. One might even say that the adolescent organization can offer a kind of *sine qua non* for the kinds of exploration and experimentation that promote a sense of identity that is both internally reliant on, and allied with, good enough relationships with good enough internal parents, yet one which is also distinct from these parents, to the point that the individual can feel confident in something called his or her own self, confident in a capacity to come into one's own. During adolescence, to draw any clear distinction between what might be called mental "order" and mental "disorder" is always a challenging and subtle business, defying ready categories or formulations, which is why living or working with this age group presents such an alarming, and at the same time such a rewarding, challenge.

References

Armstrong, D. (2005). *Organization in the Mind: Psychoanalysis group relations and organizational consultancy*. London: Karnac.

Bion, W.R. (1962). *Learning from Experience*. London: Karnac, 1979 [unpublished lecture].

Britton, R. (2003). *Sex, Death and the Superego: Experiences in Psychoanalysis*. London: Karnac.

Byatt, A.S. (1985). *Still life*. London: Chatto & Windus.

Eliot, G. (1972). *Middlemarch*. Reprinted. Harmondsworth: Penguin, 1985.

Freud, A. (1958). Adolescence. *Psychoanalytic Study of the Child, 13*: 255–278.

Freud, S. (1905). Three Essays on the Theory of Sexuality, S.E., 20. London: Hogarth, 1955.

Freud, S. (1933). The Dissection of the Psychical Personality. S.E., 22. London: Hogarth, 1955.

Green, A. & Kohon, G. (2005). *Love and its Vicissitudes*. London: Routledge.

Jones, E. (1922). Some problems of adolescence. *British Journal of Psychology, 13*: 31–34.

Lichtenstein, H. (1964). The role of narcissism in the emergence and maintenance of a primary identity. *International Journal of Psychoanalysis, 45*: 49–56.

Meltzer, D. (1973). *Sexual States of Mind*. Strathtay, Perthshire: Clunie.

O'Shaughnessy, E. (1999). Relating to the super-ego. *International Journal of Psychoanalysis, 80*: 861–870.

Pick, I. (1988). Adolescence: its impact on patient and analyst. *International Review of Psychoanalysis, 15*, 2: 187–194.

Pushkin A.S. (1831). *Eugene Onegin*, C. Johnston (Trans.). Harmondsworth: Penguin, 1979.

Rhode, M. (2004). The lost child. Whose is the face in the mirror? Lecture in series on Narcissism through the Life Cycle, Institute of Psychoanalysis, December 2004.

Segal, H. (1964). *Introduction to the Work of Melanie Klein*. London: Heinemann.

Shakespeare, W. (1593). *Venus and Adonis*. In: C. Burrow (Ed.), *William Shakespeare: The Complete Sonnets & Poems*. Oxford: Oxford University Press, 2002.

Shakespeare, W. (1623). *Macbeth*. The Arden Shakespeare. London: Methuen, 1963.

Steiner, J. (2006). Seeing and being seen: narcissistic pride and narcissistic humiliation. *International Journal of Psychoanalysis* (in press).

CHAPTER FIVE

Facing towards or turning away from destructive narcissism

Denis Flynn and Helga Skostad

Introduction

In severely disturbed adolescents who self-harm and are suicidal there are movements between periods of destructive behaviour and periods of relating in an object-directed way that have a different emotionally-connected quality. At times the adolescent is seen almost literally to face towards or into something destructive and narcissistic and to be held or captured by it, like in the myth of Narcissus. At other times they can shrug it off and turn away from it to get on with life and their development (Joseph, 1989).

In adolescence features of narcissism are ever-present. Intense, self-interested, or over-valued views of oneself, one's body, or ideas and capacities and so on, arise quite easily, fluidly and continuously. And they collapse equally easily, often into despair, disillusion and contradictory states of feeling, sometimes characterized by loss of self-esteem or hope, often leaving the adolescent ridden with guilt and self-loathing. Such shifts, indeed swings, continue until some more secure internal sense of identity and sense of personal value is established as part of the developmental task of adolescence (Flynn, 2004).

Positive and negative aspects of narcissism

Idealizations, some of which are distinctively narcissistic, also play a role in adolescent development. These, in part mixed with and related to object choice, influence the formation of the ego-ideal. In this type of "adolescent idealization" there can be rapid progress not just to a better integration of a sense of body and self, but to a high level of investment in aesthetic, ethical and cultural values (Kernberg, 1991). Some analysts (Grunberger, 1979, 1991; Baranger, 1991; Winnicott, 1965) highlight the reconstitution of the lost omnipotence of infancy and childhood as a central feature of narcissism in adolescence. This, along with new specific powers of body and mind, infuse the adolescent's new aims with added strength and direction (Freud, 1905; Flynn, 2004, ch.10; Grunberger, 1991). Psychoanalytic treatment may in part provide a period of time for the adolescent to enter into a process in which they reconstitute their lost omnipotence, and as such gives hope (Grunberger, 1991). Many analysts, for example Moses and Eglé Laufer, have for this reason emphasized the importance of offering treatment in periods of increased severe disturbance and for potentially suicidal adolescents. Also importantly, early treatment recognizes the reality of the present risk (Laufer, M. & Laufer, M.E., 1984; Laufer, M. 1995; Anderson, 1999; Flynn, 2004).

Angry, hateful and destructive elements, however hidden or played down, are evident at times in every adolescent, may become internalized, and, along with more positive introjections, form part of the developing personality. William Hazlitt in his splendid essay *On the Pleasure of Hating* (1826), pointed to the satisfaction we all take in hating, a feature that is abundantly evident in the "freedom of mind" that adolescents have. Hazlitt writes, "So it is, that there is a secret affinity, a hankering after evil in the human mind ... [which] ... takes a perverse, but a fortunate delight in mischief, since it is a never-failing source of satisfaction. Pure good soon grows insipid, wants variety and spirit. Pain is bitter-sweet, which never surfeits. Love turns, with a little indulgence, to indifference or disgust: hatred alone is immortal" (Hazlitt, 1826, p. 105). He further writes, "Nature seems (the more we look into it) made up of antipathies: without something to hate, we should lose the very spring of thought and action." Hazlitt ironically prefigures the view of both Segal and Winnicott in this area, that creativity in adolescence occurs as a result of facing and working through what we hate or dislike. Viewing this in developmental terms, to move on towards adulthood the adolescent has to reject and abandon aspects of earlier attachments.

Before looking at Rosenfeld's concept of destructive narcissism, we shall spell out from Freud's complex theory of narcissism some themes that link libidinal and destructive narcissism. Key features of libidinal narcissism are also present in destructive narcissism, and a question we want to consider is, to what extent does one lead to the other? For Freud, narcissism is first a libidinal stage of development, and is a process characterized by the infant taking him/herself as a love object or sexual object. This stage is an early and primitive state of mind in which "hitherto dissociated sexual instincts come together into a single unity and cathect the ego as an object" (Freud, 1911, 1913), and it is characterized by delusive states. Importantly then, in later terms narcissistic defences unify unconscious defences in an organized way.

Freud also sees narcissism as close to, but not actually as, a perversion, in that a person treats his/her own body in the same way in which the body of a sexual object is treated (Freud, 1914, 1917). When the narcissist views him/herself as love-object, that involves an "idealization" of him/herself, leading to relationships based in narcissistic identifications and to the sexualization of thought processes (Freud, 1913, p. 89; Meltzer, 1973, p. 51–63). In "narcissistic identification" the melancholic has withdrawn his libido from the object by narcissistic identification with the lost sexual object, and thereby sets up the object in the ego itself (Freud, 1914, p. 94–96; 1916, p. 427). Importantly, this leads, in Klein's later terms, to a description of "narcissistic states" as a withdrawal from reality towards an idealized internalized object, and of "narcissistic object relations" as an excessive use of projective identification that leads the person to be trapped in a world made up of projected aspects of themselves (Segal & Bell, 1991).

Although Freud did not explicitly view narcissism as characterized by destructiveness, as Rosenfeld and others later did, and indeed mainly pointed to elements of self-love characterizing narcissism, the more negative and potentially destructive elements are there in his theories from the start, especially for those aspects of narcissism that are close to perverse and delusive states of mind. These elements are implicit in the division Freud makes between narcissistic types of object choice and "anaclitic" or "attachment types" of object choice (in the German *Anlehnungstypus*, literally "leaning-on types"). Freud (in 1914) makes a distinction (which he introduced only four years earlier and later dropped) between sexual instincts and ego instincts. He writes that in their early object choice, infants "derive their sexual objects from their experiences of satisfaction ... *in connection with vital functions which serve the purpose of self-preservation*" (my italics), and "the sexual instincts are attached to the satisfaction of the ego instincts" (Freud, 1914, p. 87). Examples of how the development of sexual instincts is linked to the satisfaction of ego instincts might be, for example, the way that feeding at the breast makes the breast become a sexual object; how eating food and being looked after, which we get pleasure or pain from, makes the carer become libidinally invested as good or bad. In an important footnote Freud points out that "the 'attachment' indicated by the term is that of the sexual instincts to the ego-instincts, not of the child to its mother", that is, not by the object choice (Freud, 1914, p. 87). However, in defining narcissistic types of object-choice, Freud merely points out the difference of object choice, that is "seeking themselves as love object", without explicitly making the important correlative point he has just implied, namely that in narcissistic object choice there is a failure to connect sexual instincts and ego instincts. Put in other words, in narcissistic choice the libidinal sexual instincts choose the self as object and fail "to lean on" (*Anlehnen*) the ego instincts. There is a disconnection, to use the words he had just used, from the "vital functions which serve the purpose of self-preservation (Freud, 1914, p. 87). This distinction would have made a clear connection between Freud's theory and Rosenfeld's theory of destructive narcissism, which still relies in part on Freud's libido theory. It shows how destructiveness can follow a moving away from reality considerations and from the reality principle. It especially makes clear how narcissism sometimes leads to thoughts and actions, prevalent in highly disturbed adolescents, which threaten self-preservation of body and mind, which can then lead to self-harm and suicide.

In the myth of Narcissus, here taken from *Tales from Ovid* translated by Ted Hughes, we can see the destructive pull of narcissism (Hughes, 1997). Narcissus, lying by the pool, is drawn by a "craving unfamiliar"—a libidinal craving—to the beauty of his own image.

His self-love intensifies, fixing him in the position and captivating him, pulling him further and further into himself. The scene then begins to change to one of selftorture, and he goes into a delusive state that he cannot pull himself out of, despite the lack of any real satisfaction. He becomes overcome by impotent grief, because he realizes that he is in love with himself, and is torturing himself by trying to grasp hold of and possess his own image in the water. This leads him to choose deliberate self-harm, and death comes because of the loss of his perfect self image.

> *Then he ripped off his shirt,*
> *And beat his bare chest with white fists.*
> *The skin flushed under the blows.*
> *When Narcissus saw this*
> *In the image returned to perfection*
> *Where the pool had calmed –*
> *It was too much for him.*
> *… He melted – consumed*
> *By his love. (p. 82–83)*
> *… So finally death*
> *Closed the eyes that had loved themselves too much (p. 84).*

His human form was lost and transformed, so that all that was left was the Narcissus flower—pretty and plentiful, living but now inanimate, and a transient reminder of an image that although temporarily "perfect" would not survive (Freud, 1916).

Moira

I would now like to give an example from an assessment (DF), to show an adolescent who faces towards, then attempts to turn away again from, more destructive tendencies, in subtle shifts of movement between narcissistic states and more object-relating states of mind. Moira, aged 17, had a history of severe anorexia, some depression and obsessional symptoms, and more or less continuous suicidal ideation that she threatened to act on. During extensive treatment of her eating problems she had developed patterns of severe self-harm, had made deep cuts and taken serious overdoses.

> At assessment Moira was pleasant and poised, but worryingly thin. She talked in a slow way with a relatively deep voice, telling me she had recently reached her target weight. She had thought her problems would get better if she gained more weight, but found this was not so. As she talked, with some help and prompting from me, about the problems she was having, particularly her self-harm, there was a hint of excitement about the cutting of her limbs and her stomach. She also said "It's funny, yunnah [*chummy, colloquial*], but I also get pleasure [*drawn out*] from eating too much and then vomiting [*with a rapid tripping onomatopoeia*] afterwards [*slowing down again to being more measured*]."
>
> From this and other descriptions of cutting, and how she related to staff in crises, I had a sense of her perverse enjoyment at "getting staff going" by her sudden acting out. I thought there was a significant pattern of getting pleasure from pain, not just in her eating problems but also in her self harm and social relationships. This sado-masochistic element formed a central part of her internal world.
>
> At one point, as she described her stepfather's fury in enforcing control over her and her younger brothers, she crouched over crying and said in a flat distracted tone, "They might as well have killed me". She told me she remembered thinking that he would come into her room and kill her.
>
> One could see in this possible links between her disturbed outer world and her inner world, where destructiveness had such a part. Indeed, it was only much later that it emerged that the stepfather, although seemingly the most caring and responsive to the children, has been sexually inappropriate and abusive to her as a child, and still exercised a tight control over her as an adolescent. We also knew from reports that there were major problems in relations with her mother, exacerbated by her mother relinquishing her responsibility towards Moira, while still caring for her brothers, for fear of the impact that

Moira's self-harm might have on them. Indeed the local workers described her mother as having a personality disorder, and
in our contact her neediness had eclipsed consideration of her
daughter. There had also been considerable marital disharmony
and perhaps also physical violence from the time Moira was a
small child.

Moira now told me that her symptoms and overt problems
had started from the age of 11 with imitative dieting: "A friend
was very much into dieting," she told me, "and I wanted to
be close to her and share everything with her." Being like the
friend was like being in Narcissus's image, an escape from her
family, inner conflicts and her emerging sexuality.

Despite the fact that her increasingly severe self-harming cut
short or prevented any real progress, there were small signs of
wanting to change. She was in tears and spoke about "wanting
to do what other girls can do". There was clearly some struggle
and some depressive pain, that is, a wish to make something
better, but unconscious guilt and pain about being unable to
achieve this. But Moira also said she continued to have a wish
to die, and when this wish came she banged her head or her
fist against the wall. Finally she said, "I don't know if I want
treatment … I'll find it hard … but I do want to understand
myself."

Before her second assessment, after three weeks, she had
taken another serious overdose. When I questioned what her
intention had been Moira replied quite flatly and prosaically,
"I want to destroy my body". She then told me with cold spite-
fulness and excitement, "I won't do it all at once, I'll destroy
parts of my body bit by bit". She said she felt her body was
"repulsive and ugly", and she "couldn't stand being touched".
She said cold-bloodedly she did "'want to understand", but this
would mean she could not self-harm, "which I want to continue
to do".

Moira appeared to teeter continuously on the edge of a negative
therapeutic reaction to past and possible future treatment. Her
assessment and then subsequent admission were characterized by a
pattern alternating between looking for understanding and wishing
to make some use of treatment, and then turning away from reality

and facing deeper and deeper into a narcissistic retreat or enclave, dominated by destructive impulses centred on her body (Steiner, 1993; O'Shaughnessy, 1992a, 1992b). At times she was more in touch and working, at other times in a deceptive illusory state, immersing herself in an anal world—a kind of "claustrum" in Meltzer's terms (1992). Her destructiveness seemed idealized, as if she could manage loss and violent enactments around her by identifying with a sado-masochistic internal object that abused her, starved her and cancelled out her own life-directed vital interests. At times it was difficult to gauge whether her wish for treatment was genuine, or whether we in the treatment team were being seduced by her plausible talking, her show of emotion, and the supposed "tragic romanticism" of her condition. After some months of treatment with some degree of struggle to change, she again "faced into" the destructive narcissism that underlay her problems, her psychoanalytic treatment stopped, and she needed acute psychiatric and medical care (Day & Flynn, 2003).

Rosenfeld's "destructive narcissism"

We shall now turn to spell out some aspects of Rosenfeld's theories of destructive narcissism (1965; 1971; 1978; 1987) that are relevant to this assessment, the longer case example, and many other cases. Unlike Freud, who thought that narcissistic patients had no capacity for transference and so react to treatment with indifference, Rosenfeld thought transference was possible with narcissistic patients. In his early work Rosenfeld (1965), following Klein, stressed the impact of omnipotence and idealization in narcissistic object relations, which can stimulate destructiveness. The impact of omnipotence in narcissistic object relations is that the object is omnipotently incorporated and treated as the infant's possession, and good and bad parts of the self can be projected into it, so that they are lost or diffused. A highly idealized self-image dominates the analytic situation and anything interfering with this picture is rigorously defended against and omnipotently denied. In treatment defences build up against dependence, as it implies love and stimulates envy, which then disturbs the process of treatment itself. Clinical progress depends on the degree to which the patient is gradually able to acknowledge the relationship with the psychotherapist and the treatment team, and hence accept some dependence, including accepting analysis of omnipotence, idealization, and denigration, and the taking up of powerful envy.

Rosenfeld's later work (*Impasse and Interpretation*, 1987) emphasizes the need to differentiate the positive side of self-idealization from its negative side, and outlines the specifically destructive aspects of early narcissism. He develops the concept of "destructive narcissism" from his earlier papers by adding that objects are not just held omnipotently, which prevents contact with dependence and reality, and is therefore harmful, but also that "omnipotent destructive parts of the self" are themselves idealized, and therefore incorporated into the narcissistic character structure. There is an overwhelming wish to destroy the analyst, who becomes via the transference the object, and the source, of life and goodness. For periods this destructive side can remain disguised, and narcissism partly has this function of hiding awareness of destructiveness and envy. But the patient can become extremely frightened of the destructiveness that is revealed by the analytic work. It can lead to further self-destructive thoughts and enactments, and the patient may then become depressed and suicidal.

We can see with Moira, and shall see with Michelle described next, that in such patients at times the destructive aspects of the self are idealized and submitted to, and they capture and trap the positive dependent aspects of the self. An arrogant attitude (in Bion's sense, denying deep needs) is assumed, and the patient's internal world becomes near psychotic and perverse, and takes on the form of a gang, like the Mafia, dominating the weak, keeping itself in power and maintaining a "corrupt" status quo (Bion, 1957; Steiner, 1993).

As Rosenfeld and others have shown, a psychotic delusional structure develops in the internal world of the patient, dominated by an omnipotent or omniscient extremely ruthless part of the self, with the freedom to engage in any sadistic or violent activity. There is a danger of an acute psychotic state if the dependent part of the patient, which is the sanest part of his personality, is persuaded to turn away from the external world and give up entirely to the dominance of the delusional structure.

There is a strong interactive impact between such patients and the therapist and whole treatment team. Steiner has emphasised that projective identification is crucial to a coherent understanding of narcissistic states: he shows that in projective identification the subject relates to the object, not as a separate person with his own characteristics, but as if he is relating to himself (Steiner, 1993). He may ignore aspects of the object that do not fit the projection or he may control and force, or persuade, the object to enact the role required of him. The patient may then believe or assume that the therapist too idealizes the narcissistic relationship, and this may mean the work of both therapist and patient progressively becomes destroyed. An example of this was a 20-year-old girl in the adolescent unit, who used to severely burn her legs with acid and even take her dressings off while the wounds were healing to further the damage by repeated use of acid. The striking thing in the light of such evident and persistent destructiveness was how her therapist was continuously persuaded to believe this girl's own plaintive cries about her "neediness" and was persuaded about how loveable she really was—an example of the command and control the girl could negatively exercise over her caring objects, both internal and external. In this case the work broke down again amid recriminations, leaving the therapist and other workers badly affected by the power of the girl's despair.

In much work with adolescents the picture is not so bleak and there is an opportunity to undo such organized patterns of defences, and allow space for other types of idealization and relating emotionally. The following clinical example (HS) will look at this. It concerns the treatment of an adolescent girl who moved in and out of different narcissistic states, some more libidinal, some more destructive. These alternated with more thoughtful states of mind where she related and used what was offered.

Michelle

Michelle is a 16-year-old girl whom I saw twice weekly during her inpatient stay at a therapeutic community. Prior to that she was on a psychiatric ward for a year because of anorectic symptoms and dangerous self-harm. She had frequently cut herself and taken overdoses. The main concern, however, was her addictive self-strangulation.

Until the age of two Michelle was brought up on her own by her mother, who later married and had three more children. Michelle, who hated her stepfather, felt deeply betrayed by her mother. She experienced her as playing mind-games and giving messages she could not understand. When she was 12, her mother invited Michelle's birth father to meet his daughter for the first time. He flooded her with gifts, which she found increasingly strange, but she was unable to withdraw. She developed obsessional mechanisms and started to self-harm. While on the psychiatric ward her disturbance had increased and she appeared psychotic. She wanted to jump out of a window believing she could fly.

Michelle is a pretty young woman, of small stature and slightly underweight, with curly blond hair. The nurses called her "Little Princess" because she was so precious and easily hurt. Her overall feeling was of not being listened to and she desperately said "I have an invisible voice". "Little Princess" also referred to the importance her looks had for her. Everybody had to wait when she was in the bathroom, doing her hair and her make-up.

> In her assessment Michelle told me that she urgently needed help. She was unconcerned about her self-harm, but feared her head would drive her mad. She could not bear her thoughts creating havoc in her mind and she gave me an experience of how this felt by the way in which she spoke. To give an example of this, she said: "Do I have an eating disorder? No—yes—I need to weigh less, but I do not want to lose weight. This is not called an eating disorder, or is it? Would you call this an eating disorder?"
>
> She got completely preoccupied with what name I would give her condition and wanted an answer from me. However, if I called it an eating disorder, according to her thoughts this would not be true, she did not have one; if I did not call it eating disorder, then she thought that I would not see she had a problem.
>
> I said she showed me vividly how maddening her thoughts were; they made her so confused that she wanted me to cure her instantly by putting a name to her state, but she also realized that this would not help her feel understood. She calmed down.
>
> Michelle described a mind and body she did not own herself. Her thoughts seemed to be made up of voices from others.

Her view of herself was how others saw her. She did not know how to think about herself. She wanted her own experience recognized and needed me to do this. She seemed able to listen to me.

However, then the atmosphere changed and I found myself increasingly confused. She told me that yesterday she had wanted to cut herself. When I asked her about it, she said condescendingly that she could not remember. Then followed a confusing account of the other children in the kitchen and of her mother washing her hair and using her as a model for a course in manicure, giving her artificial fingernails.

It seemed that after a moment, when she felt understood, Michelle was pulled away from thinking with me, into a state in which self-harm was not taken seriously. She became superior and I found myself confused. She seemed to describe a narcissistic relationship, in which she and a mother object are entangled with each other, which protects her from jealousy and envy. She need not share her mother, because she has given her body to her and mother has given hers in return. They are inside each other through mutual projective identification, one body and one soul. However, it is not a blissful togetherness; it is a couple driving each other mad.

I will now give an impression of the first months of treatment before presenting some detailed clinical material. I want to show how I came to know about the internal objects which dominated her in her states of destructive narcissism.

In the first months, Michelle came to her sessions in an anxious state: she did not have the money for shampoo, the shower in the hospital only dripped, and so on. I was expected to resolve all those problems. To my surprise, she relaxed at my interpretations. However, I soon realized that she wanted me to be her voice: I was meant to tell the nurses what she needed. When she believed that I was her voice, her anxiety lessened. She calmed down in sessions, and, significantly, I did as well. I needed to make a conscious effort to be aware that this was not the whole story. In fact she demonstrated this herself, in a chilling aspect to her appearance: she often wore a black scarf, giving me no chance to see whether she had marks of strangulation on her neck. Somehow I knew I should be wary and listen out for warning signs and yet there was a pull to trust her blindly. I started to wonder whether I was being subjected to a mind game, similar to the one she felt subjected to by her mother.

This picture, and its resonance in me, showed, I think, that Michelle was in projective identification with a seductive internal object. It lured her into the belief that everything was fine even though she somewhere knew better. In turn, I had to fight being lured into this false belief. This kind of internal object attacked her sanity and my own thinking mind it made her believe that strangling herself was safe and the best way to get rid of pain. I came to understand it as the force that pulled her back into destructive narcissism and an idealization of her self-attacks.

I now want to describe material following my first break. While I was away Michelle decided to join the family for a two week holiday. She returned in a distressed but withdrawn state, leaving everybody anxious.

She started her session by telling me flippantly that her break was brilliant. She had managed not to wash her hair. Her mother put a lotion on her hair which made it lighter, and she was meant to leave it for the whole day: this was "really good". She met a plastic surgeon who injected something into her scars to make them disappear: this was also "really good". For a moment she became upset: she was not sure whether he really did it well. But then she reassured herself: he must be a good surgeon, after all he was a friend of her mother's. I said she was not sure whether I had done something good or bad to her. I went away and she took the opportunity to have a holiday with her family, which was an achievement. But it seemed that we should not think any further about what she really felt. Had I allowed something awful and cruel to happen? She replied she was fed up with interpretations about my break. Her break was fine. I said, maybe it was too much to ask her to tell me painful things in our first session back; she must think me mad for wanting this. She went silent and I thought there was a battle going on inside her. Suddenly she started to talk and a real despair emerged. Her younger sister was self-confident while she often felt so small and shy; she could not stand it. She could not bear seeing her stepfather play with her siblings: she also wanted a father. She cried bitterly.

In her next session she told me, in a matter-of-fact way, that she had strangled herself. She could not bear what she was feeling; it was such a relief to lose consciousness. Another patient had said it wasn't dangerous. Staff should not make such a fuss, it was perfectly safe. She put a rope around her neck and pulled it tight, she lost consciousness and came round again. I caught myself thinking, at least she didn't tie a knot in the rope ... and then, I should take this very seriously. I said that in the same way as she strangled herself and made herself unconscious, she was now strangling her own thinking mind and trying to do the same with mine. Should we really go along with her version that such an attack on herself caused no harm? Very convincingly, she replied that something that made her calmer could not be self-harm. I told her that I thought she was aware of the danger and would think I was crazy and uncaring if I didn't get worried. She fell silent but eventually said she didn't think she would die, but was worried she was damaging her brain and would not remember things. I said she wanted to have her own mind, remember and feel things, but when she did, she felt filled up with something awful and the only way out she saw was to strangle herself.

In my absence, she involved herself with people—mother, the surgeon—who interfered with her body and she became confused as to whether this was helpful or not. Once back, she was torn whether to remain with an abusive internal object or return to a thoughtful one, which she eventually did.

Over the next months, a different more libidinal narcissism, in the service of her development, emerged. I felt that she tried to find her own mind: she did not want to swallow what others had said. However, she was far from allowing separateness; everyone was to follow her in her thinking. Sessions showed a typical pattern. She talked a lot, but when I tried to say something, she shouted: I should listen, it was her session, she wanted to talk. At the end of such sessions, she became anxious and apologized several times, wanting reassurance that I did not hate her. In fact, I was more relieved than angry. She seemed to develop her own ideas, which was crucial for her. If I listened and gave her space, she became calmer and thoughtful. One day she said smilingly that I had picked her up late.

When I replied that she might have thought I didn't want to see her, she answered "No, it just means we have different times". In the same session she said that her mother confused her; whenever she talked about herself, mother said she had the same experience. "Can't I have my own?" she wondered. Her own thoughts and feelings became important for her and I was not allowed to intervene. This alternated with moments when she related to me and felt real pain. I will relate some clinical material from this time:

> She came to her session crying and shouting. An adult patient had started to teach her yoga, but Gina, another patient of mine, had organized, behind her back, to join in. In the group she had complained that Gina had not asked her. The group therapist's response was that she wanted a special relationship with the adult patient. How could he say that, he was completely wrong, she didn't want a special relationship! Whenever I tried to say something she shouted this was not the point, had I not listened? She thought I was her therapist and I didn't even listen to her. I finally managed to say that there were two people in the room who weren't listened to. She felt I did not listen, but I was not allowed to finish a sentence. She seemed to feel threatened whenever I opened my mouth, as if I wanted to wipe her out. She began to cry and told me that this was exactly what happened with yoga. Gina had sat down opposite the yoga teacher, placing Michelle's mat far away. She had enjoyed being on her own with the teacher so much! Never before had an adult just wanted to teach her. She now became painfully aware that Gina was my patient too.
>
> The next session she told me that she had put her name on her mat, so that nobody could take it, but she had also agreed with Gina to share yoga. Suddenly she became upset: Gina had lice. She moved to another chair in my room and declared it as her chair.

Here she seemed to fight for her place with me. Although she shouted me down and could not tolerate me having my own thoughts, she needed my presence to find her own thoughts and voice and to make sense of her feelings. When she felt I listened she could use me to think about herself.

I will now describe material from a later period, when she started to talk about memories of abusive situations and fears of having been sexually abused. Although she often felt unable to speak she managed to turn to me again and again, fighting the pull to strangle herself.

This session, the final one I will describe, was preceded by others in which she twisted what I said, took it as proof that I talked rubbish and that therefore she could not talk to me, even though she would need to.

> The session started with the same pattern and I eventually put to her that something strange was happening. She seemed to have something on her mind but then didn't get it out of her mouth. Instead we were sidetracked, nearly ending up in an argument, and not talking about the real issues. She now told me that she had slept with somebody at a party her mother had organized. Her stepfather had shown a fatherly reaction (she smiled): he was very angry as he thought the boy took advantage of her by making her drunk. Her stepfather was wrong; she had wanted to sleep with this boy, she took advantage of his wish to take advantage. Her mother had thought this was fine, and had slipped a condom in her bag. She would meet this boy tomorrow (which I knew meant missing the routine and structures in the hospital day). She explained why it was really important to meet him. I said I should be made to believe that this was fine and be manipulated into going along with it. She was furious: if I didn't take that back, she would leave. I said she thought it would be best for the two of us to join in this view and not listen to the warning that somebody was taken advantage of. If I just went along with this I would not take seriously her relief about the firm fatherly voice saying this was not on. I had expected her to shout at me. To my surprise, she told me that she hadn't used the condom and was worried now about diseases. She then got upset and started to talk about her father.

Over the next sessions, it emerged that she was deeply suspicious as to why her mother had introduced her to him when she was 12 and had never met him before. She thought mother must have known that he was "mad". He had made her drunk, had given her beer in a baby bottle, behaved like a child, saying, "Oh, I want your chocolate." She felt terribly confused about all this.

Developing her own mind and finding her own voice also meant that she started to separate from and confront the abusive internal object, which did not want her to speak to me and, over and over again, tried to seduce her into stopping any thinking.

Eventually, she remembered how her father had wanted her and another girl to take photos of each other, dressed in knickers and bras. He said he would crawl under a blanket and not watch. But the blanket had holes in it. She even believed him when he said he wouldn't look at the photos when developing them. How stupid she had been!

It became clear in this session how her wish to be seen and admired, a libidinal aspect of narcissism, became hijacked by a cruel object that attacked her capacity to think. This cruel object found an ally in the young girl who wanted to be desired, and could not tolerate the exclusion from the parental couple and her envy and jealousy when she saw her siblings being cared for. We can also see how traumatic childhood events and confusions have contributed to the development of destructive narcissism in her. In the case of Michelle, and other such cases, we can see moves from destructive narcissism, to libidinal narcissism and to object relating, which progressively have enabled her to continue her adolescent development.

Conclusion

In conclusion we can say that tolerating separateness and dependence, which are both necessary for relating to an object, is part of the struggle of adolescence. Very disturbed adolescents, who often have experienced traumatic events, cannot tolerate separateness. They are often intensely involved with parental objects, in love-hate relationships, and unable to disentangle from them. When faced with feelings of exclusion, they retreat into a state of projective identification with highly destructive internal objects. One gets the impression that those objects do not allow them to separate, and imprison them in a state of destructive narcissism. When we address both the destructive elements and the imprisonment this can allow for more libidinal narcissistic elements to come through. The adolescent who is more aware of the control the destructive pull has, tries to develop his own mind. Although this at times is accompanied by omnipotence and omniscience, therapeutically it is necessary to see the positive movements amid the angry outbursts or periods of negative despair, and to tolerate what may be directed at the psychotherapist in the transference. The shifts in more positive directions, even when there is a forward and backward flow in the process, can help the adolescent to confront the internal abusive system and foster their wish to develop emotionally in a fuller sense and to find their own mind.

References

Abram, J. (1996). *The Language of Winnicott*. London: Karnac.

Anderson, R. (1999). Suicidal behaviour and its meaning in adolescence. In: R. Anderson & A. Dartington (Eds.), *Facing It Out: Clinical Perspectives on Adolescent Disturbance*. London: Duckworth.

Baranger, W. (1991). Narcissism in Freud. In: J. Sandler, E.S. Person & P. Fonagy, (Eds.), *Freud's On Narcissism: An Introduction*. New Haven, CT: Yale University Press.

Bion, W. (1957). On Arrogance. In: *Second Thoughts*. London: Karnac, 1967.

Day, L. & Flynn, D. (Eds.) (2003). *The Internal and External Worlds of Children and Adolescents: Collaborative Therapeutic Care*. London: Karnac.

Flynn, D. (2004). *Severe Emotional Disturbance in Children and Adolescents: Psychotherapy in Applied Contexts*. Hove: Brunner Routledge.

Freud, S. (1905). *Three Essays on the Theory of Sexuality*, S.E., 7: 125–243.

Freud, S. (1911). *Psycho-analytical Notes on an Autobiographical Case of Paranoia (Schreber)*, S.E., 12: 3–82.

Freud, S. (1913). *Totem and Taboo*. S.E., 13: 9–82.

Freud, S. (1914). On Narcissism. S.E., 14: 73–102.

Freud, S. (1916). On Transience. S.E., 14: 304–307.

Freud, S. (1916–17). *Introductory Lectures on Psychoanalysis* S.E., 15: 13–463.

Grunberger, B. (1979). *Narcissism: Psychoanalytic Essays*. Madison, CT: International Universities Press.

Grunberger, B. (1991). Narcissism and the Analytic Situation. In: J. Sandler, E.S. Person & P. Fonagy (Eds.), *Freud's On Narcissism: An Introduction*. New Haven: Yale University Press.

Hazlitt, W. (1826). *On the Pleasure of Hating*. Reprinted Harmondsworth: Penguin, 2004.

Hughes, T. (1997). *Tales from Ovid* (translated). London: Faber and Faber.

Joseph, B. (1989). Addiction to near death. In: E. Bott Spillius & M. Feldman (Eds.), *Psychic Equilibrium and Psychic Change*. New Library of Psychoanalysis. London: Routledge.

Kernberg, O. (1991). A contemporary reading of "On Narcissism", In: J. Sandler, E.S. Person & P. Fonagy (Eds.), *Freud's On Narcissism: An Introduction*. New Haven, CT: Yale University Press.

Laufer, M. (Ed.) (1995). *The Suicidal Adolescent*. London: Karnac.

Laufer, M. & Laufer, M.E. (1984). *Adolescence and Developmental Breakdown: a Psychoanalytic View*. New Haven, CT: Yale University Press.

Meltzer, D. (1973). *Sexual States of Mind*. Strathtay, Perthshire: Clunie.

Meltzer, D. (1992). *The Claustrum*. Strathtay, Perthshire: Clunie.

O'Shaughnessy, E. (1992a). Enclaves and Excursions. *International Journal of Psychoanalysis*, 73: 603–611.

O'Shaughnessy, E. (1992b). Psychosis: not thinking in a bizarre world, In: R. Anderson, (Ed.), *Clinical Lectures on Klein and Bion*. New Library of Psychoanalysis. London: Routledge.

Rosenfeld, H.A. (1965). *Psychotic States*. London: Maresfield.

Rosenfeld, H.A. (1971). A clinical approach to the psychoanalytic theory of the life and death instincts: an investigation into the aggressive aspects of narcissism. *International Journal of Psychoanalysis*, 52: 169–78.

Rosenfeld, H.A. (1978). Notes on the pathology and psychoanalytic treatment of some borderline patients. *International Journal of Psychoanalysis*, 59: 215–221.

Rosenfeld, H.A. (1987). *Impasse and Interpretation*. London: Tavistock.

Steiner, J. (1993). *Psychic Retreats*. New Library of Psychoanalysis. London: Routledge.

Segal, H. (1986). *Delusion and Artistic Creativity and Other Psychoanalytic Essays*. London: Free Association.

Segal, H. & Bell, D. (1991). The Theory of narcissism in the work of Freud and Klein. In: J. Sandler, E.S. Person & P. Fonagy (Eds.), *Freud's On Narcissism: An Introduction*. New Haven, CT: Yale University Press.

Winnicott, D.W. (1963c). Communicating and not communicating leading to a study of certain opposites. In: *The Maturational Processes and the Facilitating Environment*. London: Hogarth, 1965.

Winnicott, D.W. (1965). *The MaturationalProcesses and the Facilitating Environment*. London: Hogarth.

Winnicott, D.W. (1971). *Playing and Reality*. London: Penguin.

PART III

ADULTHOOD

CHAPTER SIX

Mourning or melancholia: What's love got to do with it?

Eileen McGinley

W hether a person is able to deal with facing loss in its many guises, either predominantly through the processes of mourning, or through melancholic, depressive solutions, is something Freud recognized, in a ground-breaking way, was a measure of the nature of the development of the personality. As in so many other instances, Freud could see beyond the symptoms of a disorder, in this case depression, with their connotations of pathology, to how these symptoms gave us a better understanding of the functioning of the personality and its structure.

Freud postulated that although there were different pre-conditions for whether the loss of a loved object was faced either by mourning, or by depression, it was still the loss of a loved object that was common to both. The pre-conditions that can lead to one outcome or another involve several factors. They include the state of the ego when it meets with the loss, including the degree of maturity and integration of the ego and its functions. It also involves the nature of the ego's relationship with its objects, both external and internal. In depression, ego functioning is immature and the object relationships are predominantly of a narcissistic type. Freud postulated that the ego, rather than being able to abandon its object choice, instead splits, and regresses to narcissistic mechanisms, and takes the lost object into the ego itself. A process of identification with the object is set up, described by the now famous phrase, "Thus the shadow of the object fell upon the ego." This poetic description however somewhat belies the damaging effects to the ego of these processes, as the ego becomes altered through splitting and through identification with the attributes of the lost object.

Freud also seemed to be implying in *Mourning and Melancholia* that depression of a melancholic type could be seen as a pathological form of mourning, which raised the possibility that, under certain therapeutic conditions, there could be a shift from depression to mourning as a way of dealing with loss. We might think today that this shift could be achieved through circumstances that lead to improving the state of the ego, either through enhancing its maturation and integration, or by ameliorating the damage done to the ego through its identification with the lost object. This would be to promote the process of disidentification through which the ego is freed up and the potential for relating to new objects is enhanced.

But if this shift from a melancholic position to one of mourning a loved object can be achieved, then this must also involve a process of mourning in respect of the alterations to the ego itself, as well as a mourning in respect of relinquishing the object. That is, that both relinquishing the lost object, and disidentification involves a mourning process. Freud showed that the economics of the process of acceptance that the object no longer exists involves a respect for reality and its acceptance. However, this acceptance is never immediate, is only achieved slowly bit by bit, at great expense of time and cathectic energy, and he added, "In the meantime, the existence of the lost object is psychically prolonged." This is important when we consider how the connection to the lost object through identification still comes to exert considerable influence on the ego through identification with its properties, psychological and physical, even when there is acceptance that the object is lost. The work of analysis will be to make both of these unconscious processes more explicit, and involves the unravelling of the entanglement between the ego and the objects it has become identified with. This involves recognising what belongs to the self and what belongs to the object.

In considering the conditions that lead to the formation of depression, we have to remember that for the initial establishment of these pathological states, the person suffering from depression must have had no other recourse to dealing with the mental pain, anxiety and anguish attendant with the loss in any other way. Here, the work of Klein on the psychogenesis of manic-depressive states is relevant and illuminating (Klein, 1935; 1940).

Klein proposed that it was the establishment of a stable internal good object that determined the outcome of whether losses in later life were worked through predominantly by processes of mourning or predominantly by depressive identification with the object. She writes, "This first and fundamental external loss of a *real* loved object, which is experienced through the loss of the breast before and after weaning, will only result in later life in a depressive state if at this early period of development the infant has failed to establish its *loved* object within its ego."

What Klein alludes to is the failure for the infant to establish within its ego a loved object that has the attributes of a "good" object, which has serious consequences on psychic development and which sets up psycho-pathogenic processes, including depression. This allows for further consideration of the circumstances that lead to a failure of an infant's psychic development. This includes consideration of the innate qualities of the ego, but also the real nature of the external objects, and the external environment. The work in particular of Bion and Winnicott has greatly influenced our contemporary understanding of the circumstances which can lead to damage to the infant and child's psychic and cognitive development from the lack of a containing object, particularly important for the transformation of anxieties from being unbearable to bearable (Bion, 1962; Winnicott, 1965).

Different pathogenic consequences can result from deprivations in the containing properties of the early environment. These include the hypertrophy and over-dependence on projective-identificatory mechanisms (Rosenfeld, 1987) and to detrimental effects on the development of the capacity to symbolize and mentalize. (Segal, 1957; Fonagy, 1991). The over-use of primitive mental mechanisms may also be provoked as a defensive response to the infant being excessively projected into by her early objects. In this respect, the inconsistency of containment and attunement to the infant's needs may be particularly disruptive to its capacity to develop a stable sense of self, and a stable identity. Where the maternal object has been psychotic or borderline, there may have been very disturbing alterations to the maternal functioning, so that the infant is met with both an inconsistent object and also an inconsistent container. The problems with containment, in particular the transformation of affect laden experiences, can result in the infant having to resort to increasingly more violent projection to try to get through to the mother, or the infant being excessively projected into, and "no entry" defences set up against this (Williams, 1997). These situations are rarely absolute, so that there may also be moments of more helpful containment and transformation of the child's experience. Different types of identifications may therefore exist side by side, which although they may represent different versions or aspects of the same object, may be expressed or related to as if they are different object relationships.

If we return to Klein's statement that in situations that lead to depression in the infant and later adult life, there is a failure to establish the loved object, we might ask what she is meaning by loved. Klein described the situation in early infancy when object loss can lead to mourning as the depressive position. This is the constellation of anxieties, distressed feelings, and defences that are connected with the growing recognition and acceptance of a whole object relationship, when the object that stimulates our love, desire for and admiration, is recognized as being the same object that also stimulates our hatred, frustrates and, importantly, is separate from us. This process involves the dynamics of love and concern, sorrow and grief for harm done to the object in phantasy and reality through hatred and aggression, but also sorrow and grief at the state of the object and the state of the self. When concern and love for the object can be recognised as being part of the experience of loss, this stimulates reparative wishes towards the object, but also towards the self. This process allows for the ongoing evaluation and assessment of the real qualities of the object, and the reliability of the external world. It enhances the distinction between what belongs to the object and what belongs to the self. This is in marked contrast to identificatory processes which do not allow for this working through. In contrast to melancholic identifications, when the loss of the object can be accepted, slowly bit by bit, further work can be done on the maturation of the ego as the process of disidentification and individuation proceed.

The depressive position, as Klein postulates, heralds the growing capacity to master both loving and hateful impulses and emotions, and to tolerate ambivalence. When this does not develop, then love and hate of the object are kept very separate, split and projected. There is a tendency to deny separateness of self and object, and instead, narcissistic object relationships based on omnipotence come to dominate the personality.

Also, while the infant is in a state where there is little resistance to identifying with this object, it means that what is loved and identified with does not depend on whether the attributes of the objects are good or bad. If the object which is installed is early life is based on an identification with a depressed or ill mother, whose attributes include a limited capacity for containment, or a malignant type of containment, then the infant is incapable, because of the immaturity of the ego and its defences, of becoming separate from this object. Loss of the object of dependency is too bound up at this stage with the preservation of the ego. Until the ego has matured further, then relinquishing the object can be feared as bringing about a psychic catastrophe (Steiner, 1993). There is also the paradoxical situation that while the ego is identified with a poorly containing object, it cannot contain and transform the anxieties involved in relinquishing this object. This would also link to Bion's idea that when the infant faces a container which blocks the projections of the infant's anxieties, that this is experienced not as a passive process, but as being actively hated by the object (Bion, 1962). The container become like a deadening, malignantly misunderstanding or toxic object, unwilling to accept the projections of the infant's disturbance (Green, 1986).

If we consider that in both mourning and melancholia that it is the loss of a loved object that the ego is trying to deal with, one question might be, what has happened to the love for the object in depression? By the time we see patients in psychoanalytic treatment suffering from depression, the ego has become greatly altered, and also damaged by the depressive process. The experience of being identified with the lost object is described by the patient as like being invaded by the object, like a parasite lodged within the psyche, like being possessed by a malign ghost, or like being consumed and controlled by the object. It is as if both subject and object are locked together, not so much in a loving relationship, but in a very destructive, violent, cruel, and sado-masochistic interaction. The person's predominant internal perception is of hating their internal objects, and being hated by them, and having a limited capacity for loving. So what has been the fate of the more loving and helpful aspects of both the self and object in these situations? Even if splitting and projection of the loving aspects has occurred, where do they now reside, and why do the libidinal aims become so immobilized?

This question is in part answered by the fact that some of the libidinal aims find expression in the narcissistic object relationships which are set up through narcissistic identification with the object. These relationships can become highly organized into pathological organizations of the personality which can become addictive and difficult to relinquish. Rosenfeld's work (1988) on destructive narcissism has in particular shown that what may be loved about objects in the narcissistic disorders are their destructive qualities, which is also relevant to narcissistic melancholic identifications. Betty Joseph, in her paper (1982) on *Addiction to Near Death*, tackles another aspect of depression, which is the pleasure gained from the torment of depression, and of tormenting the object, aspects of depression that are both painful to recognize and difficult to relinquish.

The libidinal aims can also find expression through the development of hysterical symptomatology. Freud had been first interested in the process of identification from his very early work on hysteria. As early as 1900, he wrote, "Identification is not simple imitation, but assimilation on the basis of a similar aetiological pretension; it expresses a resemblance as is derived from a common element which remains in the unconscious. This common element is a phantasy." He added, referring to hysterical symptoms that "... the symptom is a defence against this identification and against the sexual wish it presupposes." Later, he also noted (1921) that several different identifications can exist side by side in conflict with each other. The hysterical identifications seem to particularly defend against oedipal conflicts that cannot be worked through a process of mourning. Consideration of these different types of identifications is relevant for some of the clinical material I would like to consider today.

The body plays a large part in the presentation of this patient. She is a large woman, and she considers herself overweight, and that the propensity to "heaviness" is inherited from her mother. She dislikes the look of her body, and is suspicious of any man who likes her as she is, fearing in her mind that he might prefer her body to her as a person. This split between her representation of her body from her representation of herself leads to quite severe dissociation between her body and mind.

I would like to present some clinical material to illustrate how we might try and understand her better by thinking of whom she brings to analysis with her for help.

Clinical material

The patient, Ms A, is a woman who first came for psychoanalysis after her mother was hospitalized following a suicide attempt. Ms A thought she had had an idyllic childhood, a view that was apparently only shattered by her mother's illness. She spoke initially with very little sympathy about her mother's disturbance; she expressed more how she had felt betrayed that her mother should have tried killing herself without telling her. Both parents could be depressed, and seemed very resentful for different reasons of their own parents. Her father was prone to severe outburst of temper and shouting, but she has always presented this in a very idealized way, and that she is just like her father. There were obviously shameful "secrets in the family" and she had an early dream in her analysis of the family secrets being found out, and her family being sent away as outsiders, outcasts from the rest of society who could not bear to look at them.

Despite quite considerable difficulties in working with her, she had found the analysis helpful, even describing it as a life-line. She became increasingly successful in her work, but became quickly resentful, tired, unappreciated. She also tended to become "one of the boys", and had a very low self-worth concerning her feminine identity. She hated her body, the way it looked, but this was changing.

Her analysis had been a very stormy one, and she nearly always avoided me and acted out around my breaks, either by taking long breaks herself, missing many sessions with the lead up to a break, and then being very shocked at my absence. After she made several trips overseas, when I kept her analysis available for her, the attraction of escaping to another country had lost its appeal.

The sessions I will present occurred about five years into her analysis. I would like to present firstly a sequence of sessions to show some of the rapid shifts in her thinking, the nature of some of her identifications and her defensive manoeuvres whereby I think she brings aspects of her objects, particularly her mother, to analysis in a reparative way (Rey, 1988). I would also like to show how her narcissistic identifications hindered the more dependent and needy infantile aspects of her ego from being helped.

Session one

She returned on a Friday after missing nearly five weeks of her analysis. Work commitments meant that she had talked about and planned to miss three out of five sessions during this week, but she had not come to any of them. I would get a telephone message each day, usually left on my answering machine, and timed during the session before hers. She would mumble in a low voice that she had the flu, or a headache, or a cold, or had slept in, or had slept through her alarm. I eventually wrote to her, saying that I was concerned that she was finding no time for herself, or her analysis, despite her having made arrangements that she could attend some of them.

Significant factors prior to this prolonged absence were that an increase in her analytic fees were due to start that month, agreed on before the summer break, and I had also changed some of her session times by five minutes, which she correctly thought was due to me accommodating a new patient.

When she came into the session, she fumbled in her bag, and I thought she was looking for her cheque to pay for her bill which was weeks overdue. Instead, she was looking for a tissue, and asked if I had one, and took one from the box on my table. She started by saying that when she got my letter, it had sobered her up. It made her realize that her focus had been all wrong. She seemed to try to reassure me that she now wanted to make time for her analysis, for this to be her focus now. After a brief pause she told me what a terrible few weeks she had had. She had been shouting again at her team; they all hated her. She then told me that she was buying her mother a flat, and how ungrateful her mother was. She also did not have a flat mate, she needed to advertise for one, but she could not get round to doing anything. After another pause she repeated that she had made such a mistake, but could make some time now.

I said to her that it had been very difficult for her to turn any of her attention to coming and seeing me, particularly having to accommodate and make adjustments for a new time.

She did not respond to this directly, but repeated that the weeks had been awful, that she was worried that she had alienated her staff, felt that they all hated her, and that she had been shouting at everyone. I suggested that she had spared me her shouting by not coming, but perhaps it was really me that she wanted to shout at and not her staff. After a short pause, she said that she thought it was to do with her mother. Her mother had told her, in the way she usually did, that she did not really mean to tell her, but that she had not wanted a third child. She had thought of aborting her, but had not. She thought her mother never really cared for her. She asked what kind of person would want to abort her.

I said to her that when I had changed the time of her sessions, she had thought that I was having another patient, like a third child, and that she had not been to any of her sessions since the start of the new times. I think she had wanted to abort her analysis, along with my new baby.

She turned on her side, I thought in more contact with me and more towards me, and said that she had spoken to her sister, H, about her mother and told her that she thought their mother did not really want her, did not have time for her.

I suggested that she turned to her sister, H, in the session because she was her older sister, and that she hoped that H knew something about feeling pushed out by her when she was born, just as she was feeling pushed out now by my new patient, worried that I would not have enough time for her. She replied, again in an indirect way, that she thought that her mother was jealous of her being her father's favourite, because of her secret relationship with her own father. I said that seeing me having a new patient had also come as a shock to her, as it made possible that there might be a father somewhere who was being kept out of sight from her, rather like a secret relationship which she was not a party to, and perhaps this was more shocking if she wanted to be my favourite patient.

She became quite tearful, and said she had made a terrible mistake. She felt so much on her own and the only people she had helping her were people she had to pay. I said that I thought she was not just talking about money, but that she knew there was a price to pay to come and see me, and sometimes she was persuaded that the price was just too high for her. But I got the impression that she was now regretting this, and was wanting to try to get back to the possibility of something better with me again, and not to give up her place, either to one of her sister's or even to her father. At the end of the session she repeated the new time of her next session and wished me a good weekend.

Discussion

I felt in this session that I had to be sensitive to her persecutory anxieties over returning to see me after such a prolonged break from her analysis, and her fears whether she had tried my patience to breaking point, and whether I would want her back. She keeps me still waiting for her, waiting for her to pay my bill, waiting for something from me, and some sign that I still want her. She presents in a complex way, in which she seems quite fragile, needing me to give her tissues, perhaps as a sign of my friendliness, and yet I experience this as something rather exaggerated and even disarming. My letter to her seemed to be experienced as helpful, something which "sobered her up", as if she had been in an intoxicated state, expressed usually by manic acting out. She could also allow herself to turn at least some of her attention back on me and her analysis, though this was done in a very tentative way.

It was interesting to me that when I took up in a more direct way her identification with a mother who wanted to abort her, and linked this with her wish to abort the third object, she seemed able to tolerate this, and was even relieved. I thought there was a movement from a more paranoid atmosphere at the beginning of the session from her fear of being aborted, to a more depressive position of her fear that her mother did not have time for her. Her identification with the aborted object, which was acted out by her abandoning her analysis, and me, causes her to lose any contact with me as a potentially good object and someone wanting to help her work. It was however, very unusual indeed for her to turn to her sister in a helpful way, and she had also tried keeping some links to me by phone. I think in this way she kept my attention in some way on her, and her on me, without having to see anyone else. She still cannot tolerate too much direct links to her own hatred and aggression provoked by the new, more triangular situation, where she is not the total focus of my attention. It is her mother's jealousy of her, not her jealousy of her mother with the new baby; it is her own secret relationship with her father which has been her focus when she turns away from her mother or feels that her mother turns away from her.

Another aspect of this I would like to consider is that I think she may also be attacked by her own ego, when she is more cooperative in her analysis, as this gap also occurred when she had been appreciating her analysis more and had been coming more regularly to her sessions.

Session two

A Monday session. She came 10 minutes late, and went to the toilet before the start of the session. She explained that she had come by car that day, and that she could not find a place to park, though she had been up and down the street. Friends had given her the car and had only charged her £100. She had had a difficult weekend, she was buying her mother a house, well actually a flat, and the solicitor rang to say that there was a conflict of interests for him, and he told her she would need another solicitor. He had made it seem very dramatic. She rang her mother, who was in a panic. She told her mother that she should phone the senior partner. Mother did and rang the patient back to say that she had made it alright, and had even managed to negotiate a better deal to get the flat for less. With contempt, she said the way her mother was talking, anyone would think that she was buying the flat and not her, that it was her suggestion that she speak to the senior partner, but she said she would have thought about it anyway. She knew she felt very resentful but did not know why.

I said that there was lot in what she said of circumstances where people were negotiating what was the proper price to pay for things, what was a going rate, and this also included what she was paying for her sessions, which were going up this month. She sounded very shocked and said that she thought the fees had already gone up. I asked her what she meant, as we had arranged that the new fee would start after the summer break. She explained what the bill was in July, and she thought that it must be the new fee, it had seemed so much. She had calculated it was the increased fee. She felt sick.

She told me that she had already promised her mother that she was buying her flat; she could not go back on that now. She was sure my fees had already gone up. She paused and then said she thought my fees were only going up a much smaller amount. She could not pay. She did not have the money. I picked up her sense of shock, and also outrage, that she had come to believe that the fee was more what she wished it would be, than what it was, and she was now feeling that both I and her mother were making unreasonable demands on her. She continued in the same resentful, furious and anxious way, that she just could not afford it. She did not have a flat mate, and she would need to advertise for one. She never had any money for herself. I thought she was feeling trapped, that she could not stand up to her mother's voice when she told her that she must buy her a flat, even although her sisters had managed to resist this, and she had told me that there was something poetic about this. But there was a battle with me over what she should and could be paying for her sessions, that had been avoided by her missing so many of her sessions, and that there was a conflict of interests between what she wanted to pay, and what she thought was a more correct fee.

She left the session fuming with anger.

Discussion

This difficult session follows the session after which the patient felt helped and was grateful that I had helped her to regain the focus of her analysis. I had felt provoked at the beginning of her session by her lateness and her not bringing her cheque, and felt that I had jumped in with my interpretation about her fees, not really interpreting well what the situation was. I was left with the anxiety of not knowing whether I was being too greedy; was I asking too much from her, was I being too demanding? But there was also the idea of a conflict of interests and a fight over who possessed the mother, who owned her flat as it were, and a split between a greedy object who demanded and wanted too much, alternately projected into me and her mother. It was never her wanting or demanding anything. It was her mother who was ungrateful, not her. I thought she was also in a manic identification with her father; she was buying the flat for her mother as he had done, so why was her mother not grateful for this. I thought she may also have thought that if she bought the flat she would have been more in control of the analysis; it would have been her space and not mine, which she had to wait to return to after a weekend break.

I also felt full of doubts about the truthfulness of what she was saying to me about her bill, and the new fees, as there had already been a struggle over what a reasonable fee was for her to pay me. There was a very strong sense of "How could you do this to me?" which was very unsettling. Another element was that there was also something potentially reparative and generous in her wish to buy her mother a flat, and I could feel sympathy for her feeling that her mother was never grateful for her approaches to her. Yet there was something suspicious behind her generosity, and there was a repetitive pattern to her making all these generous gestures to everyone, but no one appreciating them. There was never any question in her mind with her involvement in how this state of affairs came about.

Session three

In the final session of this sequence, she came to her session in a much more sober mood. She had asked her sister whether she loved their mother. Her sister had replied that she had not felt the same after she had tried killing herself. I said she now felt that she was like her mother in some way, that she was worried about what I thought of her after she had attempted to abort her analysis, like a suicide, killing me off in her mind when I had turned so unacceptable to her. She replied that she did not understand how her mother could have done it. I thought that she had to begin again to turn her thoughts to what state of mind her mother might have been in that she could try to kill herself, as if nothing mattered to her, but that her mother might also now feel deeply ashamed and regret her actions, and find it very difficult to face her children after what she had done. But the quality of "How could she?" also reminded me of the tone she took with me when I did something she found unacceptable, like raising her fees, or changing her session time. She wanted me to be able to have some doubts and regrets too.

She replied that she felt ashamed all the time, ashamed all her life; she felt shame and regret about everything. I said I thought she was now becoming very vague and generalizing, she did feel ashamed of some things, but I also knew that she valued and appreciated other aspects of herself, and me but that she did not often stand up for these. There was a long silence, but I thought she seemed more sober. There were only a few moments left and her mobile phone rang, playing the tune of the national anthem of the country where she was born. She got up and switched it off, not saying anything.

With some hesitation, I said she was not ashamed of letting people know that she had connections to the home of her birth, ones she even valued and was proud of, but that she tended to keep that very hidden from me, and even from herself. She said, with some questioning, trying to be dismissive, that perhaps that was only superficial. I replied that perhaps it was only superficial if in her mind and attitude her attachment to the tune was only superficial, only a bit of a joke but with no substance or meaning, but I did not think that was what she believed.

Discussion

I thought she did have great doubts at times as to whether my attachment to her and her to me was only superficial or whether it had more depth and substance and could survive her attacks on it. I thought that some of her manic protestations were unconvincing, and I suspected that behind a lot of her protestations to the contrary she wished to continue with her analysis. I wondered whether it was the acknowledgement of this, her need and even appreciation of me that could not be talked about. There also seemed a more adolescent quality to her rebelliousness, like she had been at school, but she may have felt that I was also missing the point, and this was not producing the desired effect. But what was the desired effect? To provoke me, to force me to engage with her, albeit in this very sado-masochistic way? By projecting her anger and hatred of the situation she was placed in, she would provoke these reactions in me. I wondered if this provided a familiar situation of certainty for her when what she was confronted by was her uncertainty about me, and of the future of her analysis.

There also seemed an issue of how to save face, that it seemed quite humiliating to climb down from her "high horse" position, while she still may have believed that I would adopt a superior attitude over her. There did not seem much room for ordinary errors and regrets, and learning from one's mistakes. I think I may also have missed the importance of her statement that she felt ashamed all her life. I seemed to want to hear this as an exaggeration over her feeling ashamed of some of her behaviour towards me and herself, but she may have been trying to convey a deeper sense of shame over an internal situation that was difficult to bear, and difficult also for me to try to explore further. There could be something so provocative about her negativity, like lying and thinking and then telling me that she could give up smoking for the sake of her analysis, but she was not going to, that I often lost touch with something more painful.

We see different aspects to her inner world. We see a belief that she has been promised something by the landlord, a permanent place which she need never leave, the idyllic place of her childhood, which she is only shocked out of when her mother (and me in the transference) acts in ways that expose our separateness and independence from her. We see her turning against her sexual mother, and an abusive, aggressive sexualised couple becomes idealized. There is no room left for any love: it is by now only a world of hatred, and a fight for possession of her objects, who cast her out, abandoned like Oedipus. For moments she recovers her equilibrium with my help, and then I can address not just her anxiety, but her hatred, and how she loses her sense of having loved either her mother or her father, and perhaps more importantly, having been loved by them. I thought she brought both identifications with her mother and her father together in this session. In a way she is positioned between them, or as Britton (2003) puts it, is in on the act.

Conclusion

Ms A seemed to be predominantly identified with her objects in a depressive way. These identifications were often very concrete, and somatically expressed and operated at a paranoid-schizoid level of functioning. Her identification seemed to be predominantly with a psychotically depressed attacking maternal object, and a depressed, irritable and explosive paternal object. At other times, working in the transference, a glimpse of more whole object functioning, belonging to more depressive position functioning, was seen but this quickly moved to hysterical identifications with her oedipal objects when she was confronted with relating to objects in a triangular way. These identifications belong to more pathological narcissistic mechanisms, with the characteristics of pathological organizations of the personality and borderline position functioning.

Her hysterical identifications trapped her in her oedipal illusions which prevented her facing, and accepting, and therefore working through her Oedipus complex, one of the facts of life. Instead of mourning and separating from her oedipal parents, she identified with them in an hysterical identification with a sado-masochistic version of the sexual link between them. In this way she expressed her knowledge of the triangular situation of the Oedipus complex, but at the same time defended herself against her own conscious awareness of her exclusion from the couple. By identifying with what she saw as the aggressive aspects of her oedipal parents against her, she came to idealize her aggression towards them. But what became lost in these identificatory processes, was her love for both her real objects and the possibility of a more loving link between her objects. These solutions maintained a link to her objects, but in a cruel, rather than in a loving way, though at times this may be all she could hold onto to maintain a very precarious psychic equilibrium. Her melancholic, narcissistic and hysterical identifications supported a fragile ego, yet also weakened her ego functions at the same time, and limited the potential for psychic development.

She seemed particularly persecuted by aspects of her analysis. Failures of containment, including my lack of understanding, were felt as my aggression towards her and my rejection of her in hostility, which she greatly feared. My interpretations also exposed her to my separateness from her, and she was particularly sensitive to the presence of a third object, which greatly disturbed her. Her experience of me as a new, third object, and not just the transference object of her primitive and narcissistic fantasies also disturbed her psychic equilibrium. The truthfulness or helpfulness of the interpretation, whether good or bad, was then not paramount, but more significant for what effect the interpretation had on her. While she had to limit her capacity to internalise and introject interpretations by various mechanisms, she limited the potential for introjecting not just the hated and confusing aspects of my interpretations, but also their containing aspects. This meant that a psychic apparatus for the containment and regulation of affects, that would make it more possible for her to bear the disturbing effects of any interpretation, was also difficult for her to internalize and identify with.

There was also a psychic situation for her where, as Freud put it in *Mourning and Melancholia*, while her ego remained split and fragmented, she had little resistance to processes of identifying with her loved objects, as opposed to relating to her objects. This made the intimate transference situation of an analysis a particularly hazardous process to negotiate while her ego remained immature, and while projective processes dominated the interactions between her and her objects. It meant that the analytic situation was one she not only sought, for containment from me as a good object, but which she also had to escape from when she was persecuted by fears of me either taking her over or re-projecting unbearable experiences back into her.

In summary, loving our objects goes hand in hand with the certain knowledge of their death and losing them. Freud was sympathetic to the very human dilemmas associated with the relinquishment of any loved object, but also to the potential benefits. He wrote, "It is remarkable that this painful unpleasure (referring to the mourning process) is taken as a matter of course by us. The fact is, however, that when the work of mourning is completed, the ego becomes free and uninhibited again." Why some people become trapped in deadening identifications with their lost objects, while others can relinquish and mourn them, remains of central importance for psychoanalysis today, 100 years from the publication of Freud's great masterpiece.

References

Bion, W.R. (1962). A theory of thinking. *International Journal of Psychoanalysis*, 43: 306–310. Reprinted in *Second Thoughts*. London: Heinemann 1967, 110–119.

Britton, R. (1999). Getting in on the act: the hysterical solution. *International Journal of Psychoanalysis*, 80: 1–14.

Fonagy, P. (1991). Thinking about thinking: some clinical and theoretical considerations in the treatment of a borderline patient. *International Journal of Psychoanalysis*, 72: 639–656.

Freud. S. (1900). *The Interpretation of Dreams*. S.E., 4: 150.

Freud, S. (1917). Mourning and Melancholia. S.E., 14: 237–258.

Freud, S. (1921). *Group Psychology and the Analysis of the Ego*. S.E., 18.

Green, A. (1987). The dead mother. In: *On Private Madness*. London: Karnac.

Joseph, B. (1982). Addiction to near death. *International Journal of Psychoanalysis, 63*: 449–456. Reprinted in E.B. Spillius & M. Feldman (Eds.), *Psychic Equilibrium and Psychic Change: Selected papers of Betty Joseph*. London: Tavistock/Routledge, 1989.

Klein, M. (1935). A contribution to the psychogenesis of manic-depressive states. *International Journal of Psychoanalysis, 16*: 145–174. Reprinted in *The Writings of Melanie Klein, 1*. London: Hogarth, 1975, 262–289.

Klein, M. (1940). Mourning and its relation to manic depressive states. *International Journal of Psychoanalysis, 21*: 125–153. Reprinted in *The Writings of Melanie Klein, 1*, London: Hogarth, 1975, 344–369.

Rey, J.H. (1988). That which patients bring to analysis. *International Journal of Psychoanalysis, 69*: 457–470. Reprinted in *Universals of Psychoanalysis in the Treatment of Psychotic and Borderline States*. London: Karnac, 1994, 229–248.

Rosenfeld, H. (1987). Destructive narcissism and the death instinct. In: *Impasse and Interpretation*. London: Tavistock, 105–132.

Rosenfeld, H. (1987). Projective identification in clinical practice. In: *Impasse and Interpretation*. London: Tavistock, 157–190.

Segal, H. (1957). Notes on symbol formation. *International Journal of Psychoanalysis, 38*: 391–397. Reprinted in *The Work of Hanna Segal*. New York: Jason Aronson, 1981, 121–130.

Steiner, J. (1993). The paranoid-schizoid and depressive positions. In: *Psychic Retreats, Pathological Organisations in Psychotic, Neurotic and Borderline Patients*. London: Routledge, 25–39.

Williams, G. (1997). Reflections on some dynamics of eating disorders: no entry defences and foreign bodies. *International Journal of Psychoanalysis, 78*: 927–941.

Winnicott, D.W. (1965). *The Maturational Process and the Facilitating Environment*. London: Hogarth.

CHAPTER SEVEN

Reconsidering narcissism from a contemporary, complex psychoanalytic view

Stefano Bolognini

Introduction

It is no easy task to reconstruct the historical vicissitudes of narcissism as a psychoanalytic concept and it is not my intention to write a scholastic review of a topic which really merits a more extended treatise in itself. Undoubtedly, Freud's (1914) conception of primary and secondary narcissism is still fully valid. As is well known, by primary narcissism Freud initially meant investment of libido in the self—which at that time he called the "ego" (Hartmann, 1950)—during an intermediate phase of sexual development, between autoerotism and object relations. Only later is part of this energy invested in objects. He subsequently applied the term to a primitive, undifferentiated, objectless state, which corresponds to an intra-uterine condition that the subject regains while sleeping.

Secondary narcissism, on the other hand, has four components:

a. Possible forms of return (pathological and regressive, even during wakefulness) of libido to the ego from the objects previously invested. This aspect is closely linked to psychotic pathologies, with particular reference to certain forms of schizophrenia.

b. A physiological quantity of libido investment in the ego, which remains there even in the object-cathexis phase. This aspect concerns above all the normal functioning regime of the ego and the self.

c. The creation of a psychic agency, the ego ideal, which is structurally consolidated and constantly active in providing narcissistic valuation criteria for the self.

d. The unconscious cathexis of the precipitates of lost objects which have been internalized in the ego, as described by Freud in *Mourning and Melancholia* (1916). This is why these internal items have such importance, value and influence on the psyche of the subject, though he does not know it.

In this paper, I will attempt to provide, by means of case histories, a "live" sample of a possible contemporary view of narcissism. This overview of the topic expressly considers the works of many authors who, for reasons of time and space, will not be listed. It consists of an ideal series of contributors ranging from Freud (cited above) to Grunberger (1971), Chasseguet Smirgel (1975), Kohut (1971, 1984), Green (1983), and the analysts of the self. All their contributions have been of seminal importance. Metaphorically speaking, I believe that each author has placed a significant brick to create the analytic house in which we live and work.

Contemporary psychoanalysis seems to have understood the usefulness of distinguishing, both dynamically and developmentally, the processes of constitution and growth of human beings, also (but not only) in the light of the development of their narcissistic order and equilibrium. For example, in clinical practice it has become quite natural for all analysts to distinguish accurately between healthy and unhealthy narcissism in order to choose from among the various treatment strategies available. In other words, we sometimes wonder whether the complacent self-assurance of a patient towards some aspects of himself is a providential strong-point in an otherwise poor, confused or depreciative self-representation or whether, by contrast, it constitutes a damaging and unrealistic presumption, which prevents the individual behaving intelligently and living a "normal" existence. Alternatively, in other cases, we might wonder whether a patient's apparent view of himself as an inadequate failure actually conceals his own secret ideal image of himself, omnipotent and megalomaniac; a repository for a residual narcissistic surplus that tyrannizes and disqualifies a real self that can never make the grade. And so on.

There is in any case a tendency in present-day psychoanalysis to recover and comprehend the patient's lost sense of self, whatever it may be, and gradually to gain a clearer perception of its healthy or unhealthy basis. Acceptability or lovability of one's own self by others, but also by oneself, is what I would call "necessary narcissism" or perhaps it could be described as the "minimum living narcissism" (as in minimum living wage). This issue seems to have taken on greater importance and now ranks with those traditionally investigated in psychoanalytic writings on the theme. It is linked, for example, to:

1. The subject's attitude to invest libido in objects (instead of confining himself to loving, considering, and appreciating only himself).
2. His capacity to distinguish himself from the object (instead of confusing himself with it).
3. One's own sense of self, whether it be cohesive, fragmented, or split (Kohut has written some truly important works on this functional parameter).
4. The realistic acquisition of a sense of one's own limitations and proportions (with all the problems linked to megalomania, omnipotence, and immortality fantasies, etc.).
5. Representability and the stability of one's own internal self-representation (an area of research investigated by the pioneers of the concept of self, such as Edith Jacobson (1964) and later taken up again in recent years by French analysts (e.g., Botella, 2001) when investigating *"figurabilité"*.
6. The tendency to project onto the outside world elements which are representative of the self in order to confirm to oneself one's own centrality (thus increasing the representation of the self really with a view to reducing or partially denying the existence of the non-self, the "other", so dear to French authors).

All these aspects—which I have chosen rather arbitrarily (the list is by no means exhaustive)—are involved in what we might call "the narcissistic dimension". However, each item is different and has been described and dealt with by various authors in the course of a century of psychoanalysis.

There is also a growing tendency in contemporary psychoanalysis to take up a relational and interpsychic stance in the treatment of narcissistic problems, without however losing sight of the carefully refined descriptions given by authors examining such problems from an intrapsychic viewpoint. Over and beyond learned disquisitions of a theoretical nature, this change of viewpoint has an important impact on the technical prospects of analytic treatment. For example, new light can be shed on the difficulties encountered by the individual in the necessary phases of "mirroring" of the self in the mother's face and/or mind. This topic has been investigated by Winnicott (1967), Lacan (1949), Bion (1970), and Kohut (1971), with contributions on "mirroring", "the mirror phase", "reverie", and "specular transference", respectively.

From a more relational viewpoint, thinking about what was lacking in the constitution of the mother-baby dyad and which potential psychic developments in that field might benefit from or be impaired by the analyst's various internal and external attitudes, triggers off a process of shared partial transformation which may change the internal state of the self by means of analytic interaction (analysis with the self). Here, the game is still "open", i.e., analytic interaction would produce substantial changes in internal object relations and might on occasions introduce new items into the composition of the patient's internal world, by means of new, transformative introjections of the analyst/object interrelation.

On the other hand, we may feel that *"les jeux sont faits"*, as regards introjection at the level of the self (or the ego to use Freud's language of the time). These same difficulties could then be studied and described from a more radically intrapsychic viewpoint. Here we would focus on the present functional situation, taken as permanent, and depend to a greater extent on the reading of internal reality by the conscious ego components of the analytic couple (analysis with the ego; relations between the patient's ego and the analyst's ego). The analytic work is one of recognition aimed especially at the level of the secondary process. What changes in this viewpoint is the way in which the subject's central ego may see and evaluate his own internal world and relate to it, whereas the composition of his internal object world would not be considered substantially changeable.

Figuratively speaking, we could say that in adopting the first stance, the analyst works to try to induce changes in all those travelling in the car, whereas when using the second, he feels he can influence only the driver.

It is my thesis that present-day analysts, regardless of their declared and conscious following of this or that theoretical school of thought, manage quite successfully to integrate these various observational and technical viewpoints. I also believe that narcissistic pathologies—including defective or excessive narcissistic resources, evaporation of narcissistic necessary "glue" or crystallization and rigid fixation of narcissistic investment in the self or the object—may today be treated using a variety of conceptual and operative instruments which have been made available by the wealth of literature on the topic.

For narcissism, as for all other sectors of our discipline, the task before us in the near future is to integrate the existing contributions on the question, even at the expense of gradually abandoning absolute and exclusive transference devotion toward one author or another.

I shall present two very different clinical cases. The first one is representative of "excessive" narcissistic pathologies, the second of "defective". These descriptions refer to the functional outcomes of the respective pathological processes, not to their pathogenesis.

Egidio

Egidio is a 38-year-old doctor whom I would describe as more grandiose than ambitious. There is something archaic about his narcissism which brings to mind "majesty": "his majesty the baby", as if he had an indisputable grandeur conferred on him by nature now and forever.

In actual fact, at work and as regards his career, he is somewhat inconclusive; more of a dreamer than a constructively ambitious careerist. Since he finds it hard to accept dependency, his career is hampered by continual disputes with his superiors. These conflicts are not specifically Oedipal in character, but more generally narcissistic, being aimed at possible paternal, maternal and fraternal equivalents. He criticizes both his colleagues and superiors, constantly referring to idealized alternative objects, unconscious representatives of his ego ideal. With these he has purely fantasy relations, but uses them to create an internal alliance and pour scorn on the real people he deals with everyday.

For example, the things his superiors do are not merely wrong, but also sordid and ludicrous, whereas "in America" (or "in Paris" or "in Frankfurt" etc.) "they work to much higher standards" and so on. Thus, he regards the world from the dizzy heights of his "majestic throne"/high-chair, and passes judgement on it. The world, however, cares little or nothing for him, which he finds highly frustrating.

Egidio cannot bear it when his father, mother or brothers telephone him at 8 a.m. to ask him for advice about which medicine they should take when they are ill.

"What?! How dare they?! What can they be thinking of?!"

He treats the other members of his family badly, feeling fully justified because of their supposed lack of respect for him. He talks to me about it, clearly taking for granted my total agreement with his point of view.

This brings to mind the narcissistic transference toward the self-object described by Kohut, according to whom in many cases the emergence of repressed grandiosity such as this is of itself an important therapeutic event heralding change. Kohut has shown that in certain cases these developments may form part of a process which leads to a resolution of the grandiose aspects "through lysis".

Egidio seems to manifest a strong desire to remain in an intra-uterine state; it is as if he had peremptorily placed a sign saying "Do not disturb" on his bedroom door. Clearly, this warning is also meant for me should it ever occur to me to "disturb" his absolute sovereignty by showing myself as an independent and separate object or co-subject. Certainly, we have still to make contact and deal with the anxieties of separation. But I perceive that his internal position is more complex and that his majestic throne/high-chair is bolstered up and rendered slightly perverse by his fixation with the "Me over-you under" model of the anal object relation, which leads to secret pleasure, and has been confirmed by an intense self-legitimizing narcissistic valorization.

Let us pause to consider this concept.

I use the term "self-legitimising narcissistic valorisation" to describe the operation whereby a subject authorizes himself to think of as legitimate and positive an aspect or type of behaviour of his which is in many ways dystonic and dissonant in common sense terms.

This aspect or type of behaviour receives not only approval but also admiration from a secret internal source. There is "someone" or "something" that confirms from within the admirable nature of the element in question. This "fixes" and legitimizes it, secretly but certainly, so that it becomes a valid component of his image and sense of self. The anal component adds superiority and obstinacy to Egidio's attitude and the final result is a hypocritical, complacent and non-conflictual certainty of his own natural right.

With a somewhat concordant empathic set-up, with which in theory I do not fully agree (Bolognini, 1997, 2001, 2002), but which has been strongly induced by Egidio, I waited for about three years in the hope of possible developments, but little or nothing had come of it. There was no "lysis" of the grandiose component, which persisted undaunted, nor any significant changes.

However, little by little, in an atmosphere of timid, relative trust, I felt I had built a kind of base-camp from which further operations could be launched, operations which might not be in tune with his expectations. To put it another way, I had acquired a small number of credit points which I had to spend wisely.

After one particular session full of evacuative turbulence, in which aggression and persecution had invaded the analytic field, making it impossible not only to deal with these aspects but also simply to create dialogue, there is at last a more relaxed session: a bright, clear day after the storm.

I decide to tackle the question of his "indisputable right not to be disturbed".

To be honest, at first I was aware of a difficulty within myself. I felt like the child who sees the Emperor parading before his subjects in his "invisible clothes", but finds the courage to say what he thinks and exclaims: "The Emperor is naked!"

In other words, I felt the typical initial sense of the "unutterability" of things which are kept split off in the other, and which he effectively manages to mark as implicit and not to be expressed.

After the first few words, however, I manage to express myself with relative ease, clearly and in detail, summarizing what he has told me over the years concerning his haughty, complacent attitude.

I thought I had gone too far and that he would find what I had dared to say annoying and unacceptable, but to my surprise, Egidio seems to be caught off-balance and recognizes the truth of what I say.

The biggest surprise, however, comes a little later when he apparently digresses to make an association and reveals a previously unknown biographical detail: his mother is a countess (albeit a rather impoverished one), and he had always secretly admired her haughtiness, which he saw as a positive, "noble" trait. This is significantly bound up with the narcissistic investment which legitimizes and makes "obvious" and natural, for him, the position of sovereign who does not wish to be disturbed.

Thus emerges his secret idealization of a highly idealized object and we end up talking (with a certain degree of malicious delight on my part) about Hans Christian Andersen's story of *The Princess and the Pea*, a tale that used to be read in terms of the precious discovery of a noble quality, i.e., hidden royal blood.

Nowadays, however, it chiefly elicits sarcasm about the supposed inability of the narcissist to adapt to normal coexistence with other human beings.

Theoretical observations

I believe that the vignette briefly presented above reveals a possible point of connection between narcissistic cathexis and libidinal cathexis as regards aspects of the self. This point is constituted by the experience of complacency, which is the result of a blend of fixative libidinal pleasure and self-legitimizing narcissistic valorization. In other words, the subject feels pleasure, i.e., he is satisfied with something of himself, and at the same time confirms this "something of the self" as a legitimate and indisputable trait which forms part of a lasting representation of himself.

"That's just the way I am!" is the expression most often used by narcissists with great complacency. The tone is anything but neutral and the underlying notion is: "Take me or leave me, but don't think for a moment that I can, want or ought to change. I like myself just as I am!"

This self-legitimizing narcissistic valorization is usually more or less consciously supported by parental approval. To an extent, it is physiological and a necessary part of the process of identity formation of every human being. Problems arise when such valorization is quantitatively excessive and produces a prevalence of ego ideal claims over the needs of the self, is dynamically rigid, resistant and unchangeable with respect to reality, or is unconscious or implicit, which most often means split, and/or repressed.

It is not easy for the analyst to say in the session that "the Emperor is naked". As always happens when faced with a split reinforced by self-legitimizing narcissistic valorization, we have to take a leap in the dark, or at least to jump to the other side of the ditch. In this the analyst is helped by his theoretical and technical knowledge, his personal experience and dialogue with his colleagues, which enable him to shift the centre of gravity of the patient's hypersubjective *Weltanschauung* to a position shared by the community.

But there is a more subtle and instinctive factor which helps the analyst say "the Emperor is naked": namely, his protracted counter-transference experience as "his highness's loyal subject", with the high levels of frustration that it entails.

Many professions are characterized by profound impulses which may be, to varying degrees, direct or sublimated. One thinks of a certain amount of sadism in surgeons, anal obsessivity in administrators, etc. Similarly, in analysis we should not underestimate or deny the sometimes precious contribution made by our instinctive negative responses: the analyst's vendetta is the secret driving force behind our technical choices more often than we tend to realize it. It is a matter of knowing when this vendetta is blind and destructive and when, on the other hand, it is instinctively directed toward the patient's pathological narcissistic component, which mistreats the object-analyst, just as it mistreats the patient's own libidinal-affective self. The analyst's best vendetta is to make the narcissistically despotic patient more aware of himself and his way of relating to objects, by downsizing the secret prestige which some of his components enjoy—sometimes perversely.

The analyst's claim always to succeed in grasping the needy, "wounded" aspects of the patient is also one which smacks of narcissism, omnipotence and even megalomania. It is true that our patients need help, but they can sometimes hurt the analyst quite badly and there is no reason to offer oneself up on a regular basis as a latter-day St. Sebastian (as Pascal warned: "*Mais qui veut faire l'ange, fait la bête"*). On occasions, the analyst would do better to convert his physiological desire for vengeance into a useful technique.

After such a long time, I was pleased to be able to "settle my account" with Egidio. I believe I helped him divest himself of a narcissistic prestige which was archaic and anti-relational, as well as of forms of libidinal pleasure which were inadequate and brought him no benefit. Perhaps, today he feels a little less "noble", but at least he can now have a drink with his friends just like anyone else, and works better and more willingly. He is also capable of a certain affectionate self-mockery which was previously unthinkable. In this particular case, I am delighted to have taken my "revenge".

Manuela

According to my view of "necessary Oedipal narcissism" (Bolognini, 1994), Manuela is a child who has been prematurely disinvested and abandoned by her father.

In everyday speech, we talk of a "broken home" when husband and wife are separated or divorced. Thus, the problem of emotionally or physically abandoning one's children is considered almost exclusively as the lack of the basic element of a family container.

By contrast, the narcissistic wound connected to the Oedipus complex tends to be overlooked. It could be formulated as: "My father (or my mother) has another relationship, which means not only that my mother (or my father) was not enough for him (or her), but above all that I was not the apple of his (or her) eye."

One reason for the underestimation of this wound may perhaps be due to the idea—not in fact so rare among analysts—that basically the oedipal phase should be got over quickly, otherwise we might run into anomalies. I regard the process of Oedipal disillusion (the mourning of the Oedipus complex) as one of the crucial points in the separative phase of human development, alongside birth, weaning, adolescent emancipation, leaving home, one's children's marriage, retirement and so on.

In the final stage of her "Oedipal flight", Manuela did not make a soft landing. Quite the contrary, she crashed traumatically to the ground. As regards megalomaniac pretensions, I have good reason to hold her less responsible than Icarus for this outcome. By this I mean that the process of Oedipal disillusion is universal and absolutely natural, and that it requires working through in a certain length of time and in a certain way and that these elements were missing in her case.

When she was six, Manuela's father formed a new family with a new wife and a new baby girl. He kept in touch with her sporadically, more for the sake of cultivating a superficially irreproachable image of himself than out of genuine interest. He always saw her in the company of his new partner, whose reaction he feared. Since he was also a narcissistic, seductive man, his visits were always exciting, grandiose, self-centred and highly disappointing. He "topped up" his narcissistic resources, appearing grand and exciting, only to disappear again for a while.

Manuela's mother is rather poor in narcissistic resources, but her affective and concrete investment in her daughter is solid and reliable. By working hard and making sacrifices, she provided her daughter with the wherewithal to grow up, study and become a qualified biologist.

Manuela is 40 years old and alone. She has had only one secret and conflict-ridden love affair (from age 30 to 38) with Mario, an elderly director of the firm she worked for. This surrogate Oedipal father, a married man, died after a long, painful illness, thus bringing to a tragic end a relationship which had been "forbidden, secret, and impossible" in the classic way (Bolognini, 1994), but which at the narcissistic level had been as providential as rain in the desert.

From my point of view, Manuela could have, at least in part, "picked up where she left off" and continued the process which would have led her, though not without considerable effort, to work through the Oedipal dissolution. Indeed, her lover had had no intention of leaving his wife and family and Manuela had already started, even prior to his fatal illness, to experience the turbulence and narcissistic wounds which naturally form part of disillusion.

On the other hand, as regards the traumatic disappointment she had undergone in her childhood, that relationship had been partially reparative, although her lover died too soon and the narcissistic recovery was clearly insufficient.

Monday's session

Manuela has been in analysis for six months with four sessions per week. After the analyst's absence for a week, she arrives for the session with an extremely depressed expression on her face. She is pale and seems distraught.

Patient (very sadly): "I heard about Dr X's death." Dr X is an elderly biologist from a different area who had not previously been of great significance to her. (Silence.) "It's dreadful news." (Silence.) "Just like when Dr Y died." He was an elderly administrator in the same firm who had taken her on after her graduation and who died eight years ago.

   I think to myself about the strong impact a week's absence has had on her subjective experience. Rather awkwardly, I find myself, in my fantasy, "touching wood" to ward off the possibility of being the next on the list. I think of the primitive experience of deadly omnipotence of which the patient must feel herself to be the bearer, and of a sort of pernicious sorcery.

Patient: "On Saturday there's going to be a refresher course on anti-flu prophylaxis and I'm having a job to keep the two old witches at bay." There is a hint of self-irony in Manuela's sadness; she is referring to two colleagues of hers who are against the firm's programme of refresher courses, and her negative experience of them. "As usual I have asked Professor Z from the Ministry to come and give the seminar, but he is ill and I don't know how long he will be able to carry on."

   Thank God I feel all right, I think to myself. I also think that Manuela is repeating the matter which affects her eternally and profoundly, fraught with ambivalence toward the paternal object. I reflect that we are here to work on this question. In a word, I try to "think positive", but realize that there is a brooding sense of death in the air, and fantasize about being the first to explore the tomb of Tutankhamen and get out alive.

Patient: "I had two dreams. In the first, two figures were twirling in the air, but one of them was finding it hard work. Someone offers to help her by hanging a cable from the roof beams, but then gives up: the beam wouldn't have taken the weight."

Imagining the scene, I feel very sorry for Manuela, who finds it impossible to "dance" and who is supported by nothing and no one.

Patient: "In the second dream, someone has come into my house as if they had the key and stolen some jewellery and the books on the top two shelves of the bookcase, the Adelphi and Einaudi editions. And instead there were books I don't have: *Grimms' Fairy Tales*". (Silence.) "Last Saturday I came to Bologna for another conference. There was Dr D who seemed interested in me, but I put him off. He has the physique of an athlete. I'm quite the opposite. I feel ashamed of myself."

Analyst (not knowing where to start, but feeling that the moment had come to start working through the material): "Here, today, you announce various deaths: Dr X, Dr Y and even Professor Z seems unwell. Perhaps also Mario, the man you loved, and your father, who disappeared from your life at a certain point, are part of this list, which also includes me, since I disappeared from sessions for a week."

Pause; I feel that Manuela is pondering my words and her feelings.

Analyst: "It is difficult to 'twirl' with someone when you are so 'weighed down' within yourself, and if the 'structural beams'/father/analyst cannot 'take the weight'; it's impossible for a girl to learn to 'dance' without such help and support. The jewellery which should serve to make you feel pretty and feminine has also disappeared, carried off by someone who 'has the keys' to your house/self, and who can enter and leave your life all too easily without your being able to stop him. At bottom, it's all rather underhand: someone like me, who knows you well, or your father who always knows how to 'hook you up again' but then he carries off ... no! he actually 'steals' your sense of self-worth, because he makes you want and admire him."

Patient (disconsolate and sorrowful): "Yes, that's how it is. And another problem is that I don't even have a lock strong enough to keep him out of the house."

Analyst (perceiving that the patient has entered an area of shared symbolization and intends the potential metaphoric sense of the concrete items she cites): "And what about the books on the top two shelves?"

Patient: "Well, they are very good editions, the most valuable books I have, in the sense of cultural value as well."

Analyst: "It seems that the person who stole your jewels was also capable of impoverishing the 'higher' levels of your mind. In their place, you find Grimms' Fairy Tales, a metaphor for regression, for returning to infantile mental levels ... ." I have in mind the persecutory feeling of being pursued by pernicious sorcery, like in the tales where a bad spell is cast upon a kingdom or a family.

Patient (extremely depressed): "It wasn't a pleasant feeling."

Analyst: "You make me think of the general sense of impoverishment after the traumatic theft. The problem of low 'muscle tone' compared to Dr D seems to be connected to the loss of your personal 'tone' if the analyst leaves today for whatever other interests, just as your father once left home."

Patient (thoughtful and finding it easy to make associations): "When I was 14 there was a boy who took great interest in me. He was very shy and serious and never kissed me. One day he suddenly started going out with a friend of mine, a pretty blonde girl who is now his wife." (A sense of great suffering.) "He left me just like that. Something in me was wrong; he was right to go off. He was right." She is deep in thought; I continue to feel much grief for her. (Pause.) "Mario saw something pleasant in me, not because I was nice but because he was like that; he needed someone to love. My body hasn't changed. On Saturday Dr D would have been disgusted if he had had an opportunity to see what I am like."

Analyst: "It seems that my absence has re-opened an old wound linked to abandonment by a father figure. The result is that you feel subjectively that 'the beams cannot take the weight'. The fact that you are able to tell me this is important." I feel that by filling me with sorrow and desperation—in the original sense of hopelessness, the patient is taking the first steps required for her to share her experience in a way which is not totally evacuative. By experience, I know we are on the right path. Later it will be possible to start the operation of libidinal-affective replenishment and at the same time recover her narcissistic resources.

As she leaves at the end of the session, the patient's face bears an expression which, though still suffering and hesitant, contains at least the merest hint of doubtful, conflictual, but nevertheless perceptible hope.

Theoretical-clinical comment

It strikes me as important that the analyst does not only have in mind, but also samples—at least to a certain extent—both the subjective ego-syntonic experience of the patient, which is deeply depressive, and the past experience relevant to the internal objects of the patient herself: the "abandoning", or dead or deadly objects that deprive the patient of her healthy narcissism (denying it through the practical demonstration of how easy it is to abandon her), or strengthen the pathological narcissism through a reactive quest for omnipotent illusions ("objects only abandon me because I—not helpless, 'hilflosig', but on the contrary, very powerful—make them die").

Why is it important that the analyst should, at least to a certain extent, experience such a complex condition?

Because, in my opinion, patients perceive quite realistically—through words, micro-behaviour and even the technical choices of the analyst—if he/she either truly understands what they are feeling, or only deduces it; or if the higher point from which the analyst observes and assesses them is even more harmful to their physiological "necessary" narcissism, or if it offers them some repairing hope regarding this fundamental component of human nature (which, in everyday language, is known as "self-esteem" or "amour propre").

In general, I think that pointing out to patients their pathological thought patterns—for example, projections, as such—is counterproductive, given that this further injures their sense of self, which is already seriously damaged (and, most importantly, by pointing it out, you do not reduce the projective flow).

The exception is when, as in Egidio's treatment, we find a major obstacle to the elaboration of a different mental and relational position caused by fixation to a kind of pleasure.

The general concept that I would finally like to briefly summarize is that the contemporary analyst treats the analytical configurations and developments, taking into account, among other variables:

1. The basic narcissistic needs (necessary or physiological narcissism) of the patient.
2. The tolerability of his/her interventions from the point of view of the patient's narcissism: what, for the time being, can be tolerated and what cannot; what will injure, offend or humiliate the patient intolerably and what, instead, can be considered and processed by him.
3. The qualitative evolution in the narcissistic organization of the patient: which of his aspects are invested with narcissism? Are those aspects part of conscious self-representation? Do they

facilitate or impede relations with others, and will they do so in the future?

My, perhaps optimistic, hypothesis is that a shared, "collective", technical-scientific evolution is, in this sense, actually modifying most analysts, beyond their official, conscious adherence to a theoretical or other type of model. To put this simply, I think that a century of psychoanalysis has, in any case, made psychoanalysts sensitive and aware also of the basic needs and potential fragility of the self of their patients, and that the qualities of tact and respect are considered increasingly important, as much if not more than in everyday life.

References

Bion, W.R. (1970). *Attention and Interpretation*. London: Tavistock.

Bolognini, S. (1994). Tranference: erotised, erotic, loving, affectionate. *International Journal of Psychoanalysis, 75, 1*: 73–86.

Bolognini, S. (1997). Empathy and empathism. *International Journal of Psychoanalysis, 78, 2*: 279–295.

Bolognini, S. (2001). *Empathy and the Unconscious*. Psychoanalytic Quarterly, *70, 2*: 447–473.

Bolognini, S. (2002). *Psychoanalytic Empathy*. London: Free Association, 2004.

Botella, C. & Botella, S. (2001). *La Figurabilité Psychique*. Lausanne: Delachaux et Niestlé.

Chaesseguet-Smirgel, J. (1975). *L'Ideal du Moi*. Paris: Payot.

Freud, S. (1914). *On narcissism: an introduction*. S.E., 14: 67–102. London: Hogarth.

Freud, S. (1917). *Mourning and melancholia*. S.E., 14: 237–260. London: Hogarth.

Grunberger, B. (1971). *Le Narcissisme*. Paris: Payot.

Hartmann, H. (1950). Comments on the psychoanalytic theory of the ego. In: *Essays on Ego Psychology*. New York: International Universities Press, 1964, 113–141.

Jacobson, E. (1964). *The Self and the Object World*. New York: International Universities Press.

Kohut, H. (1971). *The Analysis of the Self*. New York: International Universities Press.

Kohut, H. (1974). *How Does Psychoanalysis Cure?* Chicago: University of Chicago Press.

Lacan, J. (1949). *L'etade du miroir comme formateur du moi*. In: *Ecrits*. Paris, 1966.

Winnicott, D.W. (1967). Mirror-role of mother and family in child development. In: *Playing and Reality*. London: Routledge, 1971.

CHAPTER EIGHT

A dehumanizing form of prejudice as part of a narcissistic pathological organisation

Sally Weintrobe

Introduction

We say of genuine human contact that it touches us. In puts us in touch with our feelings. Experiencing emotions such as love, empathy, pity, sadness, guilt, remorse, and shame is recognized as part of the work of mourning and facing the depressive position. Feeling emotionally touched by someone also tends to mobilize in us awareness that both we and the other person are fellow human beings and that we share common human ground. In other words, we share the problems and concerns as well as the joys of what it is to be human. We realize we are linked and connected to the other, "in it together" as it were, and not so different after all, even if only in the sense of "there but for the grace of God go I".

The recognition of sharing common human ground leads us to want to treat the other fairly, as we would wish to be treated ourselves. This involves seeing the other as entitled to as much dignity and respect as we are and, like us, as entitled to be heard as an individual. It also leads us to feel guilty and ashamed when we do not listen properly or act in good conscience towards the other.

141

Psychoanalytic work on pathological organizations (see in particular Steiner, 1993, and Rey, 1997) has led to an understanding that one of their main functions is to avoid genuine human contact with the other in order to avoid experiencing emotions, "suffering" them as Bion (1962) put it.

Pathological organizations defend against anxieties as well as emotions. The anxieties include depressive anxieties, particularly about causing damage to the other and to the relationship, and paranoid schizoid anxieties, particularly of feared damage to idealized views of the self and to idealised relationships. A pathological organization can also defend against very primitive levels of anxiety, for instance involving fears of bodily fragmentation and being in bits, collapsing, falling through space, or being trapped inside objects. The organized defensive system that makes up a pathological organization can act like a carapace or hard shell (see Anzieu, 1993; Rey, 1997, and Tustin, 1986), designed to protect the self from being assailed by these kinds of primitive anxieties. It may result in an ongoing defensive oscillation between the paranoid schizoid and the depressive positions with neither being genuinely reached before it is moved away from and avoided. Here, neither position is fully felt and there can be a phobic avoidance of anxieties and emotions felt to be "too much" to be borne and suffered. Pathological organizations involve complex and multi-layered manic defensive strategies to protect the self from "too much" anxiety and "too much" painful emotional contact with psychic reality.

It can be very difficult and often not possible to unravel what factors may have led to the formation of a particular pathological organization. Was it a survival response to trauma in childhood that has by now become a part of character? Had it a constitutional foundation? Based on some speculation but also on getting to know the patient whom I will discuss, Mrs. B, I came to think that she had suffered considerable emotional neglect by an anxious narcissistic mother. Her mother basically wanted her to be someone else, the apple in her idealized maternal eye; she did not show her much affection, interest, or understanding, and also seemed to want immunity from the anxieties inherent in being a mother with a child. I do not think Mrs. B's mother took her in sufficiently; did not make herself available to receive her projections. To survive in the rather cold environment of this relationship, Mrs. B very early on formed a hard shell around herself as protection to avoid feeling anxious and left out in the cold. Her hard shell was formed in part from phantasies based on identifying herself with her cold mother so that unconsciously she felt she mostly lived inside this cold mother and feared to separate from her and face being in the cold.

Mrs. B's hard shell seemed to be made up of feeling superior and entitled to both special treatment and anxiety-free conditions. It came across as narcissistic in character but our work gradually revealed it to involve defending against very primitive and bodily anxieties. In the paper I will argue that to maintain her hard shell and to avoid feeling touched and softened she also defended herself by the use of phantasies involving dehumanizing prejudice.

Much work has been done on exploring the complex nature of the internal object relationships involved with narcissistic pathological organizations (see in particular Rosenfeld, 1964, and Steiner, 1993). Steiner pointed out that the psychotic part of the self can include sane parts that have been corrupted and seduced. He talked of the way that cooption and corruption of sane parts could lead to the phenomenon of turning a blind eye, where reality is both seen and not seen.

My limited focus in this paper is on just one aspect of the narcissistic pathological organization, the way a seeing eye can become blinded by prejudice. I suggest that a prejudiced eye does see the other but in a way that dehumanizes the other and also erodes common ground. Being on the receiving end of this kind of eye, under the gaze of prejudice, promotes feelings of humiliation, unworthiness, and rage. The person at the end of a prejudiced gaze may actually come to feel unworthy, not entitled to proper respect, and afraid that if they stand up for themselves and assert their equal rights to human treatment in the relationship, they may be subjected to severe punishment. The object of prejudice may retain their sanity but lack courage and backbone, and be forced to the sidelines in the relationship.

In the paper I suggest that a prejudiced gaze is maintained through the operation of various phantasies that rely on splitting along the lines of dissociation. These phantasies include seeing the self as superior, particularly ideally good and moral, and the other as inferior, particularly extremely bad and immoral, seeing the bodily self as ideally clean and the body of the other as revolting, messy, and disgusting; and seeing the self as a supremely important individual while stripping the other of any individual qualities, casting them in a stereotyped way as a nondescript part of a group. These are all phantasies that elevate the self while denigrating and dehumanizing the other.

I will limit my discussion to one of many functions that dehumanization may serve for the narcissistic organization. This is to enable greed to flourish without apparent guilt and shame, and also without apparent comeback. Prejudice is designed to weaken its object and succeeds in doing so for as long as the object remains intimidated and/or agrees with the assessment that it is unworthy and bad. In discussing narcissism, I will restrict my use of the term to its more destructive forms, as described by such authors as Rosenfeld (1964), Kernberg (1975), and Green (2001). What has been termed positive, or "normal" narcissism, as described by authors such as Kohut (1984), I see as part of the lively entitlement of a lively self to a relationship with reality.

The narcissistic part of the self, discussed here as relying on an organization involving multi-layered and highly organized defensive strategies to maintain itself, not only feels entitled to adoration from the other as being special and ideal, but also feels entitled in a narcissistic way greedily to exploit the other, to treat the other as a servant, and to use the other for its own gratifications. Part of its sense of narcissistic entitlement is also to be spared conflict, guilt, and shame over this treatment of the other. However, because a sense of morality and what is fair is a natural part of being human (see Rayner, 1999), treating the other in an inhuman way necessarily leads to a situation, if faced, of conflict, and also potentially considerable anxiety about any damage caused. Because of the nature of the manic defence of rendering guilt insignificant, anxieties about damage can tend to escalate.

If the other in the relationship is dehumanized and common ground is eroded, there is less sense of anything shared with the other, and consequently less risk of feeling touched and so experiencing remorse and guilt over exploitation. Of course this is an omnipotent solution that depends on splitting and projection.

The resulting delusion is that the other is not fully human and thereby can be dissociated from. The reality is that the narcissistic part of the self has found organized ways to split off a sense of good conscience and to dehumanize the self.

This paper explores this general theme within the clinical setting of psychoanalysis. It us focus is on the use of prejudice to achieve an inner state of dehumanization, so allowing greedy exploitation of the other to continue while avoiding feeling touched by the other or feeling anxious about the fate of the self and other, thus helping to maintain the delusion that greedy exploitation can continue in a guilt- and shame-free state. In this way both closeness and distance from needed good objects can be managed and regulated.

In a prejudiced gaze, what becomes eroded is more loving empathic feelings evoked by seeing the good in the other, by feeling drawn to and close to the other, and by forming an individual tie with the other. Thinking about the other tends to become stereotyped, rigid, and not open to new experience. Prejudice results in dehumaniza-tion, but, importantly, dehumanization can also be its underlying aim. Prejudice is a highly effective way of rendering untouchable someone one also needs. However, it is not the other who is untouch-able; it is rather the self that is protected from feeling touched.

A very extreme illustration of the elimination of common human ground with prejudice at work is Primo Levi's description of the way Dr Pannwitz looked at him. Dr Pannwitz was his Nazi jailor and the chief of the chemical department at Auschwitz. On first meet-ing Dr Pannwitz, Dr Levi reasoned that if he could convince him of his credentials as a fellow chemist, he might avoid extermination. Dr Pannwitz looked at him and Primo Levi remembered, "That look was not between two men; ... [it] ... came as if across the glass window of an aquarium between two beings who live in different worlds."

This vividly conveys the dehumanizing gaze of prejudice. The other is seen but as so inferior as not to share any common ground. Self seen as superior and other seen as inferior have no points of contact. They live in different worlds that do not meet or connect. Here the splitting and projection is achieved through dissociation. Self and other are kept separate in a rigid way. They share nothing in common.

Clinical material

Mrs. B, a patient in analysis, brought a recurring dream:

> *A lord of the manor enters a room. Someone else who is there leaves.*
> *The two are not together in the room at the same time.*

Slowly, through our work together I gradually came to think this dream represented her unconscious understanding of the existence of a superior lord of the manor figure in her internal world. This figure eroded common ground between us to ensure very little emotional touching and to promote a situation where each of us was to live in segregation, actively held apart from the other. We were not to be in the same room at the same time. In her internal world an organized narcissistic part of herself treated a lively part of herself in the same way. Equally she experienced me as a cut-off superior psychoanalyst attempting to lord it over her. I will suggest that this lord of the manor figure also had a prejudiced gaze.

Mrs. B

Mrs. B was a young woman in her early twenties, very recently married. When the analysis began, she tended to be dismissive and hostile to her new husband; she felt that after all, they had little in common. The marriage seemed in jeopardy, and she had frequent thoughts of leaving.

She was actively hostile and evasive of contact for several years in the analysis. I struggled in an ongoing way to try to understand her and to take in how she might be experiencing me. It emerged that she saw me as a rather high and mighty analyst type who did not really want to be bothered with her and did not listen to her, who was not interested in my patients whom I saw as inferior to me. I also came to think she needed an experience of a mother who could accept her, including when she was hostile and evasive, and she needed to express these feelings and have them received. I often found myself locating my position with her as a child with a rather cold and distant mother, and struggling to survive. I was struck by a pervasive sense of her needing to be in control and began to notice the ways she blocked affective contact. She could also be quite superior in the way she dismissed what I said as uninteresting and rather stupid. I was aware of how difficult it was at times to maintain a balanced analytic outlook, by which I mean repairing both my heart and my mind in the face of what I could experience as considerable onslaughts against both. The cold atmosphere was particularly hard to endure. I also noticed that she would become very anxious, disagree with me vehemently, and say I was in effect a very bad analyst at moments when she was in danger of allowing herself to experience feeling herself to be understood by me.

One day, thinking over a particularly difficult and blocked session, I wondered if I had missed seeing something quite fundamental. This was that I was talking to someone who saw me through prejudiced eyes. In less extreme terms, but to illustrate the point, it was as though I was in the position of Levi being looked at by a dehumanizing Nazi in her. It struck me that there is no talking with someone who is deeply prejudiced against one. I sensed her prejudice was ego-syntonic for her and was operating as part of an underlying narcissistic pathological organization.

The ongoing countertransference situation was of being with someone who did not seem to relate to one as fully human but who nevertheless needed one badly. It was rather like being a needed but discounted servant. We never seemed to be quite in the same room together and I had an impression that anything of real significance for her was going on in her thoughts about relationships outside the room. My role was to help whatever it was that was happening out there to happen better, and I did seem noticed in this way. I found Mrs. B's lord of the manor dream helpful in thinking about this atmosphere. I think that when a lord of the manor side of her entered the room of the session, a struggling patient in her relating to a struggling analyst were forced by her lord of the manor to exit. It was the analytic couple that was forced to exit her internal analytic workroom.

I hope to illustrate the way that I thought Mrs. B attempted to keep internal objects rigidly apart through the use of prejudiced phantasies involving superiority, grievance, revulsion, and groups. I suggest these phantasies were based on a dissociative form of splitting and were aimed at achieving a state of dehumanization. This was a defence against feeling touched by emotions and anxieties that felt highly destabilizing and "too much".

At the time of the first clinical example, taken from during the first phase of the analysis, Mrs. B had begun to bring material that indicated, I thought, an unconscious understanding that she was living in a split state. Despite always coming to her sessions and for the full time, there was a chronic and ongoing feeling that she did not want to talk to me and she would express her hostility towards me openly. She very rarely showed any enthusiasm. I would detect grumpiness and also a sense of her not wanting to be bothered, and I would find myself having to take care not to enact the role of being someone who carried any hope for change. I discerned that she could play rather perversely on feelings of hope.

First clinical example

She arrived and gave me a smile as she came in. She lay down. After a short silence, she said, "Before I came here today, I thought I wanted to talk to you, but actually I find I don't. I don't have any desire to talk today." She sounded to me rather cold and disengaged and she was then silent for several minutes. I said yesterday she had said she was feeling hostile to me and that was why she did not want to talk to me, but today I sensed she was more unwilling than hostile. No, that's not quite right, she said dismissively; she was feeling hostile. There was more silence. I asked if she had felt hostile before or after what I had just said. Before, during and after, she replied. She told me a dream.

> In the first part, she was at a dinner with other people. She was given special food with some meat in it, which she started to eat, but then she left and went to the loo. Not much came out. She spent time washing herself and then went back to the dinner. She found that people had finished the main course and she thought, well at least I can have the dessert. She had fruit salad but she found bits of it dropping through the utensil she was using. Then, in a further part of the dream, she was at a party. Tom was there but on the other side of a fence. She called for Tom to come to the party but he was filled with grievances and refused. Tom started to move further off and Mrs. B climbed over the fence and followed him, saying to him, "Give up the grievances and come to the party." But Tom went further and further away, and she lost him. Then someone appeared who said, "Let Tom go."

Her associations were to her friend, a man I have called Tom. She said Tom was a very angry and depressed person who ruined his relationships, and Tom was also a control freak.

I said I thought she was telling me about two different sides of her, that she kept quite separate, like the two areas divided by a fence in her dream. One side of her wanted to talk to me and the other side of her was caught up with grievance towards me. The dream showed her wanting to appeal to the person in her who nursed grievance to give it up and join in more with the analysis, the party in her dream. Her dream image of following Tom over the fence described us just now, with me following after her, encouraging her to talk and join in with me. "Mm" she said and lapsed into silence. Then she said she was thinking of a photo of her older brother as a baby. There were hardly any pictures of her as a baby. When she asked her parents about this, they said that was natural as her brother was the first one. That was the big event. She said this with great resentment. (This material was not new. She had told me several times before about the preferential treatment she felt her brother had received.) She went on to reflect that her brother felt that her coming along had spoiled it all for him. Actually, she said, she did not know whether she or her brother had the bigger grievances. She fell into a brief silence, and then said she was thinking about stories of cruelty and torture on the TV news. She became caught up with a theme of corrupt authority and a TV programme of fascists taking over the government. "You cannot rely on any safe authority, anywhere," she said bitterly. She began to talk in a way that seemed to me chopped up and bitty about how corrupt all the governments of the world were.

I told her the session was now like part of her dream. She might have felt I gave her something meaty when I talked about the bit of her that was being rather hostile and aloof here with me, that needed all this persuading to be a part of her analysis. I considered she recognized this, but like in her dream, she then went off and washed her hands of it. I said her doubts about who was to blame and what was reliable started out by being about her personal relationships, with me, with her brother, her parents; but then her doubts became impersonal and abstract, about governments, and her thinking seemed to start getting chopped up, and harder to pick up, like bits of fruit salad. I said she felt increasingly lost when this happened. She said "Mm" in a way that sounded more thoughtful and also relieved. Here, I sensed a moment when there was more of a feeling that we could be with each other in the same room and talk to each other.

Discussion of first clinical example

One aspect of the first part of her dream was particularly important. *She missed the main meal by going off to the loo, but had dessert.* Nursing grievance is frequently accompanied by anal phantasies. I saw *going off to the loo* as representing her "control freak", part of herself, replacing a desired and needed analytic relationship (*the main meal*), with idealized self-produced products—her grievance-bound states of mind where she was grudging and withholding (*not much came out*).

Her prejudiced, grievance-bound state of mind, where she became excited by an increasing frenzy of cruelty, corruption, and cut off-ness *was* her dessert. However, here she was more openly needy about how lost this activity left her feeling, especially when it started to spiral out of control. One of the more dangerous aspects of projecting her manic side into larger and larger groups was that in this state she would become less and less able to find anything in herself or her analyst to counteract cruelty and sadism. Her individual ties with me, her wish to talk to me, and even the tie of her individual hostile grievance at the start of the session, were increasingly broken.

In this session Mrs. B became increasingly caught up with a pphantasy that she ruled the world. Links with an analyst who could contain her in the structures of reality were increasingly severed. The corruption of good authority, I would suggest, was projected into me and fuelled her grievance. Her message to me was, "Why should I talk to you or listen to you? You provide no safe authority." I thought part of her triumph was being able to sever links with her awareness of what might be called a good containing superego analyst (in the sense described by Schafer, 1960), while at the same time having it that it was the good superego that was corrupt. I sensed she started to feel hugely inflated with this activity, which was the exciting dessert that she tended to choose over the main meal of reality.

In this session she was still projecting into groups to a considerable extent and was still living under entrenched split conditions (the *fence* that divided). However, a sane part of herself appeared to be stronger than previously. Also, she seemed to listen to what I said at the end in a thoughtful way. A link was preserved with an analyst and a part of herself who could help her to think about her megalomania. In her dream imagery, this was represented by *someone who appeared and said, "Let Tom go"*.

I thought prejudice was present in this session. Her revulsion came across in a quality of, "Ugh! I don't talk to *you*. Not yesterday, today or tomorrow." Her grievance came across in her grudging withholding and her underlying accusation that I was a corrupt authority that could never be relied upon. Her use of groups came across in the way that by the end it was not me she felt was corrupt and unfair but me as one of a stereotyped group—world governments. However, despite her use of prejudice phantasies, the lively unprejudiced part of her self, grown stronger, was able to tell me about her desire to see me, to preserve a tie with me and to hear and feel contained by my final interpretation about how lost she was becoming.

It took considerable further analysis to make progress towards Mrs. B being able to look at her internal world and its objects in a more realistic way, one freer of prejudice.

Second clinical example

This clinical example is from the middle section of the analysis. Towards the end of a Friday session she told me her husband was in a European city on a business trip and not due home for another week. She had been agonizing about whether or not to fly over to join him for the weekend. The weather forecast was sunny, and, acting on impulse, she had just phoned him and suggested she came. He was very pleased and encouraged her. Then the radio forecast rain and she phoned again and told him there was no point in coming after all as it was going to rain. However, in the session she was still nagged by the thought that perhaps she should go to be with him after all.

On Monday she began by saying, it was strange, she could hear her own voice better since her cold was subsiding. Then she said, well, she did go! It had been such a struggle to decide. She left the decision whether to go right up to the last minute, and she nearly missed getting a flight. She had to leave her car in a street near a tube station far from home. She phoned her husband from Heathrow and he said, "That's great! I'll be there to meet you." They had such a good time together. She helped him with some work he had to finish on Saturday, then on Sunday the sun shone and they walked in a beautiful part of the city that revived happy memories from a previous visit. So, she concluded, it had not rained after all and the visit had been worthwhile.

I said I thought she was finding it hard to let her husband openly know she wanted to be with him. After a pause, she agreed and said she had felt up against enormous difficulty in going, with an argument raging inside her. For instance, when she planned to leave her car near the tube, she immediately considered she could not possibly leave it there as it would be damaged by vandals. This became a huge issue in her mind. But in the event it was easy to leave the car. She found her worry evaporated and then she could not understand why her decision to go had been so hard. The plane was full, and she was allocated a seat next to a man who looked, well, a bit like a sort of "Albanian refugee", and she registered a feeling of physical reluctance to sit next to him. Then she thought it was awful to feel like that about another person, and during the flight she found herself thinking about the man. Why did he look downtrodden and troubled and tired? What sort of life did he lead? Who knew what sort of difficulties he faced? She started to feel sorry for him. He fell asleep and started snoring. Her husband was there to meet her, and it was quite romantic, actually. I said, "Mm" in a way to indicate to her that I recognized it had felt intimate and good with her husband.

Then after quite a long silence, she said although she slept well last night, she could not remember any dreams, and so had none to bring me. She sounded cut off and withdrawn as she told me this. I said I wondered if she felt I was only interested in her telling me her dreams, like a dutiful patient in analysis, and not so interested in what was really important to her right now: feelings and thoughts stirred up in her by her decision to meet up with her husband and be with him. After a pause, she said she was remembering the way her mother hated to be bothered by anything and found everything too difficult. Well, she continued, she did not want to think about her mother and in any case, I was never interested in hearing about her mother. So, she concluded, she agreed with me when I said I was not interested in her. Then she said there were phone messages for her when she returned home on Sunday night. One was from a woman friend whose life was not going well at the moment and who seemed stuck in a rather chronic sort of way. This woman was also hard- up financially. She did not want the trouble of getting involved with this friend.

I said I thought she did not want the trouble if she picked up a rather chronic "hard-up" grudging side of herself. She had been like that with what I had just said, saying she agreed with me, but also concluding I was uninterested in her. I said she had told me at the beginning today that it was strange to hear her own voice. I could hear two voices in her, one wanting to tell me about her good week-end, and the other more grudging. After a silence she said she was having nice thoughts about the weekend. She then told me in more detail about her day out on Sunday with her husband; what fun they had together, and their real pleasure in their surroundings, the good food and the carefree atmosphere. She conveyed, without saying so directly, that they had rediscovered an experience of being in love. Then she said there was another phone message when she reached home, one from a new friend, whom she really liked. She returned the call and they had arranged to get together. She had been think-ing about all this in the silence, then found she did not know what to say to me, and started falling asleep. I said I was reminded of the refugee on the plane who fell asleep and whom she felt sorry for, imagining him feeling excluded, struggling and up against it. I said I thought it felt exhausting and also painful to pick up and look at her grudging side that deprived her of good experiences. I said look-ing at it did not feel sunny, but felt sad, like the rain.

Discussion of second clinical example

In this material the lively part of her self was stronger and oper-ated to loosen the hold that prejudice had on her. Her anxieties were more depressive in feel—the rain that came with the good experience—and at this stage she only wanted the good relationship if it stayed sunny and she did not have to confront pain, loss and guilt. Here, her grievance towards an ideal *object* that was failing felt like the beginning of a complaint: why could she not have the good relationship without pain (sunshine without rain)? (I am using complaint in the sense outlined in my 2004 paper which contrasts grievance and complaint. Grievance is directed towards an ideal object that had failed whereas complaint is directed to an object with eyes and ears, an object who can take one in.) She was operating a manic defence against depression, very different to megalomania, and easier to begin to discuss with her. A sense of the "Albanian refugee", as an individual, came through despite her typecasting. Her revulsion seemed to have softened to a reluctance, which she countered with pity and empathy for him. This man had projected onto him not only her lively self, denigrated, exiled, and deprived of a relationship, but also her exiled and denigrated analyst whom she was starting to feel guilty towards. She was able to withstand internal intimidation in the shape of a mafia-type group (the vandals who would attack her car) that threatened her if she asserted she wanted to give up her prejudice against a real and an affectively good and truthful relationship. I thought I was the new friend she was starting to get together with, and this faced her with many painful aspects of reality.

Third clinical example

This example is taken from the end phase of the analysis. There had been a marked general shift in the atmosphere. Also, the emotional temperature in the room had changed. Whereas before it had tended to swing from cold detachment to invitations to heated dyadic and I thought erotized exchanges, now it was affectively warmer and also more human and ordinary. I noticed my warm feelings for her survived better in this new climate and less internal work was needed to repair myself.

A more perverse excited control had given way to Mrs. B being more sad and worried. She now thought the difficulties in our relationship lay more with her than with me. This did not feel like compliance—she could be very complaint—but felt genuine. She noticed she was not feeling so chronically angry. She was much more giving and generous with material, more helpful to me and to the analytic process. I sensed her levels of competitiveness and envy had diminished.

Her relationships were flourishing, as was her work life, and she now wanted to become pregnant and have a baby. I was able to discern real people in her descriptions of friends and family, something that felt new. Before I had tended not to be able to form reliable pictures of the people she spoke of that carried any conviction as genuine. More often my pictures were vague, lacked detail and substance, and were confusing. A very important part of this change was that she was able to assert something about herself without her usual caveats of "well", "I'm not sure", "I don't know", "but on the other hand". I sensed she was at moments risking not sitting on an endless internal fence. Alongside this she became less dogmatic and controlling, and more pained by moments of insight into her way of being imperious.

However, we also faced what seemed at times to be an insurmountable difficulty. When she came to a point of very nearly openly expressing gratitude to me she veered away. Often at this sort of point she would switch to talking of feeling very grateful indeed to others. I felt in an awkward position. It did not feel right just to ignore her ongoing avoidance of gratitude when the issue could seem so present in the material. At the same time it felt wrong to take it up. I sensed she might experience my saying anything about her apparent lack of gratitude as me greedily demanding all credit for myself. I also knew from experience that guilt and shame were two emotions that Mrs. B strenuously avoided, guilt more than shame. This felt like a place where the analysis could potentially become stuck. I was subtly invited into being either a bit silent and useless or into joining in with enactments if I mentioned her avoidance of gratitude. She could hear me as a beating and punishing superego very easily and I also sensed she felt terribly, monstrously, guilty in an underlying way and could use my words to punish and beat herself with at the drop of a hat, as an omnipotent solution to how guilty she did feel for the way she took from me in an ongoing way without acknowledgement.

In one session when I felt faced yet again with this sort of dilemma and was feeling stuck in relation to these kinds of thoughts, Mrs. B said something that I thought addressed the situation directly. She told me that she was suddenly feeling terribly, terribly, guilty towards someone, a woman she had never mentioned to me before and someone she hardly knew. I sensed that at this moment she was struggling to conceptualize her difficulties with me in relation to giving and taking but also keeping them at a great distance. Mrs. B went on to tell me she was planning a big celebration party. She had led this acquaintance of hers to believe she was going to invite her to her party but then she did not get back to her, did not offer a clear invitation, and had left her dangling. She felt terrible about this. How must this poor woman be feeling? She had put this woman in the awkward position as the one to contact her if she wanted an invitation to the party. It was not fair. Here I felt more able to make a link with the transference, suggesting that she was struggling with feeling guilty for not inviting me to share in her recent success and changes by not acknowledging my help, leaving me in the awkward position as the one to take this up with her.

The next day she told me what I said had got through to her and she had thought about it. She did not elaborate. She said she felt strange, aware there was something different about her these days, but not able to explain or convey it to me. Towards the end of the session she put it that she had had a glimpse of endless different ways that she avoided me. This was hard for her to see. It must be very tiring for me. She was feeling exhausted these days.

The following day she brought a dream.

> She came to fetch her car but found it stuck in a car park. The entrance was blocked by cars parked in front. She thought, "Oh my god I can't get out." But she knew if she waited the cars would later move and then she would be able to get out. She walked out and saw an old ruined castle up on a hill. It was so old it was prehistoric. She looked out from the castle and saw an extremely beautiful view. Everything was green and the sun was shining. Her first thought was they built the castle there for the beautiful view. Then she thought, no, the real reason they built it there was so they could clearly see when enemies were approaching. Building castles upon hills is defensive strategy.

She related her dream to the thought she had had about all the different ways she avoided me. She believed the castle in her dream was her defensive castle of avoidance.

Later in this session I reminded her that the castle was ruined and very old, in fact so old it came from prehistory. I was worried she could not quite take this, that it might leave her feeling hopeless, which she often did feel, but after a long pause she said, I thought in the voice of a small child, that she wanted to tell me a very strange thought she had had that left her feeling very anxious indeed. She was thinking about wanting a baby and then about having a baby. She suddenly urgently felt she had to get away from the baby as she feared it would be so demanding it would eat her alive and kill her.

Discussion of third clinical example

I thought she had brought her representation of her altered relationship to her narcissistic pathological organization in a dream. I saw, and she did too, in her way, the castle as the manor house of the lord of the manor side of herself, a dwelling place, a psychic retreat (see Steiner, 1993) maintained by a narcissistic defensive organization. I also think the manor was manna, the narcissistic supplies her lord of the manor fed her with. The material of the session revealed that the underlying situation she faced was an extreme one: that she lived in a close identification with me, almost parked inside me. To move out was to risk what felt to her "prehistoric" i.e. barely symbolizable kinds of anxieties. In this session she was able to put into words that her fear was of annihilation, being killed by being eaten alive. I do not think in this prehistoric place she could distinguish whether she was eating the analyst mother alive or being eaten alive by the analyst mother, and I sensed this was the ruined transference, the relationship ruined by irreparable damage caused by greed. It gave me a different perspective on the importance of my surviving her ruthless levels of greed both in my heart and mind. I think these anxieties about damage and ruin in the relationship were the worst sorts of enemies she needed to be able to see approaching and to defend herself against inside her castle.

Here, I suggest that our work had deepened considerably. We had come to understand far more about the primitive anxieties that her pathological narcissistic organisation may have been protecting her against. This was a situation of ruin, I think involving phantasies of a ruined mother, destroyed by uncontained greed (perhaps initially unmet emotional hunger for contact and the anxiety that her greedy lively hunger had indeed damaged the mother), and a ruined self, left with an excess of greed and without an internal mother and internal parents to survive it and help her contain and lessen it.

She was driven to test my forgiveness about being greedily exploited to destruction. When she felt she had managed to destroy me in heart and mind she felt in danger of a psychic melancholic collapse and when she felt I had survived and was not a ruined mother, and ruined parents, her destructive greedy side then felt entitled to exploit me further.

Discussion

My focus has been the way that the narcissistic part of the self needs good objects nearby to sustain it and to sustain life that it depends on, but at the same time also exploits these objects and needs to distance itself from feeling touched in a lively way by the nearby good objects. Seeing objects through a prejudiced gaze can appear to achieve the omnipotent feat of simultaneous closeness and distance from needed, exploited, and feared good objects.

In looking at prejudice from a psychoanalytic and clinical perspective, I have focused in particular on the way that emotions stirred by feeling touched in individual and intimate individual relationships, particularly with parents, can be dissociated from. The use of groups, especially when combined with revulsion and with narrow-minded negative stereotyping, are prime ways that prejudice achieves dehumanization of both self and other.

I have suggested that prejudice within the psyche can be part of a pathological organization, operated by the narcissistic part of the self, particularly when in the grip of megalomania and intent on preserving its entitlements. It is a way of looking at the object, what one might call the gaze of prejudice, coloured by the various types of fantasy that dehumanize. The narcissistic part of the self, to maintain its narcissistic entitlement to an omnipotently constructed psychic retreat, has a rigidly prejudiced attitude towards reality in human relationships. Objects that help make links with psychic reality are prime targets of its prejudice.

One target in particular is the normal superego. Bion wrote of a "super" ego, placing itself above the superego, that was "resultant of an envious stripping or denudation of all good" (1962, p. 97). Bion's "super" ego is an abnormal superego, destructive to the ego. The narcissistic self, particularly in states of megalomania, can operate as an abnormal superego (see O'Shaughnessy, 1999, for a detailed account of the concept). It dissociates itself from the knowledge that it exploits the needed good objects and also from knowing that omnipotence is not truly creative and generative. Prejudice plays a key role in relation to these two aspects of dissociation. Prejudice, through dehumanization, fosters delusions of exploiting with no cost, and being superior and in charge within the psyche.

Prejudice aims to erode common human ground. One kind of common human ground is of particular significance with patients like Mrs. B. In all three clinical examples, she let me know something of what it is like to be with a stony, rigid, prejudiced object, someone who is deaf to one's appeals. At one level, she may have wanted to find out if I was better able to manage this situation than she had been when little and faced with a narcissistic prejudiced mother who, as I have suggested, often did not take her in and contain her projections in good enough fashion. As I came to know her better, I also came to appreciate that she and I indeed shared common human ground in that neither of us dealt terribly well with this kind of ongoing prejudiced stoniness. She needed me to be able to feel it and to manage it, in order for her to have an experience of being taken in and understood. She could see psychoanalysts as lord of the manor types staying on the far side of a fence that kept out unbearable feelings, also high up on the analytic hill, relying perhaps on our interpretations to hold ourselves together and defend ourselves in the face of inhuman treatment. If I managed to survive her prejudice, she could feel I was not quite human. If I did not manage it, she could feel I was no good to her. However, her stoniness did gradually soften considerably as she began to appreciate my efforts to take her in, at the level of her feelings and anxieties.

References

Anzieu, D. (1993). Autistic Phenomena and the Skin Ego. *Psychoanalytic Inquiry*, 13: 42–48.

Bion, W. (1962). *Learning from Experience*. London: Karnac, 1965.

Green, A. (2000). The Central Phobic Position. *International Journal of Psychoanalysis*, 81: 429–451.

Kernberg, O.F. (1974). Further Contributions to the Treatment of Narcissistic Personalities. *International Journal of Psychoanalysis*, 55: 215–240.

Kohut, H. (1984). *How Does Analysis Cure?* Chicago: University of Chicago Press.

Levi, P. (1987). *If This is a Man*. London: Abacus.

O'Shaughnessy, E. (1999). Relating to the superego. *International Journal of Psychoanalysis*, 80: 861–870.

Rayner, E. (1999). Some functions of being fair and just. *International Journal of Psychoanalysis*, 80: 477–492.

Rey, H. & Magagna, J. (1997). *Universals of Psychoanalysis in the Treatment of Psychotic and Borderline States: Factors of Space-Time and Language*. London: Free Association.

Rosenfeld, H. (1964). On the psychopathology of narcissism: a clinical approach. *International Journal of Psychoanalysis*, 45: 332–337.

Schafer, R. (1960). The loving and beloved superego in Freud's Structural Theory. *Psychoanalytic Study of the Child*, 15: 163–188.

Steiner, J. (1993). *Psychic Retreats: Pathological Organizations of the Personality in Psychotic, Neurotic and Borderline Patients*. London: Routledge.

Tustin, F. (1986). *Autistic Barriers in Neurotic Patients*. New Haven, CT: Yale University Press.

Weintrobe, S. (2004). Links between grievance, complaint and different forms of entitlement. *International Journal of Psychoanalysis*, 85: 83–96.

PART IV

OLD AGE

CHAPTER NINE

Mourning in later years: Developmental perspectives

Arturo Varchevker

> *Autumn Song in Spring*
> *... In spite of time that's so unyielding,*
> *Thirst for love is my parched burden.*
> *With grey hair, I'm always moving*
> *Toward the roses in the garden ...*
> *Treasured days of my youth and boyhood,*
> *You are gone and won't be back again!*
> *You know I'd cry if only I could,*
> *Then the tears come and I wish they'd end.*
> *But the Dawn is mine! And it's golden!*
>
> *Ruben Dario (1867–1916)*

Defining older age

We cannot escape the format of life, even if we try hard. We can say that our destination is death and that this is the terminal station of our journey. This station is part of our life and includes beliefs and fantasies about death and life after death. From a biological perspective, life in all its manifestations has a cycle from birth

163

to death, which can be interrupted or disrupted by accidental or non-accidental circumstances. We are genetically coded and our biological clocks follow the patterns imprinted in our chromosome maps.

At the same time, developments in science and better living conditions in the western world have mostly extended the length of our journey. The impact is evident in the ageing individual who experiences noticeable biological and emotional changes. These changes have an effect on the family culture and relations. There is also a considerable impact in the health system, and in society at large.

Some say that the first signs of menopause announce the beginning of "older age" in women. Discrepancies are as varied as when people try to define the average age of the mid-life crisis. There is a benign attitude that manifests itself in the expressions: "He is a wise old man", "He mellowed with age", or independent of whether she has grandchildren or not, "She is a nice granny". When the person reaches older age, people's responses are apparently caring and often they say, "You don't look your age, you look much younger". Either the person who utters the caring expression cannot deal with the view of a body that is changing or the recipient of the comment is perceived as unable to deal with his or her view of a changing body, factual age, or both. In addition we know that certain contexts make this experience easier or more distressing. In our western culture when women reach around 45 and men around 50, they have already reached the middle of adult life and tend to experience that "older age" is getting too close. It is noticeable that the effort to push it further away is fuelled by narcissistic needs which are well exploited by our consumer society. From a socio-cultural perspective, some will say that older age starts with retirement. In some countries this is at 60, in others 65. In this country now, there is a project to extend it to 70. However, "older age" acquires an unpleasant taint in relation to what is considered wrong or improper for a person of a certain age—whether this manifests in appearance, work issues, sex, relations etc. In our culture, "old" has a pejorative or negative connotation. To say that someone is "old" or "too old" is a form of disqualification or negative description. I found it useful to subdivide older age into "early", "middle" and "later" stages. At the same time it is important to acknowledge that in countries where the health and economic conditions are very low, adolescence and older age have a brief span.

In 1905, Freud stated that he did not consider that older patients could benefit from analysis. He limited the benefit of this new form of treatment to a small population that was educated, not feeble-minded and not "old", which meant people approaching 50. In fact, because his theoretical conceptions, cultural and personal preju-dices furnished these views, he gradually shifted according to fur-ther observations and theoretical developments, and to his own personal circumstances and cultural changes. Freud's theories were based on an understanding of the patient's psychopathology and the constructions he made of the child's emotional development as part of its psychic functioning. As we know, the actual treatment of children not only confirmed some of Freud's theories, but also further advanced psychoanalysis as a whole and provided a deeper understanding of the individual psyche at different stages of life and development. Nowadays, there is plenty of evidence that older people also can benefit from psychoanalysis and psychoanalytic psychotherapy, and can achieve significant psychic changes. In fact, extended longevity has contributed to the increase in productive years and this has enabled many older patients to be referred to or to seek psychoanalysis or psychoanalytic psychotherapy. As a result, in the last few decades, there has been a growing understanding and experience of this type of patient.

From birth onwards the initial weaving together of early experi-ences will become the platform for further development. A gradual integration is achieved by the interaction of external and internal experiences that strengthens or disturbs this development. The former gives rise to integration or to what Melanie Klein describes as the "depressive position" and the second to further splitting and the schizo-paranoid position.

As highlighted by Klein, the mental life of the individual is domi-nated by unconscious phantasies in interaction with the outside world, which from the very beginning of the individual's life play an essential part in the development of the personality through the use of splitting, projection and introjection and especially projective identification. These phantasies tend to be modified by the way the individual has successfully or unsuccessfully dealt with the most important and pertinent tasks of each phase of development. This facilitates the exploration of what is common to the entire life cycle and what is specific to each phase. In addition, the concept of the family life cycle, which was introduced in the 1970s, complements this frame by facilitating the exploration of how individuals at different stages of the life cycle view and interact with themselves, in terms of their biological and psychological changes, and with other family members who are at different stages of the life cycle and vice-versa. I consider the individual life cycle and family life cycle useful frames for the exploration of the individual's behaviour and phantasies. In certain circumstances this contributes to and widens our understanding of what is going on in the patient's mind and in the interaction with the analyst. In fact, previous stages of the life cycle can lead to a type of emotional platform for constructive change, but can also move in the opposite direction. This means that they can be used as a refuge to side-step or block the following stage of the life cycle.

The work of mourning

We know that when older people find it difficult to integrate the experience of ageing, painful emotions associated with loss, lack of achievement and fantasies about their future set in. Depression is one of them. This is a familiar state of mind when we consider the various possible reactions to the process of ageing. Depression acquires different forms of intensity and shape depending on the mental state of the individual and his possible psychopathology. Ogden (2002) points out: "What differentiates the melancholic from the mourner is the fact that the melancholic all along has been able to engage only in narcissistic forms of object relatedness. The narcissistic nature of the melancholic personality renders him incapable of maintaining a firm connection with the painful reality of the irrevocable loss of the object that is necessary for mourning." The main difficulty of mourning for the older patient with a very structured narcissistic personality is acknowledging any separateness of the object, when the possibility of facing loss and changes in this part of life is hampered.

At times it is not easy to differentiate the melancholic depression of older patients from a depression that is part of mourning: I do not think that the work of mourning follows a straightforward line. What we have is the type of object relations, mobilized by internal as well as external pressures, that tend to block, distort, activate or facilitate the work of mourning. The complexity of this phenomenon requires close and sensitive scrutiny.

If the individual finds it difficult to tolerate frustration or psychic pain, the tendency is for them to find ways to rid themselves of that experience through mechanisms of withdrawal and projection. Manic reactions constitute another form of evasion. Anxieties about loss and persecution can intensify and activate feelings of impotence; the individual's sense of identity feels under pressure and their struggle is not to lose it. Ongoing feelings of anger, hatred, and depression are familiar emotional ingredients that colour their reactions to these changes. When paranoid anxieties have a firm grip, the possibilities of relying on a supporting environment, family, friends, and helpers, are undermined by the amount of splitting and projection that bring about lack of trust, suspicion, and delusional persecution depending on the psychic pathology. Success or failure in negotiating and integrating them have a crucial impact, be it positive or negative at this stage of life.

In older age the main Oedipal anxieties are represented by King Laius who fears the arrival of the new generation or by Oedipus who will end in exile.

In older age, the wish to acquire a positive role as the good grandparent also fulfils the function of counteracting the feeling of empty hands and acquiring a new value that reinforces and lifts the weakened ego. When this is done under the aegis of a harsh and persecuting superego, it manifests itself in conflicts of rivalry with one's children, now the new parents or parents in law.

Older age activates considerable anxieties. Some older people feel like a boulder in others' way, useless; they feel hopeless and helpless. I think that the comparison with asylum seekers captures vividly this particular type of experience. They feel like that, or are treated as such, or both. In essence they feel unwelcome and looked down upon as if they did not belong, and they represent a threat because they are so needy. I have noticed in my clinical experience with older people, especially when they are confronted with very important changes they need or hope to make to their lives, a cloud of pessimism, scepticism and passivity descends upon them which then is enacted in the session, propelled and coloured by their psychopathology and life circumstances. When these experiences are worked through, the significant changes that can be achieved can take both patient and analyst by surprise.

This brings to mind a patient, approaching his mid-sixties, who is in his fifth year of first three and then four times a week analysis. He is an intelligent man, looks younger than his age and is physically fit. He is seeking help because of a marital crisis. His sense of omnipotence and narcissism has kept him on the move all the time. The family business, which he expanded and made very successful, ran into difficulties in recent years; this activated his wish to sell this business. But selling his business has been in his mind for at least a decade, related to his wish to change his work and life style. He mentioned this at the initial interview and it reappeared on and off throughout the treatment with different meanings. At one level it feels like a form of defeat supported by his need to maintain an image of self-sufficiency and independence. Any real change posed a degree of uncertainty and this for him has become increasingly persecuting. He fears that he will be forced into retirement and then nobody would want to have anything to do with him. In fact there have been interesting openings in the last 18 months; in practical terms this could make the move manageable and offer him the possibility to carry on working in another field that has attracted him for years, but the uncertainty that any significant change brings about, especially at this stage in his life, arouses overwhelming anxieties.

Mr. A: "I feel that I am in a void. I don't know what I want. I don't know what I am doing here or anywhere. I don't know what to say or if I am saying things for the sake of saying things. For instance, now I don't know if I want to sell it. The mere idea that I may be forced to sell, it makes me sick. I have wanted to lie on my back and read and read; to get lost reading but I fall asleep after half a page. Then I wake up and I can't sleep. I don't want to retire. I don't know if I want to be with my wife or not. She wants to have sex and I don't want to. My cousin invited us for a meal and I don't know if I want to see them. I feel I have been in this state for such a long time and I don't see it changing." I said that he was presenting to me such a discouraging and gloomy landscape which made me wonder whether he was watching how I was going to deal with it. (Pause.) "I don't think so."

(Long pause.) I commented on what appeared to be apathy or lack of interest.

Mr. A: "I don't know. I am not watching or thinking about you or anybody when I feel like this." I drew his attention to the fact that he had arrived early to his session, which was quite unusual. Therefore I had presumed that he had picked himself up from the state of mind he was describing, which suggested that perhaps he had wanted to have a proper interaction here. Furthermore, he had communicated this in a non-verbal way by how eagerly and assertively he entered the consulting room and approached the couch, but then something unexpected happened that stopped him in his tracks. I referred to the fact that I had noticed that I had omitted to change the tissue that lies on the pillow (which normally I change after every patient and I apologized as I put down a new tissue). I suggested that he felt so unwelcome and rejected when he was confronted by it that his eagerness and positive attitude had fallen into a void; now he was not interested in the potential psychoanalytic work, he had gone into some form of retirement. His initial response was to say it did not affect him, implying: I'm not affected by such a small thing. "Sorry, I don't want to be rude, but it feels nonsense."

Initially I felt uncomfortable, feeling I should have waited longer before making my interpretation. We worked further on his response and gradually, through to-ing and fro-ing, the meaning of what had happened emerged. This issue showed the links with fears about getting involved with a real change in analysis, as well as practical, important changes in his work life. His active flow of associations and intellectualizations had kept him and me going as if this was a super-analysis, supposedly feeding his narcissism and mine. His parents never had time for him as each was engaged in so many important things outside the family. I also enacted that situation because, when I omitted to change the tissue, my mind was engaged with another issue outside my patient. The understanding of this interaction not only brought to life what was going on in the present but activated in a meaningful way what many times appeared as dead history. Mr. A's present crisis was activated by the financial situation

that may force him to sell his business or make significant financial adjustments and changes. This brought alive his early experiences, his familiar defence mechanisms, the difficulties of a genuine
involvement maintained by his sense of narcissistic independence.
A recent visit to a heart specialist had reinforced and coloured his
fear of ageing and dying, even if the medical investigation showed a
normal heart condition. He is now getting closer to his father's age
when he died and this also increases his anxieties about death.

Changes at this stage of the life cycle are different from important
changes at its earlier stages. The individual often feels pressurized
to get it right because there is the awareness that life ahead is limited
and one's own resources intrude and challenge yesterday's sound
defence mechanisms, activating stronger anxieties and fears. In older
people, passivity and depression, which quite often appear or reap-
pear, are the enemies of work and liveliness. Passivity, in most cases,
manages to kidnap initiative and through hopelessness institutes a
form of control. In some cases, hyperactivity or manic behaviour at
this stage are another form of defence to avoid these issues, especially when narcissistic needs can be successfully fulfilled.

External reality of the older patient presents a landscape of
major ongoing losses—relatives, friends who have died, physical
limitations—and tend to erode, in some cases a genuine move forward. The patient may feel that he/she got stuck inside a cloud that
limits the capacity to see and connect with a good object. The first
step is to become aware of this and draw the patient's attention to
what is happening. If this does not produce any movement, the analyst has to contain the good experience trusting that something in
their interaction may open up.

Sometimes, in the psychoanalytic interaction, we travel down a
very narrow path and what happens at one moment can have a different meaning a moment later on. This applies to every analysis,
but when working with patients who are physically limited by serious illness or whose age activates a physical and mental decline, it
is important to keep in mind that what is quite painful originates
in the limitations and illness of the patient. What I wish to emphasize is that in those very painful situations the analyst is dealing
with a complex phenomenon where several parts of the patient and
the analyst become activated and this requires a close scrutiny to
prevent the analyst's empathy becoming sympathy and therefore a

form of collusion or enactment. It is for this reason that what, when and how to interpret is so difficult.

Similarities with childhood and adolescence

There are significant differences pertinent to each stage of development. In childhood and adolescence the struggles are played out in the process of growing up to their next stage of development, while in older age the process of growing up is almost paradoxical, as the process of development seems like growing down. The landscape of "older age" presents a body that starts to develop faults and gradually degenerate, accompanied by fears of losing mental faculties and the nightmarish dread of dementia and ultimately death.

Much has been written about what happens with childhood, adolescence and adulthood. Notwithstanding that, I would like to refer to some interesting similarities between childhood and adolescence on the one hand and older age on the other. We can detect certain features in adolescence that have some resemblance to the first half of older age; there are also some resemblances between childhood and the later part of older age.

In general, the initial stages of older age and puberty arouse anxieties about new physical and biological changes. An observable feature is that pubertal and menopausal changes are more noticeable in the female sex than the male. Males in both cases can be less aware of the changes or the anxieties associated with them. At times, this lack of awareness may delay the possibility of having to deal with these anxieties and the obstacles that might be in their way. These physical and biological changes tend to activate fear and excitement at different levels of the personality, and their psychic balance is called into question; in some cases easily broken. During this phase, there is an increased sense of exposure, and greater embarrassment and shame are lying in wait, both for the adolescent and the person approaching older age. As a result, their egos need to feel strong in order to cope and integrate the emotional reactions that are activated by these changes. It is as if their entire internal world has been shaken up.

It is a well known fact that when adolescents cannot integrate and cope with the anxieties related to growing up, they grab and cling to what provides a sense of strength, or to some form of escape;

usually this is done in a dramatic style that can lead to despair in those around them. Often they regain a sense of balance by defensive manoeuvres like searching for a group identity, by introjective identification with a fashionable idol, or by the use of fashionable appearances in terms of particular types of clothing, hairstyles, tattoos, and the use of drugs. All of this becomes their way of coping, a form of refuge when the ego feels overwhelmed by the experience and threatens to fall apart. Sexuality now is in three dimensions and this may be quite overwhelming; the need to hide this can further increase its disturbing effect.

For the adolescent, the struggle to establish their own identity is more demanding than we see at earlier stages of development and the need for independence and distance handicaps the possibilities of parental help, or help in general. In a different way, which in general tends to be less noticeable, the effect that the physical and biological changes have on those of older age represents a major challenge to their psychic balance. As in adolescence, physical appearance plays a major role in older age. The wish to remain important or occupy a place of importance in relation to family or immediate surroundings is very much connected with the changing roles that older age brings about. The struggle is to maintain a degree of independence, to avoid loneliness and to keep alive a sense of self-worth. To integrate the flow of a new, but now quite different, sensory experience that threatens the psychic equilibrium requires a considerable degree of integration in order to achieve a positive transformation. Bion has made a very important contribution through his conceptualizations of the phenomenon of transformation. In his theorizing, he refers to psychoanalytic observations in which the analyst is able to note the transformations of observable facts into thoughts capable of acquiring significant meaning (Grinberg, Sor & Taback de Bianchedi, 1993). These transformations could lead either to growth and positive development, or sometimes to turmoil of intense persecutory and catastrophic anxieties or pathological transformations.

The capacity to deal with these changes is supported by the way the previous early experiences of separation from the first object and the Oedipal relations have developed through the individual's life. The importance of the early interaction of the care giver and the child is also emphasized by other theoretical models. "If secure attachment and mentalization come from successful containment, insecure attachment may be seen as the infant's identification with the parent's behaviour" (Fonagy & Target, 2003). A very important role is played by the present internal and external context, which may offer some form of reverie that makes the experience more manageable or digestible.

Sexuality in old age

For men or women of a certain age openly to show in public an interest in sexuality is to be vulnerable to critical perceptions by others. It may lead people to all sorts of musings and possible reactions of disgust.

When Freud discovered the existence of infantile sexuality, it shocked the professional world and the general beliefs of his time. Even today, culturally there is uncertainty, apprehension, anxiety, and on occasions amusement, when adults are confronted with manifestations of children's sexuality. In the family, the emergence of sexuality in the adolescent daughter may arouse disturbing anxieties in the father and mother and often we see grandparents with the attitude that says: "Oh! We have gone through all that ourselves", adopting a supportive wise meta-position or persecuting one, according to their psychic balance and the anxieties that arise in them. The loss of sex drive in the couple, often more noticeable by a man's inability to sustain an erection, tends to activate early paranoid or depressive anxieties that add or re-activate further disturbances in the couple's relationship. It not only brings to a halt any form of sexual activity or intimacy but often generates a form of withdrawal or silence in their communication, and a wider gap grows like a thick wall between them. It is difficult to predict the effect of the loss of intimacy in older couples. Intimacy requires trust between the couple, and time. Sometimes couples are helped and able to adjust to this situation when they manage to develop new areas of interest. Grandchildren are a big asset in this respect, because through them the couple can regain some of their previous roles of father and mother and, in this way, find a way of getting closer, channelling their tender and loving feelings towards them ... .

We are witnessing an interesting phenomenon with the impact of new drugs, like Viagra, the use of which grew rapidly throughout the world. The real benefit is that it can bring couples together and help them to enjoy intimacy and sexual activity that had diminished or come to an end. Or it may create a manic reaction, an omnipotent belief in a never-ending youth that will keep loss and ageing out of their systems. The way these drugs are advertised is very telling: "We assure you that you will regain your sexual virility and power. You will be young again".

A couple in their mid-sixties had not expressed physical intimacy for several years because, in the case of the husband, his sexual desires were fragmented by the fear of not maintaining an erection. He imagined his wife's frustration and found it overwhelming that he might fail her or let her down. His wife also found the experience frustrating and painful. Both made considerable progress in many aspects of their lives. However, the sexual issue carried for them a strong element of embarrassment and shame at this stage of their lives. Their son and daughter had already left home. Their over-whelming concern and worry about their wellbeing was their attempt to cope with the feelings of "empty nest". The children left home, and once again they became a couple, now in quite different circumstances. The possibility of being able to bring this issue into the open in the marital therapy sessions initially brought a mixture of intense shame and embarrassment. In addition, early Oedipal anxi-eties came to the fore. We were able to work through some of these issues: first in terms of a comparison between their own Oedipal anxieties; this then led to them becoming more aware of the positive and negative complementarities present in their relationship and their mutual projections. Once this was achieved they felt empow-ered to acknowledge that there was a space to experience and work on wishes and anxieties about intimacy and sexuality even at this stage of their lives, and to normalize them. This brought an impres-sive sense of relief. It felt as if they had conquered a new exciting territory; they held hands and looked at each other in such loving ways. Subsequently, they were able to deal with more immediate losses including a decline in their physical and mental capacities and finding creative ways of supporting and dealing with them.

Idealization of the past

Idealization of the past brings with it the notion of time: time in the present and time in the past. In some cases, idealization of the past and sometimes of the future is an attempt to cope with the present.

I would like to illustrate this by using a clinical vignette. Mr. B. is in his late fifties and a couple of years ago had a very serious motor car accident that had threatened his life. He became depressed and insecure, and for this reason was referred for individual psychotherapy. He started on twice a week and after several months he agreed to come four times a week. This change was strongly resisted and resented because it clashed with his sense of independence and need to keep everything at a distance. The accident and the surgical treatment related to it was a big shock to his system and an intrusion into his sense of omnipotence. He told me at the initial interview that he had been confronted by "the real" possibility of death. Following a Christmas break, he spoke about the experience he had when he went for a visit to his home country in South America. "I had a shock when I attended a big garden party in the country house of an old friend of mine. I saw many old friends I have seen throughout the years and my first girlfriend and her family. I haven't seen her since we broke up. It was a total surprise. I looked at her repeatedly and I could not recognize her. It was horrible. I could not go and talk to her. Honestly, I felt like running away. She was my girlfriend when I was 16, 17; so pure, so beautiful. Through all these years, I kept her in my mind as she was then and I could not believe that woman with grey hair and wrinkly was her. I have kept her like a precious photograph that one looks at from time to time. In fact, whenever I needed; when I had problems with my first wife I would often turn to the photo in my mind and wrap myself up in it and fantasize different situations. I did it so many times, whenever I needed to. I still do it with S (his present partner).

A: Now she has destroyed that photograph; she has pushed you in front of the mirror and forced you to look at yourself.

Mr. B: Yes! This is exactly what had happened. It had such a disturbing effect. I don't know how to explain it. Maybe you are right in what you said.

A: It was a powerful experience and somehow you felt some form of shock. I also have the impression that you had a powerful experience in yesterday's session … .

Mr. B:　I don't know what you mean.

A:　You have perceived my interpretation as an intrusion, You felt that I was trying to spoil the image that you were so keen to sell to me and to yourself about how impressive and effective you are with your various important commitments, including analysis.

Mr. B:　I don't know. I know I left in a hurry, I did not want to be late and I needed to rush home and change for the meeting I had later on. (Pause.) I was thinking ... I have also tried to have a conversation with my older sister, but it is so difficult to talk to her. She is always busy with the grandchildren, her daughter, the house and so many things. Our conversation was interrupted like 100 times. (He then went on talking in a more animated way, about things I had heard often about, the work he has to finish, a possible trip abroad connected with work—this is a project he had been working on, a possible long weekend in Florence, some ideas he has for his son's work, etc.).

A:　You are showing me how energetic you are by taking on so many commitments, and also here, going from one subject to the next. (Pause.) I am supposed to be like an audience, admiring your display, unable to do anything else; a similar situation to the one you had with your sister.

Mr. B:　When I was there, seeing how she is with her grandchildren, and especially with her grandson, it reminded me of my mother; she is a lot like her. When one is a child ... or before I reached puberty, I was taken by the school bus from home to school and back home. At that age my parents were totally in charge, they took care of everything. They thought for me, they knew what I needed. This is why I had to struggle so hard to have my independence when I was an adolescent. I really worked hard, especially with my mother because she was so domineering. Her moods were so volatile and she did not allow anybody to disagree or take over. You have been saying that I need to keep a distance here as I keep a distance from everybody else. However, I did manage well in my life. (He went on mentioning some of his achievements.) You want me to bury my happy periods; to stop being energetic and doing things ... , like ... . (He

started to mention several of the things he has been working
on in the last few months.)

A: You perceive me as trying to either turn you into a total
dependent patient who cannot do anything for himself or
turn you into an old man who is like an invalid ready for retirement, structuring your life in such a way that it becomes
like a journey, from home to analysis and from analysis back
home.

Mr. B: Yes, this is exactly what my parents did, especially my
mother. (Pause.) It sounds an exaggeration but I feel a bit
like that. I felt that you pushed me into four times a week
and that once or twice a week would have been more than
enough with all my present commitments. (Pause.) You
know, last year, I was very depressed. I don't want to fall
into that trap.

This vignette highlights the emotional struggle to confront one's
own age when that age appears in grey or negative colours. He has
been holding onto the image of his first girlfriend like a precious
treasure that he brings to life whenever he feels pressurized and
troubled. He has disclosed how important this is for him; he is using
it in his present relationship as he did in the past with his previous
wife. The idealized image keeps him in the present with the spirit
and appearance of the past, while it helps him to keep a distance
that may, if reduced, bring him too close to reality. This means having to take full notice of a painful reality. He often refers to this in a
very rational way to show how open-minded and insightful he is.
That is more to impress me and get my admiration so we can have
a pseudo-animated analysis. He has shown a pattern of pseudo-
mourning of his losses by keeping himself at a distance. At present,
his noticeable defence is his capacity to rationalize that function as
an intellectual defence, whilst at the same time this provides a narcissistic gratification. The colourful life seems to lack the depth he
would like to see and would like others to see. Recently he has made
an important change regarding his career, which represents a big
challenge. I recognized its importance and also acknowledged his
talent and creative side. At the same time it felt important to analyse
how the excitement and manic investment feeds the narcissistic part
of his personality. His hyperactive life, the intense sports activity and

lifestyle resembles in some ways an adolescent trying to impress and make a considerable impact. Sometimes it is not easy to differentiate between his seductive and manipulative pressure; especially when insight is not used as insight and the change of topics is so fast and short lived that it is difficult to follow. My impression is that there is quite a lot in his early relationships that supports this type of development, but also there is quite a lot in his present context, in terms of age and social interaction that supports and reinforces this type of stance. It is a stance where the manic and colourful life prevails and the depressive mental photographs of the past are in constant use to justify and support this attitude. I also think that there are subtle emotional links to both his parents who suffered a great deal during their old age, and underlying ongoing fear of falling into a deep depression, as did his mother.

In the analyst's technique, it is important to assess how the patient uses reconstruction. Past recollections could be used as a rigid form of defence and manipulation in order to avoid paranoid anxieties and psychic change. Often this is activated by external change, moving house, altering a set routine etc. It is not unusual that some patients tend to cling, as it were, to a fixed photograph of the past. Sometimes the emotional and intellectual awareness does not produce good enough changes in the internal objects to produce the psychic change that may lead to changes in the external world. In these situations, the fixed view of the past has the specific function in the present of maintaining and justifying an entrenched form of relating. In this way, these patients avoid the uncomfortable experience of the old self and new self being exposed side by side, now no longer having at their disposal their idealized grandiose self and not feeling confident or sufficiently satisfied with their new reality. This fixed view of the past, which emerges in analysis as a repetitive narrative, blocks the possibility of confronting reality and genuinely starting the work of mourning—on what they leave behind and on what they were not able to do or achieve in their lives.

"We tell stories to ourselves and to others about our past, which contributes to creating a self in the present based on what we call 'memories'.... If the stories told by us are caught in an unchangeable past that repeats itself, we are self-institutionalized, inhabiting a self that is tyrannized by its past. In this case, there is no possible creativity in our lives: change cannot be imagined" (Kohon, 1999, p. 135).

It is my impression that this form of self-institutionalized state of mind is either more frequent or more noticeable in older people. It is important for the analyst to become aware of the interplay of aliveness and deadness in the transference situation, manifested by the unconscious pressure that the patient exercises to avoid confronting the possibility of change which, for conscious or unconscious reasons, feels quite threatening to the patient. Some positive move in the analysis often activates this type of defence, producing some form of negative therapeutic reaction. Sometimes it is the past viewed from a present perspective that feels too persecuting by guilt, so that now it is not possible to put it right: some of the protagonists may be dead or the future feels too gloomy, so that a cohesive integration of present, past and future is not manageable at this stage. However, if the connection with the good objects is established or re-established, it opens the possibility of integration and transformation and then leads to a favourable outcome.

The later years

> I had not thought death had undone so many
> I think we are in rats' alley
> I sat down and wept
> At my back, in a cold blast, I hear
> We who were living are now dying
> Shall I at least set my lands in order?
>
> The Waste Land, T.S. Eliot

The very much appreciated achievement of extending the lifespan of the individual through better living conditions and scientific achievements brings with it considerable problems. As people live longer the incidence of physical and mental illness (depression, dementia) increases. This puts a considerable emotional pressure on individuals facing this stage of the life cycle when they look and plan or fantasize their future. For some individuals the prospect of dependency may feel an ugly or shameful prospect. For some it is simply horrible because they cannot rely on a supportive family or social environment. For some families that take full care of, or are very involved with, the older person in his later years there could be a big emotional and financial burden. There are cultural variations that play a significant role in how this experience is lived through. At the social level it puts a considerable pressure on the health service and social services. This poses an important challenge in how to face and tackle all these different areas. Here I am focusing on the individual and the way our psychoanalytic understanding and technique can facilitate this process working through the process of ageing.

When individuals reach the later stage of older age they are confronted by greater or lesser deterioration of their physical and mental capacities; they may react with despair, passivity, anger, or acceptance. The sense of dependency and limitation that develops at this stage of their life cycle tends to bring them closer to their early experiences of childhood. As they visualize that the last steps of life are getting closer, their inner strengths and past experiences become part of the inner platform that in many cases can sustain them. It is not uncommon in the final years of the life cycle to feel that everybody has disappeared, is dead, has moved away or is not interested. When this experience is fuelled and activated by early traumatic experiences it can produce a mental state of emptiness, vacuum, or desert. The kingdom of apathy or lack of life has taken over. When this experience appears in the analysis it needs to be worked through in the transference. The possibility of discovering the meaning of this experience and establishing a historical continuity can be extremely valuable in capacitating the patient, and also the analyst, to face a very difficult future, especially in those patients who feel that death is nearby and recognize that the right time has arrived to say goodbye to life and meet death.

Even at this stage of the life cycle, for those individuals for whom loneliness had been an important feature of their life experience or for those whose bad internal objects or their destructive and self-destructive aspects had the upper hand, in spite of their efforts, there is still some hope. It brings to mind several lines by various poets that manage to convey that, even in the last steps, it is never too late for something positive to happen. The film *Wild Strawberries* by Ingmar Bergman manages to portray this in a vivid way. The film concerns an old professor who is about to celebrate 50 years as a scientist. The professor introduces himself by saying: "Our relationship with people consists of discussing and judging our neighbours' character and behaviour. For me, this has led to a voluntary withdrawal from virtually all so-called social intercourse. Owing to this,

I have become somewhat lonely in my old age, the days of my life have been full of hard work and for this I am grateful. What began as a struggle to make a living, ended in a passion for science." Then he adds, "I had a peculiar and highly unpleasant dream." Dream: "During my morning walk I strayed into an unknown part of town with deserted streets and houses in disrepair." In the dream he looks at the big clock and his own wristwatch and the hands are missing. One of the meanings is that there is no time left. The windows and doors of the houses are shut. The scene conveys a sense of loneliness and isolation. He is confronted by an ugly figure of a man who appears to be mute and blind and who, when he tries to touch him, collapses. He can hear the sound of bells from a nearby church, another reference to time. There is a funeral carriage and a coffin, and a hand emerging from the coffin tries to grab him and pull him towards the coffin; it is probably the hand of the dead figure which collapsed as he tried to touch it. Later on in the film, the protagonist is in a reflective mood about the past and says: "Wild strawberries. It is possible I became a bit sentimental. Perhaps I was a bit tired and felt a trifle melancholy … I don't know how it came, but clarity of the present shaped into an even clearer image of memory which appears before my eyes with the force of actual events."

At this stage of life, the individual may face a crossroads: it is "now or never" "the last chance to put one's house in order" and, therefore, it is crucial to connect or re-connect with a life given strength coming from outside or from within to help them to put their internal house in order. Even in the last stage, then, it is possible to find some satisfaction or mental peace in saying hello to death and goodbye to life, like the professor in Bergman's film did before closing his eyes. However, it would be an idealization of psychoanalysis to say that every possible patient can benefit from it and that psychoanalysis would be the treatment of choice for every type of patient. Here I am arguing that some older patients can benefit from psychoanalysis and that we as psychoanalysts can deepen our understanding through such an exploration.

Conclusion

The transition in each stage of development brings about changes and losses; they are like normal crisis points. The passage from one stage of development to the next one is a progressive move. Some of these transitions are experienced or perceived by the patient as catastrophic (Bion, 1965), and, as in major catastrophic events it is important to be in touch with one view that is the pre-catastrophic, pre-transition and the other view that is post-catastrophic, post-transition. What is crucially important is to take notice of how these two views manifest themselves in the present. This should high-light previous developments in terms of their capacity for mourn-ing losses and coping with future new developments. Of course there are constitutional factors and interactive contexts that influ-ence and play a part. All this acquires a distinct quality in older age, in the way that life and death instincts come into play in relation to physical and mental changes, and family and socio-cultural pres-sures. Another aspect that is worth noticing is Oedipal anxieties: they acquire a different dimension. Now it is the father's throne that he feels is threatened, the emphasis is on Laius as well as the later years of Oedipus, which bring forward the fear of exile.

In addition, differences between male and female at the anatomi-cal, developmental and socio-cultural level may make it harder for men than for women to embark on the work of mourning.

In older age, history acquires particular significance, in terms of what life goals have been or have not been achieved. The way the individual can understand and make sense of history and establish a cohesive continuity to deal with the anxieties aroused by ageing is extremely important. The capacity to mourn early dreams not achieved, unfulfilled passions, and personal and family expecta-tions, is crucial at this stage of life.

The theoretical and technical psychoanalytic frame does not change when working with older patients. I highlighted the impor-tance for the analyst not to lose his psychoanalytic balance when the pressure to do so can be considerable. In relation to this I drew atten-tion to situations where substantial losses in several contexts com-bine to make the process of mourning and integration more difficult: a gloomy cloud wrap patient and analyst. I underlined how difficult and important it is for the analyst not to lose emotional and cognitive sight of the significant positive psychoanalytic changes or achieve-ments the patient has made. Hopefully this extra containment will allow the necessary time and space for an opening that will ena-ble facing what is overwhelming and indigestible. Regaining con-tact with positive psychic experience may also activate the creative aspect of the patient. That said, it is also important that the analyst is careful to avoid falling into a form of enactment. Of course, real psychic change emerges through the patient's inner strength to take responsibility for the changes that take place in body and mind. This manifests itself in the patient's capacity to say goodbye to what is gone and to bear what has not been achieved, in order to be able to make the most of what is there. Ultimately, it is a way of fuelling liveliness and therefore supporting life when death is close; but also of having the courage to assess in those tragic circumstances if the basic quality of life is no longer there, gone forever because of mental or physical impairments.

As I have stressed throughout this presentation, each phase of development requires adequate and specific stimulation. It is obvious and more noticeable in the early stages of development when dependency needs for survival are to the forefront, but there are significant difficulties that appear in the later years, when the individual is physically and mentally losing ground or deteriorating. At this stage, the analyst's proper understanding, adequate stimulation and challenges make a significant difference and sometimes one is surprised by the quality changes that can be achieved. Otherwise, when older people are ignored, the emotional effect on them is quite intense, their passivity or self-destructiveness takes over, and their lives drift away.

References

Baranger, M., Baranger, W. & Mom, J. (1983). Process and non-process in analytic work. *International Journal of Psychoanalysis, 64*:1.

Baranger, W. & colaboradores (1980). *Aportaciones al concepto de objeto en psicoanalisis.* Buenos Aires: Amorrortu.

Baranger, W. & Baranger, M. (1969). Proceso en espiral y campo dinamico. *Revista Uruguaya de Psicoanalisis, 59.*

Bion, W.R. (1965). Transformations. In: *Seven Servants.* New York: Jason Aronson, 1977.

Bion, W.R. (1970). Attention and interpretation. In: *Seven Servants.* New York: Jason Aronson, 1977.

Britton, R. (1998). Subjectivity, objectivity and triangular space. In: *Belief and Imagination.* London: Routledge.

Britton, R. (2003). Narcissism, Part III. In: *Sex, Death and the Superego.* London: Karnac.

Britton, R. (2003). *Sex, Death, and the Superego.* London: Karnac.

Davenhill, R. (Ed.) (2007). *Looking Into Later Life.* The Tavistock Clinic Series. London: Karnac.

Dario, R. *Selected Writings.* Harmondsworth: Penguin, 2006.

Grinberg, L., Sor, D. & Taback de Bianchedi, E. (1993). *New Introduction to the Work of Bion.* New York: Jason Aronson.

Ferro, A. (2005). *Seeds of Illness, Seeds of Recovery.* The New Library of Psychoanalysis. London: Routledge.

Fonagy, P. & Target, M. (2003). *Psychoanalytic Theories.* London : Whurr.

Freud, S. (1914). On Narcissism: An Introduction. S.E., 14: 67–102.

Freud, S. (1917e). Mourning and Melancholia. S.E., 14.

Hildebrand, P. (1982). Psychotherapy with older patients. *British Journal of Medical Psychology, 55*: 19–28.

Jacques, E. (1965). Death and the Midlife Crisis. *International Journal of Psychoanalysis, 46*: 502–514.

Joseph, B. (1989). On passivity and aggression: their relationship. In: E. Spillius, & M. Feldman, (Eds.), *Psychic Equilibrium and Psychic Change: Selected Papers of Betty Joseph, 1989.* London: Routledge.

Joseph, B. (1998). Transference: the total situation. In: E. Spillius & M. Feldman, (Eds.), *Psychic Equilibrium and Psychic Change: Selected Papers of Betty Joseph, 1989.* London: Routledge.

Joseph, B. (1998). Psychic change and the psychoanalytic process. In: E. Spillius & M. Feldman, (Eds.), *Psychic Equilibrium and Psychic Change: Selected Papers of Betty Joseph, 1989.* London: Routledge.

King, P. (1980). The life cycle as indicated by the nature of the transference in the psychoanalysis of the middle aged and elderly. *International Journal of Psycho-analysis, 611*: 153–160.

Kohon, G. (1999). The Aztecs, Masada and the compulsion to repeat. In: *No Lost Certainties to be Recovered.* London: Karnac.

Laufer, E. (2006). Transformation in the analytic process and in the normal development in adolescents. *European Psychoanalytical Federation, 60*: 10–22.

Ogden, T.H. (1999). Analysing forms of aliveness and deadness of the transference-counter-transference. In: G. Kohon (Ed.), *The Dead Mother: the work of André Green.* London: Routledge.

Ogden, T.H. (2002). A new reading of the origins of object relations theory. *International Journal of Psychoanalysis, 83*: 4, 767–782.

Plotkin, F. (2000). Treatment of the older adult: the impact on the psychoanalyst. *Journal of the American Psychoanalytical Association, 48*: 4, 1591–1616.

Puget, J. (2006). The use of the past in the present in the clinical setting. *International Journal of Psychoanalysis, 87*: 6, 1691–1707.

Riesenberg-Malcom, R. (1999). *On Bearing Unbearable States of Mind.* London: Routledge.

Segal, H. (1958). Fear of death: notes on analysis of an old man. *International Journal of Psychoanalysis, 39*: 178–181.

Schafer, R. (2003). *Bad Feelings.* London: Karnac.

Valenstein, A.F. (2000). The older patient in psychoanalysis. *Journal of the American Psychoanalytical Association, 48*: 4, 1563–1589.

Waddell, M. (2002). *Inside Lives.* London: Karnac.

CHAPTER TEN

His majesty the ego: The tragic narcissism of King Lear's "crawl towards death"

Ken Robinson

The critics of Shakespeare have long been alive to his depiction of the ways that his heroes, especially his tragic heroes, relate to the roles that they occupy within their society and family. Each of the heroes moves with ease within his role until something happens to dislocate his relation to that role. The tragedy flows from there. In a very fine essay on character and role in the tragedies Peter Ure writes: "It is the character faced with his role, forced to decide about it, the quality of his response, that Shakespeare shows us, not just his performance in the role ... It is often because we are made aware of the gap, not the consonance, between the man and the office, that the situation becomes profound and exciting, and permits rich inferences about what the hero's inward self is like" (Ure, 1963). I would like to add that, in the four major tragedies at least, Shakespeare portrays heroes who are faced with their roles at different developmental stages, from the adolescent prince faced with the role of avenger to the old man who retires from his role as king and has to reinterpret his role as father.

I shall be focussing on *King Lear* and Shakespeare's portrayal of the painful tragedy of retirement when the ego is narcissistically fragile. Confronted with the loss of the equilibrium that he has hitherto managed both through his role as king and father, and through his narcissistic use of his objects, and confronted too by his inexorable development towards death, he is haunted by his fear of frailty, depression, madness and disintegration.

For Freud "creative writers are valuable allies", none more so than Shakespeare. The writer, in Freud's words, "directs his attention to the unconscious in his own mind, he listens to its possible developments and lends them artistic expression instead of suppressing them by conscious criticism. Thus he experiences from himself what we learn from others—the laws which the activities of this unconscious must obey. But he need not state these laws, nor even be clearly aware of them; as a result of the tolerance of his intelligence, they are incorporated within his creations. We discover these laws by analysing his writings just as we find them from cases of real illness." In this paper I shall not press Shakespeare into Freud's service but present the insights of Freud and Shakespeare side by side. The most germane area of Freud for my purposes is *Mourning and Melancholia*, which I treat as part of his developing concern with narcissism.

Freud did not deal substantively in his writings with the psychology of old age. I shall preface my remarks on *Mourning and Melancholia*, therefore, with a few words about the later psychoanalytic treatment of retirement and old age.

In his diary entry for 1 August 1991 Tony Benn, then 66 years old, wrote:

> The days, the weeks, the months race by and there is a part of me now that is just longing for retirement and another part that knows that, if I do retire, I'd sit about, do nothing, be depressed, be a hypochondriac. I am kept going by a combination of an interest in the job and the fear of what would happen if I stopped.

In the event, of course, he could retire. Tony Benn's diaries provide a normative narrative of being able to reinterpret his relation to his role, face retirement and come to terms with the vicissitudes of ageing. But here Benn puts his finger on an all too obvious danger of retirement: the loss of a role which has been a source of self-esteem. This role might well have become so essential that to lose it is to risk depression and collapse. Of course its loss will probably bring with it associated losses—most obviously work colleagues.

Those who have approached problems in old age from a psychoanalytic perspective have also been alert to the dangers associated with the loss of role in retirement. Pearl King, for example, has written of a 63-year-old woman whose job in charge of a children's home had become the central source of her own sense of worth and identity. So narcissistically invested was her role that her image of herself and her ontological security depended on it. She was referred in an acute state of anxiety as she approached retirement. Such patients are able to use their professional roles and successes in work to protect their impoverished or immature egos and to counteract their fear of failure, their fear of narcissistic wounds, and the consequent disintegration of their brittle ego-structure (King, 1980).

Negotiating retirement and the loss of an established role, at work, in the family, and in society, is one of the developmental tasks of advancing years. Where there has been an unhealthy narcissistic investment of role, to step aside from it is to feel that the self is depleted or its integrity threatened. Another task is to acknowledge and accept the ageing body and mortality. Tony Benn recognizes not only that depression involves withdrawal of interest or cathexis from the external world and the redirecting of that interest onto the self but that hypochondriacal cathexis of the body (or part of the body) becomes more likely in old age in the face of a struggle to come to terms with diminishing physical prowess, ill-health and ultimately death. I wish to add that the part played by the body in depression is not limited to hypochondriasis. Where the individual has been unable adequately to surmount the narcissistic wound of not being in total control of his own body, the process of ageing brings the danger of depression. I shall be emphasizing the importance of the individual's system of self-esteem regulation in negotiating old age. I shall concentrate on the threat of depression where narcissistic cathexis of role, of objects and ultimately of the body, together with underlying ambivalence towards objects and the body prevail. You will remember that for Freud the precipitating cause of melancholia is the loss of an object or ideal, and the predisposing factors are first a narcissistic relation to the lost object and second a conflictual relation to it due to ambivalence.

I now turn to Freud's psychoanalytic understanding of depression, especially as found in *Mourning and Melancholia* (1917 [1915]). Depression for Freud was a narcissistic mood state. Because the person suffering depression cannot discharge his depressed feelings towards a particular object or through any particular channel, they infect the ego functions as a whole, jaundicing all the person's relation to and perception of his world. Denial of affects or perceptions which might challenge the depressed mood ensures that it persists (Milrod, 1988). The world of the depressed man is a different world from that of the happy man. The affects generally associated with the mood of depression are loss, guilt, self-criticism, and a feeling of inferiority. Freud thought of depression as a disorder of self-esteem.

Freud's account of melancholia in *Mourning and Melancholia* deals specifically with psychotic depression. He warns against generalising it to cover depressive disorders as a whole. Freud held that people develop severe depressive disorders because of psychic loss and an impaired ability to replace the lost object. In outline, whereas in mourning the mind centres on memories of the lost object which evoke grief and sadness, in melancholy there can be no such memories because the melancholic does not know what he has lost—he might know whom but not what he has lost. Instead the melancholic gives vent to his own failings, unworthiness and suffering. As Freud puts it an object loss is transformed into an ego loss with consequent diminution of self-esteem. The work of grief consists of the slow withdrawal of cathexis from the external lost object, but in melancholia the libidinal cathexis cannot be withdrawn. The melancholic deals with his inability to renounce his attachment to the lost object by assuming its mental and/or physical characteristics, that is, by identifying with it (or more properly introjecting it)[1]. "The shadow of the object falls upon the ego." In Freud's words, "The ego wants to incorporate this object into itself, and, in accordance with the oral or cannibalistic phase of libidinal development in which it is, it wants to do so by devouring it." The intense ambivalence which characterizes the melancholic's relation to his object is expressed in the cannibalistic destruction and preservation of the object, or by the retention of the object through introjection on the basis of love and by attack on this introject on the basis of hatred.

The melancholic's ambivalence points to a developmental problem in binding aggression through love. Because this binding is insecure when an ambivalently cathected object is lost, the loss may precipitate defusion of aggression and love. In depression unbound aggression is directed at the self so relentlessly that Freud thought of melancholia as the "pure culture of the death instinct". "It often enough succeeds in driving the ego into death, if the latter does not fend off its tyrant in time by the change round into mania" (Freud, 1923). We shall see later how Shakespeare found his own solution for King Lear.

Of course, Freud himself later recognized that in mourning, too, introjection of the lost object takes place and that more generally the character of the self is built up on the basis of identification proper. In melancholia, however, introjection functions differently. The result of introjection in melancholia is an intersystemic conflict between the superego and the introject within the ego.

It will be useful for what follows to spell out in more detail the course of psychic events which lead to melancholia. We need to think of an ambivalently cathected object as the essential source of narcissistic supplies for the self (or more properly the self-representation). Its loss (or the loss of its love) is a narcissistic blow. Because the differentiation of self and object is frail, withdrawal from the wounding object is hard to bear. It feels imperative to preserve it. The object is idealized, or at least its value is exaggerated, as libido withdrawn from the self is redirected towards it. But there is a price to pay. Not only is the self impoverished as a consequence, but there is no chance of love being returned by the overvalued lost object. Libidinal investment in the self (or self-representation) is replaced by hostile cathexis. The person involved loses self-esteem. It is only possible to employ this defensive manoeuvre so long as reserves of narcissistic libido remain. When they are depleted idealization of the object gives way to devaluation of both the self and the object. We are familiar with such an attempt to preserve the lost or disillusioning object, with its adverse impact on self-regard, in a variety of circumstances: in unrequited love, for example, or in the case of the child who suffers abuse from a parent. But the melancholic goes a step further. In a last ditch defence the melancholic turns away from the external world that has so let him down, withdrawing his investment in the offending external object. Since, however, he is narcissistically unable to give up his love object he tries to keep it alive in his internal world through introjection: "The shadow of the object falls upon the ego". The problem is that when he takes in the object it is experienced as split as a result of unresolved ambivalence into a loved and a hated part, and then it is the hated part which is subject to the self-hatred which, as Freud pointed out, is characteristic of melancholia.

Although *Mourning and Melancholia* is concerned with only one type of depression it sets a framework for understanding depression more generally. Other forms of depression may also be thought of in terms of the economics of pathological self-esteem regulation and internal conflict. Whereas *Mourning and Melancholia* focuses on the consequences of the loss of narcissistic supplies from the love-object, the consequences are different when the loss is from the side of the superego or the ego (Milrod, 1988).

When, for example, the depression stems from the side of the ego, there may be too great a discrepancy between the ideal self-image we have for ourselves and our current sense of ourselves in the world. We attack ourselves for falling short of our aspirations, count ourselves a failure. This is a form of depression which we may well be likely to be more prone to with advancing years as we, for example, assess the extent to which we have achieved what we believe we should have been capable of in our careers and emotional lives or as we try to square the fact of our ageing bodies with a wished-for body-image. Unless we can reach some accommodation or find some way of protecting ourselves—by eternalizing an ideal image of ourselves through art, for example—we are condemned to the depressive realm of what W. B. Yeats, a poet much concerned with ageing, called "the foul rag-and-bone shop of the heart" (Yeats, 1950: *The Circus Animals' Desertion*).

Of course, although we can distinguish neatly between these different types of depression on the basis of the framework bequeathed to us by Freud in *Mourning and Melancholia* in real life the distinctions are not so easy to make. It is not unusual for different forms to run together or for one to be manifest, another latent and kept at bay.

Tony Benn's diary entry draws attention to the link between depression and the body through hypochondriasis. I would like to return to this briefly, both because it is especially important for old age where changes in the body and body-image have to be negotiated, and because the body figures significantly in *King Lear*. It has been suggested that although hypochondriasis may not be accompanied by depressed mood and may be without guilt or self-criticism it may often represent unconscious depression. The loss of a narcissistically cathected object may bring with it a recathexis of an earlier body image from a time when the differentiation of self and object was less mature so that the loss of the object is felt as a threatened loss of part of the self, specifically a now hypochondriacally invested organ (Asch, 1966; Ostow, 1960).

Such hypochondriasis is common in old age as, too, are psychosomatic conditions which also express difficulties in relation to a reactivated immature boundary between the bodily ego and the external world. Pearl King's patient suffered hair-loss and developed a serious skin condition which Miss King took to be linked with her body boundary (King, 1980). But there are more general connections, too, between the body and depression.

According to Freud's viewpoint, the forerunner for all object relationships is our relation to our own bodies. The ego is first and foremost a bodily ego. And its first object is its own body. The problem with this body is that it provokes unpleasure: it is experienced, as Freud put it, as "alien". Together with external stimuli which also threaten to disturb blissful homeostasis after the caesura of birth, it comes to be hated, hatred being for Freud older than love. But the infant cannot sustain life without the very world it hates. In the service of self-preservation it seeks out and libidinizes need-fulfilling objects which it takes into itself. Love now coexists with hatred. The first love relationship is to our own bodies, later there is the relationship to the mother or her substitute; but these relationships do not supersede the relationship of hatred. Much as the infant might seek to control its body and the need-fulfilling mother omnipotently, it also knows in some sense that it does not. The body has a way of disturbing wished-for blissful equilibrium and the mother has a way of being frustratingly independent and absent when she is most wanted. In reasonably healthy development the infant relinquishes at least some of its omnipotence in the movement towards object constancy and whole object love. Where this does not happen, the relation to the body remains narcissistic and ambivalent and there is a predisposition to depression in the face of an experience of bodily infirmity. In such cases the ultimate narcissistic insult is not being in omnipotent control over one's own body (Robinson, 2002). Clearly, advancing age is a danger point.

As Freud remarked in his essay *On Narcissism: an Introduction* (1914), we create ideals for ourselves in an attempt to regain the lost narcissism and omnipotence of childhood. In the case of bodily infirmity and failure to accept the limitations of our control over our bodies (including mortality), there can be a pathological denial through compensatory fantasies centred upon images of an ideal body. In so far as such fantasy constitutes a magical identification with this ideal body-image, there is an attempt to deny the ego's (and the parents') limitations and to hang on to infantile omnipotence. This may go hand in hand with regression to an early form of object relationship in which because ego-boundaries are not yet firmly established whatever seems pleasurable and strong in the outside world can be experienced as belonging to the self. These defensive operations can be working away beneath the surface for many years without too much difficulty, or indeed without any apparent difficulty, so long as their omnipotence is not severely challenged. When it is challenged depression, or hypochondriacal anxiety which represents the reverse of narcissistic inflation, may follow (Reich, 1960). Those stages of development which bring with them marked changes in the body bring particular danger: adolescence, pregnancy, mid-life and old age.

The idealized body-image may be associated with various developmental stages. It may, for example, be pre-natal. Béla Grünberger (1966) has written of the suicidal melancholic's desire to get rid of the "rags and tatters" which is their body-image to restore the pre-natal state of self-sufficiency and felicity associated with the unborn body. Or the idealized body-image may be that of a latency child. Whatever the image, "One of the essential mechanisms in depression is, in many cases, the operation of a specific body image" (Peto, 1972). The specific idealized body-image for King Lear is that of the crawling infant.

King Lear

In *On Narcissism* Freud writes of the way in which as adults we hanker after the lost narcissism that we feel we have enjoyed as a child.

We see it in our own children and treat them like "'His Majesty the Baby', as we once fancied ourselves". We attempt to achieve narcissistic omnipotence once again by proxy so that just as "illness, death, renunciation of enjoyment, restrictions on his own will, shall not touch [the child]" so they will not impinge on us. As Freud puts it: "At the most touchy point in the narcissistic system, the immortality of the ego, which is so hard pressed by reality, security is achieved by taking refuge in the child. Parental love, which is so moving and at bottom so childish, is nothing but the parents' narcissism born again, which, transformed into object-love, unmistakably reveals its former nature" (*King Lear*, 4.7.60). "Fourscore and upward" and on the verge of retirement, King Lear has no male heir to succeed him. The very beginning of the play opens this up as a potential narcissistic wound in contrast to Gloucester's capacity to beget boys within and without marriage. Lear is also subject to the increase in narcissism that comes with ageing (Gillespie, 1963). Not only does King Lear relate to Cordelia as his ideal child, he fantasies that his retirement will give him back his infantile omnipotence. He "thought to set [his] rest/On her kind nursery" (1.1.124–125). He envisaged an infantile world out of time where death does not lie in wait. Mortality is a major threat to Lear's narcissistic equilibrium, beyond his omnipotent control. As Freud noted, we are all loath to relinquish the omnipotent plenitude of being His Majesty the Baby, and, depending on how much earlier narcissistic wounds remain unhealed, we are more or less likely to wish to revert to it when we suffer injuries to our narcissism throughout the life cycle. King Lear, we are told, suffers not simply from "the infirmity of his age", but "hath ever but slenderly known himself" (1.1.294–295). We might say that his cathexis of his objects is so narcissistic and that he has such a marked inability to put himself in others' shoes and to see himself as they might see him that he has been unable to know himself. Old age and impending dependency sit ill with but also fuel his display of narcissistic omnipotence. His whole bearing at the beginning of the play, together with the script he has in mind for the apportioning of his kingdom between his daughters, speaks of what Freud, in *Creative Writers and Daydreaming* (1908 [1907]) thought of as "the true heroic feeling ...: 'Nothing can happen to *me*!'". In this "revealing characteristic of invulnerability", Freud writes, "We can immediately recognize His Majesty the Ego, the hero alike of every day-dream and of every story." When Cordelia fails to play the part that Lear has scripted for her she denies him the fantasied nursery world of His Majesty the Baby. Instead of being able to crawl in it as the baby in defensive safety he has to find another solution to the painful reality of the "crawl toward death". He heroically attempts to assert himself as His Majesty the Ego. He clings to his omnipotence with all the defensive resources at his disposal in order to stave off recognition of his frailty, rooted in the body, and to avoid feared depression, madness and disintegration.

At the outset of the play King Lear has occupied two roles: king and father. He is about to negotiate radical changes in both: handing over the office of king and the power associated with it and handing over his remaining unmarried daughter, his youngest and favourite daughter, Cordelia, to a husband. Since both of these roles are narcissistically invested and the changes therefore involve a difficult shift in his psychic economy, he is in trouble, all the more so when his narcissistic vision of retirement, his fantasied solution, is not realized. Unable to be His Majesty the Baby in Cordelia's nursery he regresses developmentally to an infantile mode of functioning. Anybody or anything that contradicts his wishes or sense of himself is alien. He denies their capacity to affect him. He symbolically annihilates his "sometime daughter" Cordelia (1.1.121), telling the King of France, as it happens with tragic irony, that "we/Have no such daughter, nor shall we ever see/That face of hers again" (1.1.264–266). And he banishes that other truth-teller, Kent, for daring to "come ... between the dragon and his wrath" (1.1.123). Instead of letting Kent be "the true blank of [his] eye" (1.1.160) he turns a blind eye, again with tragic irony, to what Kent tries to tell him about himself. Like the child Lear is peremptory. What he says must happen. Nothing is allowed to come "betwixt [his] sentences and [his] power/Which nor [his] nature, nor [his] place can bear" (1.1.171–172). What he wishes he must have, as he expresses in unmistakeable oral terms at the beginning of Act I, scene 4: "Let me not stay a jot for dinner; go, get it ready" (1.4.8). He loves those who serve him as need-fulfilling objects. His retinue's behaviour, as described by Goneril, expresses by proxy his own tendency to live by the pleasure principle, with poor impulse control and little or no concern for the consequences of his actions. His men, like Lear himself, do not "know themselves". They are:

Men so disordered, so debauched and bold,
That this our court, infected with their manners,
Shows like a riotous inn. Epicurism and lust
Makes it more like a tavern or a brothel
Than a graced palace (1.4.233–236).

After Cordelia and all she stands for have been cast out in a tali-onic punishment for what Lear experiences as a castration of his omnipotence, Lear is left to try to regain his narcissistic grandeur in relation to his remaining daughters, Goneril and Regan, who are all too aware of the infirmity of his age. They systematically cut him down to size by reducing the number of his retinue, ignor-ing his peremptory imperatives and putting Kent in the stocks for insubordination—an act of humiliation which Lear feels narcissisti-cally to be worse than murder. Lear defends himself with increas-ing desperation against these further castrations and depletion of himself. He cannot tolerate his frailty as an old man and the pain-ful repercussions of Cordelia's loss, as all these wounds press upon him with greater and greater force. With the increasing defusion of love and aggression he explodes with narcissistic rage, cursing his daughters with increasing severity as if in his childlike way he believes that his words might magically inflict the very wounds that they promise. He will make Goneril sterile or the victim of a "thankless child" (1.4.281), or with the help of "fen-sucked fogs" (2.2.356) he will blister Regan's beauty. Lear moves increasingly between high-handed treatment of others, rationalization of their ill-treatment of him, cunning rhetoric and abject pleading. As his narcissistic defences crack the painful affects he has sought to keep at bay, initiated by the loss of Cordelia, threaten to break through.

But what does Cordelia stand for? She stands for the heart and feeling (Latin, *cor, cordis*), which might bind aggression, and she stands for Truth, a capacity for grief. These are all qualities alien to Lear, at least for a large part of the play. They require a relation to objects as separate and independent and whole: Lear's relation to his objects is essentially narcissistic. To these we must add death. In his 1913 essay on *The Theme of the Three Caskets*, Freud argues with considerable and erudite evidence from myth (and analytically on the basis of reaction formation) that when Lear carries Cordelia's dead body on to the stage, Cordelia represents Death. He suggests that in the choice between the three sisters, "What is represented ... are the three inevitable relations that a man has with a woman ... the mother herself, the beloved one who is chosen after her pattern, and lastly the Mother Earth who receives him once more." For Freud, "It is in vain that an old man yearns for the love of woman as he had it first from his mother; the third of the Fates alone, the silent Goddess of Death, will take him into her arms."

In vain it might be but Lear nevertheless fantasizes Cordelia as the maternal figure in whose nursery he would like to "crawl toward death" (1.1.40). Through reaction formation she is also the youthful representative of death. Viewed in this way Lear's regressive yearning for Cordelia as a maternal figure is all the more poignant. In his extreme old age Lear cannot countenance his mortality and the decline of his body which signifies his progress towards death. His conflicted abdication from his role as king threatens him with acknowledgment of his own mortality and in disowning Cordelia he is as it were projecting his awareness of mortality as well as protecting himself against those other qualities she stands for.

We see in *King Lear* both the precipitating and predisposing factors for depression as described by Freud. Cordelia's disobedience represents a narcissistic object loss and Lear experiences an unresolved ambivalence towards both her (and all she stands for) and his own ageing body. Additionally, he gives up the role which he so narcissistically cathected that every inch of him has been the King. It is a role that has carried an ideal image of himself and helped hold him together. But rather than experience depression Lear defends himself at the outset of the play against anything which disturbs his narcissistic equilibrium. He does so through regression, omnipotent posturing, denial and projection. He will continue to defend himself, with increasing difficulty throughout the play. To acknowledge depression would be a blow to Lear's manhood. His defences threaten a break with reality, the madness that he fears but will ultimately embrace. By contrast Gloucester experiences grief. So does the Fool who since Cordelia's expulsion "hath much pined away" (1.4.72). In Lear's mind the Fool and Cordelia are ultimately symmetrised. It is through the Fool as Lear's "shadow" (1.4.222) that the shadow of Cordelia's loss falls upon Lear[2]. The Fool as a disowned and projected aspect of Lear takes Lear to task for his foolishness. When Lear comes too close to having to acknowledge the projected truth the Fool speaks, he threatens to whip him so as to keep what is unbearable at a manageable distance from consciousness. In this way the Fool represents the depression and self-criticism that lie in wait for Lear. We glimpse it, too, through its opposite, in Lear's restless search for a daughter who will grant him the libidinal supplies he needs to live out his last years in blissful narcissistic ignorance of himself and death, whether in the nursery or in the pretend world of still being the King.

Little by little Lear's defences crack. Unwanted feelings associated with the loss of Cordelia press in upon him in the form of the "mother", "*hysterico passio*" (2.2.246–27), or his "rising heart" (2.2.310). Lear is bitter towards them because they have the "power to shake [his] manhood" (1.4.289), to castrate him as Cordelia has. They represent for him the introjected Cordelia. He begins to acknowledge that reality is not as he wishes it to be and that there is a gap between the role he wishes to fulfil as all-powerful king and father and the man he feels himself to be, hence his cry: "Does any here know me? ... Who is it that can tell me who I am?" (1.4.217–221). It is a cry which beneath its surface irony expresses Lear's profound disturbance at his loss of his narcissistically-cathected role. Whereas Lear could initially disown Cordelia, by the time he wishes to disown Goneril he is aware that something of her will live on within him—we might say as a hated introject: she remains "[his]flesh, [his] blood, [his] daughter,/Or rather a disease that's in [his] flesh,/Which [he] must needs call [his] ... a boil,/A plague sore, or embossed carbuncle/In [his] corrupted blood" (2.2.410–414). When Regan humiliates him he comes close to acknowledging the reality of his situation as "a poor old man,/As full of grief as age, wretched in both" (2.2.461–462). But no sooner has he spoken these words than he vows that he will not weep. He would sooner his "heart ... break into a hundred thousand flaws" (2.2.473–474) and go mad than weep. Feelings are feminine for Lear. To experience them in any intensity, to weep, to be depressed, is to suffer a further castration. In order not to experience them he self-destructively castrates his own ego, cuts himself off from reality and goes mad.

This conflictual oscillation between being in touch with loss and mortality on the one hand and defensive denial on the other continues into the storm scene as Lear enters a confusional state. He sees the storm as a punishment from the Gods for "undivulged crimes" (3.2.52) and thinks of it as joining forces with Goneril and Regan to attack him, but he simultaneously regards himself as the victim of "filial ingratitude" (3.4.14) and as "more sinned against than sinning" (3.2.59). He can only get so close to his narcissistic wounds, shame, and guilt, before the loss of self-esteem that they threaten is too much and he backs off. Slowly he moves closer and closer to being in touch with the common humanity and mortality of a "poor naked wretch[…]" (3.4.28) until Kent and the Fool intervene to prevent him tearing off his clothes to render himself "unaccommodated man … a poor, bare, forked animal", as naked as Tom (3.4.105–106). He may seem to have travelled a long way from his omnipotence at the opening of the play, but at the very point of seeming to empathise with the lot of others battered by the elements, he can only see their plight as a reflection of his own as a "discarded father" (3.4.71). He refuses to see it otherwise. He somehow always remains narcissistically regal. He believes that the tempest in his own mind makes him immune to the tempest raging outside: he *is* the storm. He can never completely divest himself of his role, just as he cannot surmount his narcissistic fragility so as to face the "sovereign shame" that "elbows him" (4.3.43) due to his maltreatment of Cordelia. Although his actions towards her "sting his mind so venomously", shame prevents him being able to contact her.

The storm brings the break with reality which will continue for the rest of the play. In his madness Lear now recognizes that the omnipotence he had enjoyed as king which his court had seemed to confirm was a lie. When it came to it "the thunder would not peace at [his] bidding", nor was he "ague-proof" (4.6.101–104). Mortality clings to him: he wipes it from his hand before offering it to Gloucester. But his madness also protects him. It allows him, for example, to place himself under the guardianship of Kent, rather like the senile patient described by Grotjahn (1940) who compared himself to Lear. Grotjahn's patient's psychosis allowed him to put himself into the care of his physician and to enjoy a childlike "dependence upon a powerful, helpful, father-like person who managed some of the problems in reality and who offered him reassurance and protection". As Gloucester puts it in a passage remarkable for its insight into the defensive nature of Lear's madness:

> The King is mad: how stiff is my vile sense,
> That I stand up and have ingenious feeling
> Of my huge sorrows? Better I were distract;

> So should my thoughts be severed from my griefs,
> And woes by wrong imaginations lose
> The knowledge of themselves (4.6.274–279).

Freud thought of Lear in the last scene as being invited to "renounce love, choose death and make friends with the necessity of dying". Does he make such reconciliation, or does the break with reality function here, too, to cushion him against finally acknowledging his loss, guilt and mortality?

When he awakens and eventually recognises Cordelia, Lear, a "very foolish, fond old man ... not in [his] perfect mind", (4.7.60–63), accepts that she has cause to punish him. But Lear's remorse is no more than fleeting. The next time we see Lear and Cordelia captured by Edmund they are about to be taken off to prison. Here Lear substitutes for a harsh and dangerous reality a vision of prison in which he once more resorts to an illusionary world in which they "will sing like birds i'the cage" (5.3.9). He gathers them lyrically "into the artifice of eternity" (Yeats, 1950: *Sailing to Byzantium*), in which they will outlive "packs and sects of great ones/That ebb and flow by the moon" (5.3.18–19). Lear conjures up a world redolent of the timeless nursery of narcissism that he had wished for in retirement. He remains unable to face reality right to the end. He enters with Cordelia dead in his arms, pronouncing her "dead as earth" (5.3.259). For a moment he seems under no illusion that his "poor fool is hanged". And then in his last breath he hallucinates life on her lips, dying on a blissful delusion of life together in the nursery of the hereafter:

> Do you see this? Look on her: look, her lips.
> Look there, look there! *He dies* (5.3.309–10).

Lear's tragic narcissism has run its full course. He has had to forgo the illusion of retirement as a formal regression to being His Majesty the Baby in the timeless world of Cordelia's nursery. Unable to mourn his loss he has defended himself heroically as His Majesty the Ego with every means at his disposal to maintain the safety of his narcissistic omnipotence. He has suffered humiliation at the hands of Goneril and Regan who have denied him the compensatory pretend-world of being the king after giving up his role and his kingdom. He has, then, tried, as the Fool points out, to make his "daughters [his] mothers" (1.4.163–4) and they have beaten him. And he has tried to direct his defused aggression at those around him rather than direct it against himself and sink into melancholia. Stripped of his role and made aware of his mortality, assailed by shame and guilt, he has retreated into madness and, still searching for the nursery, he has put himself like a child into the care of others, notably Kent. Finally just when he thought that he had refound an everlasting peace with Cordelia (who now literally nurses him), she is hanged. His last line of defence is topographical regression. In *A Metapsychological Supplement to the Theory of Dreams*, written alongside *Mourning and Melancholia* over a period of 11 days from 23 April to 4 May 1915, Freud wrote of a form of hallucinatory wishful psychosis which stems from a "reaction to a loss which reality affirms, but which the ego has to deny, since it finds it insupportable. Thereupon the ego breaks off its relation to reality ... . Reality-testing is got rid of, the ... wishful phantasies are able to press forward into the system [Cs], and they are regarded as a better reality".

If Lear himself is faced with intolerable reality, the audience, too, can feel confronted with a tragic narcissism that is at the limit of what is bearable in the theatre. We are aware of Lear's depression more than he is. We are aware of it through its traces, especially through his increasingly desperate defences against it and through the externalisation of his intrapsychic conflict in his relationship with the Fool. What is most intolerable about his state of mind is to witness the power of the self-destructiveness that underlies his destructive narcissistic rage. He heaps destruction on himself in response to his failure to live up to the image of himself as in god-like omnipotent control of his own body without the compensations of narcissistic supplies from his roles as king and father. The idealized body-image specific to Lear's fight with depression—the crawling infant of the nursery, the body of His Majesty the Baby—operates as a defence against a fear of the body as fragile and subject to forces beyond the individual's control. As Freud put it, "The touchiest point in the narcissistic system [is] the immortality of the ego," which is first and foremost a bodily-ego. The fragility of the body pervades the play's language. The body in *King Lear* is represented horrifically as "tugged, wrenched, beaten, pierced, stung, scourged, dislocated, flayed, gashed, scalded, tortured and finally broken on the rack" (Spurgeon, 1935). Lear's ultimate act of self-destructiveness is madness. Even though it does allow him to die blissfully emparadised in Cordelia's arms, we, the audience know by tragic irony that he is self-deluded.

I have tried not to impose *Mourning and Melancholia* onto *King Lear* which has its own emphasis. It is not so much that King Lear finds it difficult to mourn but that he finds it too painful to suffer depression. He resorts to pathological self-esteem regulation rather than face inner and outer reality. I think, however, that Shakespeare did intuitively understand the framework that Freud was to provide us with in *Mourning and Melancholia* and his related works on narcissism. He understood that insofar as the narcissistic person is in imagination eternally His Majesty the Baby he is more likely to find old age hard to adjust to. *King Lear* is Shakespeare's tragedy of old age and narcissism.

Notes

1. It has long been recognised that Freud's use of "introjection" and "identification" and cognate terms can be confusing. For clarification see, for example, Glover (1947), Rapaport (1967 [1957]) and Meissner, W.W. (1970; 1971; 1972).
2. The roles of Lear and the Fool have sometimes been doubled in the theatre, though they do not seem to have been in the first performances (*King Lear*, Ed. R.A. Foakes, p. 50–51).

References

Benn, T. (2002). *Free at Last!: Diaries 1991–2001*. R. Winstone (Ed.). London: Hutchinson.

Freud, S. (1907 [1906]). Delusions and Dreams in Jensen's *Gradiva*. S.E., 9. London: Hogarth.

Freud, S. (1908 [1907]). Creative Writers and Daydreaming. S.E., 9. London: Hogarth.

Freud, S. (1913). The Theme of the Three Caskets. S.E., 12. London: Hogarth.

Freud, S. (1914). On Narcissism: An Introduction. S.E., 14. London: Hogarth.

Freud, S. (1917 [1915]). A Metapsychological Supplement to the Theory of Dreams. S.E., 14. London: Hogarth.

Freud, S. (1917 [1915]). Mourning and melancholia. S.E., 14. London: Hogarth.

Freud, S. (1923). The Ego and the Id. S.E., 19. London: Hogarth.

Gillespie, W. (1963). Some regressive phenomena in old age. *British Journal of Medical Psychology.*

Glover, E. (1947). *Basic Mental Concepts: Their Clinical and Theoretical Value.* London: Imago.

Grotjahn, M. (1940). Psychoanalytic investigation of a seventy-one-year-old man with senile dementia. *Psychoanayticl Quarterly, 9:* 80–97.

Grunberger, B. (1966). The suicide of the melancholic. In: *Narcissism.* New York: International Universities Press.

King, P. (1980). The life cycle as indicated by the nature of the transference in the psychoanalysis of the middle-aged and elderly. *International Journal of Psychoanalysis, 61:* 153–160.

Meissner, W.W. (1970). Notes on identification—I. Origins in Freud. *Psychoanalytic Quarterly, 39:* 563–589.

Meissner, W.W. (1971). Notes on identification—II. Clarification of related concepts. *Psychoanalytic Quarterly, 40:* 277–302.

Meissner, W.W. (1972). Notes on identification—III. The concept of identification. *Psychoanalytic Quarterly, 41:* 224–260.

Milrod, D. (1988). A current view of the psychoanalytic theory of depression—with notes on the role of identification, orality, and anxiety. *Psychoanalytic Study of the Child, 43:* 83–99.

Ostow, M. (1960). The psychic function of depression: A study in energetics. *Psychoanalytic Quarterly, 29:* 355–394.

Peto, A. (1972). Body image and depression. *International Journal of Psychoanalysis, 53:* 259–263.

Rapaport. D. (1967 [1957]). A theoretical analysis of the superego concept. In: M.M. Gill (Ed.), *The Collected Papers of David Rapaport.* New York: Basic.

Reich, A. (1960). Pathologic forms of self-esteem regulation. *Psychoanalytic Study of the Child, 15:* 215–232.

Robinson, K. (2002). The character of the exception as a defense against deformity. In: *Psychoanalytic Study of the Child, 57:* 305–326.

Shakespeare, W. (1997). R.A. Foakes (Ed.), *King Lear.* London: Thomas Nelson.

Solms, M. & Kaplan-Solms, K. (2000). *Clinical Studies in Neuro-Psychoanalysis: Introduction to a Depth Neuropsychology*. London: Karnac.

Spurgeon, C. (1935). *Shakespeare's Imagery and What It Tells Us*. Cambridge: Cambridge University Press.

Ure, P. (1963). Character and role from *Richard III* to *Hamlet*. In: *Hamlet, Stratford-upon-Avon Studies 5*. London: Edward Arnold.

Yeats, W.B. (1950). *The Collected Poems*. London: Macmillan.

PART V

CULTURE

CHAPTER ELEVEN

States of narcissism[1]

Margaret and Michael Rustin

In this paper, we develop the view that narcissistic states of mind are primarily to be understood as defences against mental pain arising from states of dependency and relationship. We argue that they are liable to emerge whenever the context of secure relationships on which human beings depend for their development becomes seriously deficient, or, even worse, threatens their well-being. This can be the case when relationships are impoverished in infancy and childhood, but also when this occurs in adult life, in the primary situation of the family, or in the wider life of a society. When they feel that others are indifferent or threatening to them, individuals can become absorbed largely in themselves, and withdraw feeling and attention from others. Narcissism is thus a strategy for psychic survival in situations of severe emotional impoverishment or danger. We will describe these modes of psychological defence in two clinical psychoanalytic examples, in order to locate the concepts we are using in the context which is primary for psychoanalytically-based discussion.

We will discuss different forms of narcissism as these manifest themselves in society. Narcissism manifests itself in identification with collectivities, which give apparent strength and support to a fragile or damaged sense of individual identity, as well as in the psychic defences of excessive individualism. We will discuss the consequences of war, terrorism and the collapse of social bonds, in generating extreme kinds of identification with groups. We will also examine the ways in which"'regimes of individualization", which force individuals to regulate and measure their own performance by criteria imposed on them, may lead to "psychic retreats" (Steiner, 1993) into narcissistic self-regard, and may detract from creative relationships with others. And, related to this, we shall look at situations where individuals and work-groups are exposed to intolerable anxiety and feelings of persecution, and are given inadequate support in responding to it. We hold that in these situations narcissistic defences are adopted which lead to mindlessness, and the phenomenon John Steiner (1993, chapter ten) has described as "turning a blind eye". Although consumer and life style cultures no doubt engender more obvious kinds of narcissistic self-preoccupation, we will give less attention to these than to the kinds of narcissistic defence against anxiety which we have referred to above.

Psychoanalytic theories of narcissism

Psychoanalytic debate about narcissism is as old as psychoanalysis itself, and its development as a concept reflects broader theoretical shifts in the field, certainly so far as psychoanalysis in Britain is concerned. We hold that narcissism, referring to a sense of the self as an object of care and love, is in one sense a state of mind necessary for development and psychic survival, and in another, a pathological defence against relationships and dependencies perceived with fear, hostility, or envy. We will clarify the differences between these two senses of the term, to show how this idea can be used to identify states of well-being and ill-being for individuals, for societies, and for groups and institutions which exist in the spaces between the two.

The origins and nature of narcissism has been a disputed area in psychoanalytical theory. Freud set out an idea of a primary narcissism, which as Laplanche & Pontalis (1973, p. 256) put it, "is supposed to be characterised by the total absence of any relationship to the outside world, and by the lack of differentiation between ego and id; intra-uterine existence is taken to be its prototypical form, while sleep is deemed to be a more or less successful imitation of that ideal model."[2] Klein and her colleagues rejected this idea. "For many years I have held the view," she wrote, "that auto-erotism and narcissism are in the young infant contemporaneous with the first relation to objects—external and internalised. I shall restate my hypothesis: autoerotism and narcissism include the love for and relation to an internalised good object which in phantasy forms part of the loved body and self. It is to this internalised object that in auto-erotic gratification and narcissistic states a withdrawal takes place. Concurrently, from birth onwards, a relation to objects, primarily the mother (her breast) is present. This hypothesis contradicts Freud's concept of auto-erotic and narcissistic stages which preclude an object relation" (Klein, 1952, p. 51). Thus in Klein's view, the infant self is from the beginning constituted by the introjective and projective processes by which it relates to others.[3] Klein acknowledged, however, that Freud's position was complex, and sought to show that his ideas about identification anticipated her position.

Of course there are differences between the object-relations of infants in the first months after birth, and those which develop subsequently, and many psychoanalytic theorists, Klein included, sought to clarify this process of development. In a book first published in France in 1971, the Hungarian-French psychoanalyst Bela Grunberger (1978) wrote about narcissistic states as a necessary starting point in the development of the infant, but by this he meant not a state without any relationship to objects, but one of total infantile dependence on the care, gaze and attention of parental figures, by which the infant needs to be surrounded in its first weeks in order that its development can go forward. The infant emerges into the world needing at first to preserve as much as it can of its pre-uterine harmony with its environment. The infant's initial state of development is that, Grunberger argues, of a "monad" or "cocoon", in which the infant is not indifferent to objects, but depends on others' sensitive response to its needs and feelings.

This statement of primary developmental need is related to the ideas of "primary maternal preoccupation" (Winnicott) and "reverie" (Bion) which those leading object relations analysts, writing some years before Grunberger, held to be the precondition of the baby's development, described from the point of view of the mother's response to the infant. The infant enters the more complex and ambivalent field of object relations as it encounters the unavoidable imperfections in the fit between its own desires and needs and what can be provided for it even by the most favourable environment. If mothering is, as Winnicott put it, "good enough", and feelings of love for the infant predominate over hatred or indifference, there is every chance that the object relations which form in the infant's mind will be based on love and trust in its objects, though also unavoidably requiring more negative feelings to be included.[4]

Just as Bion saw the container-contained relation of mother and infant as a metaphor for the container-contained relationship of analyst and analysand, so Grunberger suggested that psychoanalysis initially gives analysands an experience of unconditional receptive attention, like that of a mother to a baby, providing the experience or illusion that the analysand is at the centre of everything. Analytic patients can expect, above all, to be listened to, observed and thought about in a relationship in which the analyst will not make the reciprocal demand for attention and gratification which characterizes normal social interaction. Indeed, Grunberger suggests, this experience that a patient possesses his analyst's unconditional attention is one of the basic satisfactions which the therapeutic setting provides, and is the solid ground on which the exploration of more painful aspects of experience rests. Psychoanalysis proceeds, Grunberger wrote, from narcissism into object relations, just as does the development of the human infant.

Grunberger's formulations help to resolve the disagreement between Freud's view that newborn infants were initially self-oriented, living within an illusion of self-sufficiency, and Klein, Fairbairn, and other object relations theorists' insistence that infants are oriented towards mother's presence and begin to make a relationship with her from the moment of birth, if not indeed prior to this. Whereas Freud suggests that infants depend on an illusion that those surrounding it are there to provide for them and have no purposes of their own, Grunberger with Bion sees this as an innate and necessary expectation, not an illusion. With Klein and Winnicott, Grunberger accepts that this first relationship requires the psychological as well as physical commitment of parents. Bion's theory expanded our understanding of the infant's mental experience. He proposed that infants were born with innate preconceptions.[5] A preconception "corresponds to a state of expectation. It is a state of mind adapted to receive a restricted range of phenomena. An early occurrence might be the infant's expectation of the breast. The mating of pre-conception and realisation brings into being the conception" (Bion, 1963, p. 23).

We can thus think of Grunberger and the object-relations theorists as proposing the primary dependence of human beings on a primordial relationship with others, given and accepted at first without conditions, but evolving into an interactive and reciprocal one in which infants have to accept that others in their world, besides themselves, exist in their own being, and that sharing (of mother with father, and of mother and father with other babies, real, symbolic or potential) has to be tolerated, and will sometimes be enjoyed. We think that this state of primordial dependency has relevance not only to the needs of infants, but to human development and well-being at each concentric scale of social organization.

But there is another form of narcissism quite different from the primordial emotional sunshine which is necessary to begin and sustain development. This is the pathological form of object-relation in which the self becomes object as well as subject, and in which the relational world shrinks as a result of a variety of developmental difficulties. This is Freud's concept of secondary narcissism: "a regression from an object relationship which has disappointed through either loss of the object, or some kind of slight by the object, back to narcissistic love of the ego" (Hinshelwood, 1989, p. 350), from which later ideas of narcissistic defences have developed in psychoanalytic theory.

The distinction made by Herbert Rosenfeld between libidinal and destructive forms of narcissistic object relations added a clinically vital dimension to the picture, which has been explored further by many other psychoanalytic writers. Libidinal narcissism can be understood in the conventional manner as an excess of self-love,[6] and follows the example set out in the myth of Narcissus, who was indifferent to the love of Echo, and in love with his own reflection (though he believed it to be that of another). Destructive narcissism is the outcome of the invasion of the inner world by a cruel and superior internal object, which attacks those feelings and elements of the self that might make it vulnerable or weak. The internal gang, theorized by both Rosenfeld (1987, chapter six) and Meltzer (1968), which mirrors in the inner world a gang whose members have entrusted power to a sadistic leader, is an extreme embodiment of this state of destructive narcissism. A later development of these ideas has been by post-Kleinian analysts such as Henri Rey (1994) and John Steiner (1993) who have described a concept of "border-line personality" to explain the character structures of individuals who have become identified with destructive internal objects. There is a tendency in borderline states for the individual to attack any links which makes their vulnerability apparent, or acknowledge their own negativity. As a consequence of this they cut themselves off from emotional reality and suffer for this. This kind of character structure also takes a collective or organizational form.[7]

The object relations theory of narcissism presupposes, following Melanie Klein's ideas, that the self is constructed through processes of projection and introjection from the very beginning of life. Klein held that initially fragmentary and chaotic perceptions and feelings inside the infant become ordered through the responsiveness and understanding of parents, into conceptions of the infant in relation to his emotionally significant figures. An identity is built up through internalization of parental figures, and of the infant as seen in their eyes. Where Lacan in his theory of the "mirror-stage" saw this image of the self as necessarily inauthentic, corresponding to others' desires for him, object-relations theory describes a creative and open-ended interaction between infant and parent, creating a unique experience of self in the infant, and psychic developments in parents also in consequence of their life-giving experiences.

The core stages of these developments take place in the first two years of life. Money-Kyrle (1965) following Bion, suggests that these experiences are represented in the mind in modes of increasing con-sciousness, going from concrete representation to ideographic rep-resentation, as in dreams, which is largely unconscious, to the final stage of conscious, predominantly verbal thought. He argues that psychic health and creativity depends on the continued connection between these "levels" of experience. This explains why psychoana-lysts hold that dreams are essential to psychic life, and why expres-sions in the arts provide such nourishment later on.

Psychoanalysis has given a great deal of attention to psychic defences and disorders of development, for reasons which are obvi-ous. It is however also important to keep in mind the counterparts to these disorders, which are its conceptions of psychic well-being and growth. We hold that these depend on a concept of the lively and creative relationship of individuals with their internal objects. That is, the conscious and unconscious identifications of individuals with those whose qualities and psychic functions they have internalized, and the play of developmental possibilities which these open up. Normally, psychoanalysts think of these connections in the primary context of the family, not least because it is dysfunctions and deficits in early life (whether experienced in reality or fantasy) which are so often linked to later difficulties. But our concept of internal object relations is broader than this, and extends to those individuals and objects of passionate attachment from which identities in childhood and adulthood are also constructed, beyond the primary experience of the family.

It is clear, for example, that the primary objects of attachment of many artists, so far as their working lives are concerned, are admired predecessors in their fields, or indeed the beautiful artefacts they have made. These too become internalized and the objects and subjects of internal conversation and exchange, in fact, parts of the self. As Harold Bloom pointed out in *The Anxiety of Influence* (1973), the relationships of poets with their great predecessors may well be filled with hatred and envy as well as love and admiration—there is a need for an individual artist to be able to establish his or her own identity distinct from their symbolic parents or siblings, just as the generational struggles of the Oedipus complex cannot be avoided in relations between parents and children. We think that such object relations are fundamental in all spheres of life, and that their introjection is particularly fundamental to all good experiences of education. While there are no doubt links between the primary internal objects formed in infancy, and those introjected in later life, we hold that new object relations can develop throughout the lifetime, and are not wholly determined by early experience.

Our contention is that creative dialogue between individuals and their internal objects is fundamental to life. Narcissistic defences are pathological when they prevent and impede such dialogue, and when they cause individuals to lose contact with those internal objects which give lives emotional meaning.

Clinical examples of narcissistic defences

In this psychoanalytic tradition, the most basic function of narcissistic object relations of both libidinal and destructive types is to defend individuals from the anxiety which follows the painful recognition of dependence. But if we are going to think clearly about narcissism "out of doors", that is, applied as a psychoanalytic concept outside the consulting room, it is vital to have a recognizable starting-point. This is best tackled by description of narcissistic states of mind in the clinical context, since this allows us to take note of their origin and defensive function, and to discuss whether the more precise reference which the concept of narcissism has in clinical work can be linked with its wide-ranging usage in everyday speech.

Here is a brief clinical vignette in which the pictorial quality of children's play brings out the nature of narcissism clearly.

Case vignette—a six year old boy

Paul is a six-year-old boy with severe behavioural problems at home and at school. He began three times weekly psychotherapy some time ago, and within the therapy sessions it has been possible to achieve some containment of his omnipotence and a move towards differentiation between adult and child capacities and responsibilities. There are, however, continuing serious difficulties in his external world. His mother, mostly left to bring him up on her own, is frequently overwhelmed by him, and tends to retreat from their stormy relationship to a position in which little real support is offered to Paul, who has to make do and cope with her unpredictable and recriminatory responses. At school, there is a strong commitment to helping him but this is offered on the basis that he is completely different from the other children: ordinary school expectations are set aside to an astonishing degree, and boundaries not maintained. In a sense, both parent and teachers agree to treat him as an extremely powerful, semi-monster who cannot be tamed. This unconscious dynamic is powerfully sustained within the system for a number of reasons which go well beyond Paul's own beliefs about his omnipotence and the effect of projective processes in his relationships. However, this everyday context does tend to reinforce his fears about the strength and dependability of the grown-ups in his world.

Here is an extract from a session in which Paul explores emerging from his lonely narcissistic position, represented in the play as life in the desert, and making contact with other people, represented by the farm. It follows a row in the waiting room in which mother had misunderstood Paul's efforts to tidy up, and the therapist had had to intervene for there to be any chance of protecting the space of the session from a destructive enactment between mother and Paul.

Clinical material

Paul scanned the room and then launched into resuming the play sequence of the last two weeks. The therapist was to be with the wild animals and he would be on the farm with the domestic animals. This was then reversed, and Paul put the wild animals in the sandpit on the opposite side of the room from the farm. He noticed a male figure with a rifle, and placed him with the wild animals and called him Hunter. He announced that Hunter wanted to meet the farmer, and invite him to visit the desert. The therapist, as farmer, was to respond to this invitation. Hunter and farmer start a conversation, and Hunter then remarks,"What about your wife? Bring her too." She joins them and is made to ask Hunter about his house. Hunter demonstrates that the wet sand is his bed. The farmer and his wife talk about his possibly needing a warm dry house and comfortable bed and Hunter becomes agitated and now demands that the farmer give him a pig and some horses to live in the desert. There is negotiation about price and the farmer asks Hunter why he wants to buy these animals. Hunter explains, "Having domestic animals means being rich." The farmer's wife (the therapist speaking) wonders if the animals might provide company for Hunter, who looks surprised at this idea.

When the therapist commented that she would like to think with him about this story, Paul looked annoyed, but then turned to the dolls' house, announcing that this was the farmhouse. The therapist felt that his hasty change of focus was to prevent thought and understanding. However he then removed the toy poultry to his desert home, saying that they had patches of grass attached and so grass could grow in the desert if he had lots of them. He agreed with the therapist's comment that he wanted something to grow and develop but at this point said urgently that he needed to go to the toilet. He spent a long time there doing a poo (as he frequently does) and in the remaining minutes of the session he fluctuated between wanting to leave "Right now!" once his therapist had mentioned the coming end of the session, and pausing to help her to drain the sodden sandpit, looking sad. He held her hand on the way downstairs and ran to embrace his mother, who was taken aback but made a space for them to look at a book together.

Discussion

The hunter in the desert does not any longer feel content to be in his one-person predatory world, surviving in his lonely state by aggressive assaults. Instead, he is attracted by the domestic world of the farmer and his wife, a couple who belong together, and by their farm where things grow—the farmyard bird figures are actually family groups of hen and chicks, duck and ducklings etc., so they represent not just grass growing, but small creatures being together with their mother.

Hunter's move towards this kind of place causes him much anxiety, and there are two points at which he retreats again to narcissistic omnipotence—firstly the animals are desired as possessions, as wealth, he says, not as company. Later, after the conversation about the grass, he urgently needs the toilet. We might suggest that he has taken in something very big in the session and it is too much to hold on to. But he is using the clinic toilet to deposit this unmanageable problem (that is, leaving it in the care of his therapist for future work), and thus while he demands to leave immediately once the end of the session is mentioned—that is, to claim he does not need her time and help—in fact he then manages to stay and help to clear up, and to share the sadness of the separation with her, using her to support him in re-finding his mother.

The defensive function of narcissistic omnipotence is clearly visible in this sequence—when Paul feels alone, like Hunter, it takes a lot of courage to go in the direction of the human family. Only the presence of an emotionally responsive other, the farmer's wife, the therapist, makes it possible for needs to be acknowledged. Desire for and dependence on a mother figure also usher in awareness of the Oedipal triangle, in which the farmer and his wife are seen together in Hunter's mind, and this enormous idea can only begin to be absorbed if there is access to a therapist who knows what a huge psychological task this is for this little boy.

This view of narcissistic defences as those employed when the individual feels that containment is absent (and this of course can be a consequence of either the limitations of the available environment or of attacks on the object or a mixture of both) is a good starting point for thinking about narcissism in the social context. For example, we talk loosely of the "me-generation" and of consumerist modes of being which are organized around aggrandisement of the self through possessions (like Paul's notion of wealth, perhaps). Are we noting at a societal level something akin to the unprotected isolated world of Hunter where relationships cannot be depended on or are being actively attacked and where desperate solace is then sought? Another instance we might consider—is the extraordinary growth of demands for plastic surgery: evidence of a belief that only the mirror will offer the individual the comfort of recognition? That is, that the Narcissus-self has only himself to turn to at the end of the day? It seems likely that the seduction of visual communication more generally, expressed in its most pathological and deadly form in the photographing of violent acts for their later enjoyment, on the streets and in Abu Ghraib, also constitutes a temptation to narcissism in modern societies, displacing attention away from internal reality and from the psychic conflict inseparable from relationships.

A second clinical example: An adolescent fluctuating between narcissistic arrogance and toleration of a dependent link

Adolescents are often described by adults as suffering from an excess of narcissism. Their anxious self-preoccupation with their looks, their clothes and other marks of being suitably cool are easily scoffed at, and they often seem to have almost no capacity to take account of other people's point of view, though this familiar adult complaint misses the dynamic function of this ignoring of others' wishes and needs. It is precisely in order to evade awareness of the needy part of the self that the adolescents' stance can seem so maddeningly out of touch with the realities of their dependence. However, in another chapter Margot Waddell argues persuasively that narcissism is not a disease of adolescence. This is because normal adolescent developmental processes inevitably pose great strain. Becoming one's own person is a difficult task, and the adolescent years are the time in our lives when acquiring an individual identity is the dominant theme.

Nonetheless, clinical work with adolescents provides rich opportunities to explore the distinction between different forms of narcissism. The destructive narcissism referred to above is exemplified by the following vignette, in which an arrogant state of mind is revealed to put at risk the patient's capacity for developing.

Mary is a 20-year-old student. She has been talking to her therapist about her hope of being given a place on a particular module within her art foundation course that would enable her to concentrate on an art form which is of long-term interest to her. It had emerged that she had decided to take a day off from college to work on a piece of required course-work and she then revealed that this was the very day on which places on her desired and oversubscribed module would be allocated. Realizing that she might have given the impression that she had little commitment to the course, she was precipitated into a terrible panic about being punished by not being selected for her preferred option. "A disaster", as she put it. She began to be aware of her secret conviction that she would always be the favoured student whatever she did (just as she secretly believed that her parents should forever provide for her wishes, whatever they might be, and place her in a privileged position vis-a-vis her siblings), and of her dread and rage that this was a delusion about to be exposed. Her therapist felt assailed by doubt about the quality of work she had done with her, and expected to be criticized by her supervisor, or by a hostile inner critic. Here we see emerging the destructive superiority at the heart of this young woman's narcissistic state of mind, and how it disturbs the therapist through her experience in the countertransference.

In the session that followed the one in which Mary's punctured and fragile narcissism had been the focus of the work, her therapist was treated to a startling demonstration of how little she could appreciate her efforts. It was almost half-way through the session before she revealed in a casual and offhand way that she had in fact been given a place on the course she wanted. The therapist's contribution in the previous session to helping Mary think was set aside and her pained anxiety about this situation rather cruelly exploited by her being kept in the dark. Mary then described her "odd" weekend and her Monday tutorial.

The crux of the matter was that she had had good feedback on the essay draft, but had since written 1000 words over the required length. She commented airily that this would not matter, but then mentioned in response to a question that her tutor had said the leeway allowed was about 200 words. She did not want to cut these new sections because they were so interesting, but she would have to. She then moved on to discuss the forms for university admission she needed to fill in. She became rather excited in speaking about the high level of competition for all the courses she was drawn to, and her underlying self-importance became clearer as she mentioned an event she wanted to attend at which she would be a community representative making an important local appointment. This would mean missing one of her therapy sessions.

Her therapist struggled with the feeling of being put in her place and being expected to admire Mary's many and varied talents, and to realize that treating her as one among a group of patients really did not do in her eyes. It was supposed to be self-evident that she had much more to offer and that therefore any adaptation by her to the idea of being one among others deserving of equal care was a bit absurd, although she would go along with it to a certain extent so as not to make too much fuss.

However, while the self-destructiveness of her big-headed contempt for any demands placed on her was obvious, another line of thinking also came into view. She managed to ask whether a change of session time might be possible on the date of the important community meeting, and also mentioned that she had sent the email to her tutor to the wrong address but after discovering this had managed to find the tutor to explain matters.

The struggle for dominance between the part of herself that sees the world as awaiting her interesting contribution, her tutor as the one privileged to have her as a student, her therapist as the one who may be upset at her absence, and the different part of herself that can see the reality of her dependence on others, is at full tilt. In particular, Mary managed to wonder about why she never follows up any request or proposal to anyone if she does not get a reply. The idea that others are the losers if communication is broken off was now open to question—perhaps she might be the one losing out?

This was a very different kind of reaction from the more familiar one of angry denunciation of any friend or teacher for failing to fit in completely with her plans or expectations.

Rejecting relationships

Neville Symington (1993) describes narcissism as a relationship to what he terms "the life-giver—a mental object that the mind can opt for or refuse at a very deep level". "If being emotionally alive means to be the source of creative emotional action, there has to be a turning to the object, and this object has to be taken in." Symington regards the taking-in or repudiation of the life-giver as a choice, whether for the infant in relation to its mother's breast, to other persons later in life, or in a relationship between patient and therapist. Because there is an element of choice and intention in this even for infants, we can argue that there is an inborn element in individuals' decisions to choose or reject "the life-giver"—a relationship outside the self. But whether this is chosen or rejected also depends greatly on the qualities of the life-giver itself, on the receptiveness and engagement of parents, other persons, or the wider social environment. Where sources of emotional nourishment are lacking, or are felt to be toxic, whether in families or societies, links with others will be rejected, and narcissistic defences are liable to be chosen in their place.

Shakespeare was in no doubt about the functions of narcissistic defences as responses to the anxieties of failed dependency. Many of the destructive narcissists in his plays—individuals who have made evil their good—are depicted as bastard sons, deprived of a due place in a family's affections and succession:—Edmund in *King Lear*, Don John in *Much Ado about Nothing*; or as having been deprived of their share of affection and respect through deformity—Richard of Gloucester. Less destructive forms of self-love are located in figures who have enjoyed some recognition, but have still been left ultimately disappointed and alone—Jaques in *As You Like It*, and Malvolio in *Twelfth Night* are examples of this. Beatrice and Benedick move as the crux of the action of *Much Ado About Nothing*, from states of libidinal narcissism as defences against their fears of rejection by the other, to accepting the risks of love, in the course of facing up to the power of destructive narcissism embodied in the male gang of Benedick's soldier friends. Orsino and Olivia in *Twelfth Night* escape from their self-made narcissistic enclaves because of Viola's capacity for love for both of them. Feste in that play is able to bear his own isolation and deprivation, and provide the benign gaze[8] that the couples around him need if they are to get together. Brutus' disappointed libidinal narcissism—why must he share Caesar's love with Anthony?—pitches him into a world in which he is destroyed by others' hatreds. Shylock seeks for respect and recognition, but being denied it by the Christians embraces murderous revenge. The psychological and social anatomy of different forms of narcissistic defence is explored to the fullest degree in Shakespeare's work.

Narcissism "out of doors"

In the wider world, narcissistic defences manifest themselves in the formation of individuals' character, and perhaps also in the transmission of "character ideals" through various media of communication. It seems that the "celebrity culture" which has been so amplified by modern mass media is one such manifestation, in which the admiring gaze of publics gives more gratification to some individuals than mundane lived relationships, and where celebrities attract identifications from audiences who we may feel are at risk at times of substituting a virtual for an actual relational and emotional life.

Collective narcissism

The emergence of narcissistic characters and character-ideals is one form of contemporary narcissism, and may be the result of the slow attrition of the dense social ties that were sustained by extended families, and in spatially-confined lives, and also of the waning of religious beliefs which involve acceptance of the finiteness and dependent state of the individual. But perhaps more significant than such changes of individual character is the expression of narcissism through group-identifications, which can become an apparent safe-haven for threatened identities. Where anxieties about dependency become severe, they may find expression not so much in individuals' withdrawal from social relationships, but rather in massive projections by individuals into group identities, on which are conferred a fantasied strength which individuals and families are felt to lack. A narcissistic illusion of strength and self-sufficiency is created when an imaginary group identity can be constructed and sustained by antagonism to other groups which can be defined as enemies, as rivals within a competitive struggle (for local territory or jobs), or as inferiors into whom unbearable anxieties can be dumped by projective identification. These two forms of narcissistic defence can be and often are combined. A leader embodies a narcissistic (often destructively narcissistic) character with whom followers can identify, and a fantasied form of group identity provides an imaginary social membership in which individuals can both find and lose themselves.

These may be the narcissistic character formations which take place at the level of wider society, in response to anxieties about dependency. What are the anxieties that give rise to these, and how might they be analogous to the deficit situations which we have suggested predispose to narcissistic character defences in infancy and childhood?

We can think of a psychologically secure social condition as one in which individuals believe that their wider environment ensures their physical security, is relatively predictable and mild in its impact on them, and can be seen to represent benign human or divine intentions, perhaps believed in over generations. The texturing of the symbolic landscape of American Indians or Australian aboriginal peoples with sacred symbols of place, time, aspects of the landscape, and natural species of plants and animals, is such an instance. The cultivation of countrysides like those of Europe, and the furnishing of cities and their buildings and spaces over centuries,[9] can be seen as an equivalent engagement with the environment, perceived and constructed as a benign constant presence, a backdrop for more complex states of "object relationship" which unavoidably involve competition, conflict, renewal and decay. The Green movement now perceives the relation between human beings and their environment as being placed at risk, by the greed of materialist society and by its damage to the natural world, which can be seen as a destructive kind of narcissism in its disregard for the needs of future generations.

We can see how important these primitively narcissistic guarantees of well-being are when we observe what takes place when they are destroyed or placed under severe threat. Both Australian Aboriginal and American Indian peoples have found it almost impossible to survive as creative communities faced with the loss of their territorial sense of homeland.

It seems to be when the elementary foundations of trust in others and in the wider society become eroded that pathological identifications of a narcissistic type come into existence. Take for example a situation such as that in the former Yugoslavia, where peoples who had lived side-by-side in peace for decades developed intense separatist identifications of themselves as Serbs, Croats or Kosovans, once the deployment of indiscriminate violence eroded basic trust in neighbours, and once the foundations of prosperity and the hope of future material improvement had collapsed. Similarly, in 1930s Germany the precondition for the rise of the Nazis was both humiliation in war and catastrophic economic collapse, Hitler embodying in his personality a pathologically vengeful response to both. He represented both a destructively narcissistic character-type with which people identified themselves, and at the same time fashioned collective group identities—the German people, the Nazi party, the Aryan race—into which individuals could project themselves in fantasy. His charismatic power reflected and amplified these projections.

The racial and radical nationalist movements of contemporary Europe are milder versions of the same phenomenon. The identities of communities which feel themselves to have been deeply damaged are upheld in opposition to incomers who are perceived to threaten them by their very difference, apart from more tangible kinds of competition for jobs and other resources. It is where existing forms of dependence and relationship are perceived to have failed, and groups face declining rather than rising opportunities, that defences of a collective narcissistic kind are most often resorted to. It is the subjective experience of damage and threat which give rise to acute kinds of anxiety, and for this reason that downward mobility rather than an objective level of poverty is most likely to give rise to antagonism towards those perceived as outsiders.[10]

It follows from our view that narcissism is a defence against the anxieties of failed dependence that attention should be focused on the social relationships which sustain well-being, or fail to do so, rather than on the narcissistic symptoms themselves. The disruption which the invasion of Iraq has caused to existing social relations and dependencies there (basic law and order, electricity and water supplies, policing, the availability of work) is what has made it a disaster far exceeding the immediate injuries of war. The defences of destructive narcissism embodied in terrorism, and the counter-terrorism of states, follow from such fracturing of the social order as night follows day. Suicide bombers embody destructive narcissism to an extreme degree, sometimes believing themselves to be destined to become angels in heaven through their violent acts. The political philosopher Thomas Hobbes was correct in his view that the first and main responsibility of sovereign states is to maintain the peace, since without peace no benign kind of social order is possible. Organized wars between states may appear to be exceptions, where governments succeed in insulating their civilian populations from direct damage, but few peoples are insulated from the wars which their governments engage in.[11] It follows from this argument that the only thing that could secure, for example, the peace and security of Israel would be—it has always been—the creation of a prosperous Palestinian state side-by-side with it, and as economically and socially interdependent with it as possible. A newspaper photograph some time ago of an infant Palestinian horticultural industry, located in handed-over Israeli installations in Gaza, reminded one that people who live in glasshouses do not usually throw stones.

In social environments where basic assurances of respect and security are maintained, in other words where universal and fundamental narcissistic needs are attended to, space is created for the development of "object relationships" within the social realm. That is, for the development of individual identities, sustained by a sufficiency of solidarity, and a variety of collective identities which can be allowed to be complex and non-exclusive. In other words, collective identities in which different parts of the self can be invested, and the internal and external conflict which follows from difference can be tolerated both by individuals and the groups to which they belong. It is where respect and recognition are in short supply, or are denied to significant groups in society, that extreme forms of narcissistic defence emerge, since in these circumstances individuals are fearful to expose themselves to risk, and group identities become shelters against hostility, or more primitively the fear of annihilation.

Narcissism and the life of contemporary institutions

Let us now look not at individual patients, nor states, but at the civil institutions that lie between them, and link the one to the other.

What reason might there be for thinking that contemporary social institutions undermine dependence on "objects", and bring forth narcissistic defences against this loss of relationships, or of Symington's 'life-giver'?

An example: The culture of universities

We might take as one instance the kinds of relationship which academics and scholars have to their 'internal objects', by which we refer to the internal objects of their professional lives, their fields of research and their students. We think there is reason to suppose that relations between these internal objects are now being damaged, by insistence that they be manipulated for instrumental purposes, rather than cultivated and enjoyed for their intrinsic value. We refer here to the command and control systems of the Research Assessment Exercise, which demand that academics measure and evaluate themselves, turn their gaze on themselves, and on their "publications", their cvs and, away from the primary objects of work, their students and their research field.

The modularization and unitization of university curricula has the same implication. Students' relationship to a field of study as it is slowly illuminated over years as a course proceeds, under the guidance of known and trusted teachers, and within a supportive group of fellow-students, may be cut off by the premature insistence that competencies and outcomes must frequently be demonstrated, and by the fact that teachers have only fleeting responsibility in "unitized" systems for the work of individual students.

Thus instead of academics and students being expected to devote themselves to their studies, they are required to convert their objects of study prematurely into tokens of narcissistic worth, both on their own behalf and on behalf of their departments. Of course, there were always assessments, and separate components of courses, and recognition sought for scholarly work. But it is different when assessment looms ever larger, and when fields of study are packaged as "units" and "modules" with ever more uniform "programme specifications" and "learning outcomes", to make their outcomes fully negotiable. The end point is the emergence of numerical "credits", an educational currency signifying the triumph of exchange values over use values.

One might expect this to produce inhabitants of universities who are less intensely attached to their fields of study, to each other, and to their students, than they would be in an environment which assigned more value to freely-chosen commitments to the various "internal objects" of this form of life.[12]

We have given an academic instance of this process because it strikes us so forcibly, from our own experience. Other regimes of inspection and audit in the public sector have similar consequences in the formation of narcissistic defences.

The welfare system

The refocusing of attention of health workers, teachers and managers on the evaluation and measurement of their work, especially in ratings of its relative worth, has implications for the commitments of employees. Attention becomes transferred from the real internal and external objects of work—that is, on fields of knowledge and skill, and the human subjects who are meant to benefit from their application—to the task of making an impression on inspectors and regulators, who are deemed to represent the interests of service-users and the public at large. Considerable powers are wielded by these new functionaries, who form a tier in a new system of governance. This is not so much by the issuing of direct instructions, still less by the exercise of responsible authority, but is instead accomplished through the issuing of reports in print or on websites, the compiling of league tables of competitive merit from these, and a culture of naming and shaming which follows.

We are interested here not so much in the consequences of these systems for the performance of institutions, as on their internal effects on the states of mind of their members, though this must clearly affect performance too. They coercively require individuals and work teams to worry about how well they meet the evaluation criteria imposed on them, although the fit of these with the actual tasks they purport to measure may miss much of the point of what they do. Too often, what *can* be measured takes precedence over what would *need* to be measured if evaluation were to be meaningful.

An enlarged number of functionaries gain income and power from administering these procedures, exercising powers of judging the work of others without, as managers do, having to take responsibility for it and them. This might itself be described as conducive to a kind of "borderline" state of mind, cut off from a sentient relationship with those being worked with. But this heightened superego also becomes internalized within individual members, who become their own persecutors, driven to worry about how they appear to, and are valued or devalued by, others outside the primary relationships of their work.

Everything has to be looked at in a kind of mirror, unresponsive and rigid in its reflection as mirrors are, but unlike conventional mirrors in being selective in what it chooses to capture and reflect of what is in front of it. This heightened superego generates as its concomitant a heightened narcissism in individual subjects.

The internal object of the field of knowledge, the work-task, and the human partners in the work, are displaced by their self-serving presentations for others often perceived primarily as persecutors, sometimes abetted by managers who are felt to have in this respect betrayed those who they are responsible for sustaining.

If inspection systems were dialogic, exploratory, and facilitative of a culture of learning from experience, there might be more benefits from this exposure to external scrutiny. Such accountability is in itself a reasonable and necessary concomitant of the public funding of services in a democracy. But they often do not have this character. Their aim is usually to monitor conformity to rigid benchmarks, made standard and comparable for reasons of supposed equity, not to recognize relevant differences or to support innovation and change. This "audit culture" (Power, 1994; Strathern, 2000; Rustin, M.J., 2004), often justified by the ideology of "evidence-based practice", unsurprisingly is little interested in the evidence-base for the good and harm caused by its own practices.

Why is it the case that there is so much distrust of practices which depend on relationships, and a preference for outputs which can be measured and regulated in impersonal ways? In some fields of policy, it seems to be because the human circumstances being coped with by services are too painful, and arouse too much guilt. A striking example of this is the Victoria Climbié case, where a young girl in a form of foster care was killed by one of her foster parents, while a care system comprising social workers, nurses, doctors, and police failed to take notice and act on what should have been apparent to them (Cooper, 2005; Rustin, M.E., 2005; Rustin, M.J., 2004).

There was a widespread and well-documented failure to respond to the emotional reality of the situation as the catastrophe unfolded. Although the inquiry which was set up in response to the failures tried to engage with the human situation, its main outcome was a demand for yet more regulations and indicators. Individuals caught up in these systems often seem to respond by psychological withdrawal, and by maintaining a state of mindlessness, a "borderline state of mind" closely related to narcissism, since self-protection and survival becomes a primary concern.[13]

But more widely, an attack on the very idea of dependency and relationship has continued unbroken since the beginnings of Thatcherism, with its explicit assault on the "dependency culture" and summarized in Thatcher's famous aphorism, "There is no such thing as society". Earlier, in its first phase, this ideology of self-interest and self-regard was promoted as a moral crusade. Narcissism became desirable in itself. Now it is advocated as an unavoidable precondition of economic survival in conditions of global competition. Unless everyone—now even one-year olds, it appears, in the latest guidelines for the education of young children in day care,—shapes up, we will all go under. Possessive, competitive individualism, with a mixture of a stern helping-hand and stinging punishments for the inadequate or unwilling, is now promoted not so much as morally desirable in itself, as for the general good. If everyone does the best they can for themselves and their families— this is to be encouraged by providing greater "choice" in health and education—everyone will in the end benefit.

Or will they? Is the real problem not that the alternative ethos which would give priority to social ties, the idea of an environment which would provide respect, security, and beauty for all, now has no effective public or political expression? It should be possible to base an alternative theory and critique of institutions and their practices on the contrast we have been drawing between narcissistic and relational states of mind.

Acknowledgement

With thanks to Josephine Roger and Samantha Gaynor for permission to quote clinical material.

Notes

1. This paper was first given at a psychoanalysis and history seminar at the Institute of Historical Research, University of London, on November 16, 2005, and in the British Psychoanalytical Society Lecture Series on Narcissism on November 26, 2005.

2. Freud wrote, "Children love themselves first, and it is only later that they learn to love others and to sacrifice something of their own ego to others. Even those people whom a child seems to love from the beginning are loved by him at first because he needs them and cannot do without them—once again from egoistic motives. Not until later does the impulse to love make itself independent of egotism. It is literally true that *his egotism has taught him to love*" Freud, SE 15, p. 204 (1915–16).

3. Klein later wrote (1957, p. 52–53), "The hypothesis that a stage extending over several months precedes object relations implies that—except for the libido attached to the infant's own body—impulses, phantasies, anxieties and defences either are not present in him, or are not related to an object, that is to say they would operate *in vacuo*. The analysis of very young children has taught me that there is no instinctual urge, no anxiety situation, no mental process which does not involve objects, external or internal; in other words, object relations are at the centre of emotional life. Furthermore, love and hatred, phantasies, anxieties and defences are also operative from the beginning and are *ab initio* indivisibly linked with object relations. This insight showed me many phenomena in a new light" *Envy and Gratitude*, p. 52–53, 1957). Julia Kristeva (2003, p. 58) describes this passage as a "declaration [which] sets forth the parameters of Klein's debate with Freudian theory".

4. Michael Balint (1969) also criticized Freud's idea of primary narcissism, arguing that the idea of primary love better fitted the facts of infants' total dependence on the adaptation of their environment to them. Balint was also critical of the emphasis on negative feelings in early Kleinian thinking, holding with other "Independent School" psychoanalysts that severe negativity, and "secondary narcissism", were usually the outcome of environmental failures.

5. Recent developmental research has given empirical support for this view. Infants turn out to be able to recognize and prefer their mothers' sound and smell to those of strangers within a few minutes of birth. Sarah Blaffer Hrdy (2000) has described the species survival needs which were once met in hunter-gatherer societies by the instant bonding of mothers and their babies, and the behavioural

resources which evolution conferred on infants (usually attractive appearance, disturbing cries, pleasure-giving responses) to bring this about.

6. "O, you are sick of self-love, Malvolio, and taste with a distempered appetite" (*Twelfth Night*, I v, 89).

7. A narcissistic character structure may be the consequence of a harsh internal superego, for societies as well as individuals. Kleinian theory combined the concept of the ego ideal and the superego, the crucial issue being the harshness or otherwise of the internalized superego. Narcissism is a defence against excessive persecutory and/or depressive anxiety. Modern societies liberate and stimulate desires, and then seek to repress the consequences of this for social cohesion and inclusion. The popular and media reaction to catastrophes such as the Bulger or Climbié murders, in 1993 and 2000, and the combination of ultra-individualism with repression in the criminal justice system of the USA and increasingly Britain are witness to this conjunction. Those delegated the responsibility for "care and control" of the excluded bear the full brunt of projections of the persecutory and depressive anxieties produced in this situation. Borderline states of mind are a defence against these anxieties.

8. This is particularly beautifully represented in Ben Kingsley's performance of this role in Trevor Nunn's film of *Twelfth Night*.

9. After all, if buildings are not maintained and repaired in every generation, they will become ruins.

10. What about the basic narcissistic needs of incomers, whether migrants or refugees? One should note that many collective migrations take place because these needs have not been met "at home", where war, famine or social disorganization may have deprived communities of basic security and subsistence. Familiar locations and their cultures are then exchanged for the hope of more basic securities in a new environment, though what has then been lost is also missed and mourned. What is needed in places of settlement is to combine the basic guarantees of human rights to all individuals on a universalistic basis, with the acceptance of cultural differences.

11. However, where wars are fought at an apparently safe distance, they may paradoxically increase feelings of solidarity and mutual dependence, though at the cost of undiscriminating hatred directed towards enemies.

12. One indicator of this state of affairs is an increasing incidence of plagiarism. Some universities now feel they have to designate "academic integrity weeks" to remedy a problem which formerly

arose only on an individual scale. One university has even set up an institute to advise others on the issue! The availability of information on the internet which contributes to this situation, for all of its benefits can also detract from the value of human relationships in education.

13. These borderline states of mind are discussed in Froggatt (2003), Cooper & Lousada (2005), and Anderson, Hindle et al. (2003).

References

Anderson, J., Cohn, N., Hindle, D., Ironside, L., Philps, J., Rustin, M.E. & Rustin, M.J. (2003). Borderline organisations: reflections from child psychotherapy Research. Unpublished.

Balint, M. (1937). Early developmental states of the ego. Primary object love. In: *Primary Love and Psychoanalytic Technique*. London: Hogarth, 1952.

Balint, M. (1968). *The Basic Fault, Part 2: Primary narcissism and primary love*. Evanston, IL: Northwestern University Press.

Bloom, H. (1973). *The Anxiety of Influence: a Theory of Poetry*. Oxford: Oxford University Press.

Cooper, A. (2005). Surface and depth in the Victoria Climbié Report. *Child and Family Social Work, 10*, 1.

Cooper, A. & Lousada, J. (2005). *Borderline Welfare: Feeling and Fear of Feeling in the Modern Welfare State*. London: Karnac.

Freud, S. (1914). *On Narcissism: an Introduction*. S.E., 14. London: Hogarth.

Freud, S. (1916–17). *Introductory Lectures on Psychoanalysis*. S.E., 15 and 16. London: Hogarth.

Froggatt, L. (2003). *Love, Hate and Welfare*. Bristol: Policy.

Grunberger, B. (1971). *Narcissism*. International Universities Press, 1978.

Grunberger, B. (1989). *New Essays on Narcissism*. London: Free Association.

Hinshelwood, R.D. (1989). *A Dictionary of Kleinian Thought*. London: Free Association.

Hrdy, S.B. (2000). *Mother Nature*. New York: Vintage.

Klein, M. (1952). The origins of transference. In: *Envy and Gratitude and other Works 1946–1963*. London: Hogarth, 1975.

Klein, M. (1957). Envy and gratitude. In: *Envy and Gratitude and other Works 1946–1963*. London: Hogarth, 1975.

Kristeva, J. (2001). *Melanie Klein*. New York: Columbia University Press.

Laplanche, J. & Pontalis, J.B. (1988). *The Language of Psychoanalysis*. London: Karnac.

Meltzer, D. (1968). Terror, persecution and dread. *International Journal of Psychoanalysis*, 49, 396–400.

Money-Kyrle, R. (1965). Success and failure in mental maturations. In: *The Collected Papers of Roger Money-Kyrle*. Strathtay, Perthshire: Clunie, 1978.

Power, M. (1994). *The Audit Explosion*. Demos.

Rey, H. (1994). *Universals of Psychoanalysis in the Treatment of Psychotic and Borderline States*. London: Free Association.

Rosenfeld, H. (1971). A clinical approach to the psychoanalytic theory of the life and death instincts: an investigation into the aggressive aspects of narcissism. *International Journal of Psychoanalysis, 52*, 169–178.

Rustin, M.J. (2004). Rethinking the Audit Culture. *Soundings* 28.

Rustin, M.E. (2005). Conceptual analysis of critical moments in Victoria Climbié's life. In: *Child and Family Social Work, 10*, 1.

Rustin, M.J. (2004). Learning from the Victoria Climbié Inquiry. *Journal of Social Work Practice, 18*, 1, 9–18.

Steiner, J. (1993). *Psychic Retreats: Pathological Organisations in Psychotic, Neurotic and Borderline Patients*. London: Routledge.

Strathern, M. (Ed.) (2000). *Audit Cultures*. London: Routledge.

Symington, N. (1993). *Narcissism: a New Theory*. London: Karnac.

INDEX

235